ACCOUNTS ASSISTANT
PRACTICAL EXPERIENCE
USING QUICKBOOKS ONLINE

Step by step guide

STERLING LIBS FCCA, FCPA

PRACTICAL WORK EXPERIENCE IN ACCOUNTANCY

If lack of practical work experience in accountancy is stopping you from getting your ideal accounting job and if you are really struggling and are just unsure what to do next, this book will help you sort that problem out.

If you are getting lots of rejection from recruitment agencies and employers due to lack of practical work experience, then you've got yourself something really good to help you kickstart your accountancy work experience practice.

If you are tired of working in a non-accounting related role and want to kickstart your accounting career, then this will help you get started.

If you want to learn how to properly do month-end account procedures, preparing yearend accounts, file a corporation tax return and annual accounts to Companies House and prepare management accounts, this book is definitely for you.

This book is a combination of the Accounts Payable Work Experience using QuickBooks online (APWE QB) and Accounts Receivable Work Experience Using QuickBooks online (ARWE QB) both written by the same author, with additional practical information on Month end accounting procedures and the filing of statutory accounts and returns (UK only) to Companies House and HMRC.

So, if you already have the APWE QB and ARWE QB, it might not be necessary to have this book also. You could however consider instead getting - HOW TO DO MONTH END ACCOUNTING PROCEDURES also by the same Author and also (if you are in the UK) – HOW TO PREPARE AND FILE YEAREND ACCOUNTS (UK Edition) also by the same Author as well as ACCOUNTING JOB QUESTIONS AND ANSWERS – Trainee Accountants Handbook.

The Author can be contacted by sending an email to sterling@sterlinglibs.com

Your Role as an Accountant

An accountant performs financial functions related to the collection, accuracy, recording, analysis and presentation of a business, organization or company's financial operations.

The accountant usually has a variety of administrative roles within a company's operations. In a smaller business, an accountant's role may consist of primarily financial data collection, entry and report generation.

Middle to larger sized companies may utilize an accountant as an adviser and financial interpreter, who may present the company's financial data to people within and outside of the business. Generally, the accountant can also deal with third parties, such as vendors (Suppliers), customers and financial institutions.

https://smallbusiness.chron.com/role-accountant-play-business-operations-411.html

Table of Contents

"People are like bicycles, they keep their balance only as they move forward"

Albert Einstein

NOTE TO THE READER

This step by step guide is designed to provide practical information on how to work as an Accountant using QuickBooks Online accounting software.

Every effort has been made to make this book as complete and accurate as possible. However, no assurance is given that the information is comprehensive in its coverage or that it is suitable for dealing with your particular situation. Accordingly, the information provided should not be relied upon as a substitute for independent research. It is sold with the understanding that the publisher and author are not engaged in rendering any accounting, legal, or other professional advice nor do they have any responsibility for updating or revising any information presented herein.

No representation or warranty (express or implied) is given as to the accuracy or completeness of the information contained in this book, and, to the extent permitted by law, the Author/publisher, its members, employees and agents do not accept or assume any liability, responsibility or duty of care for any consequences of you or anyone else acting, or refraining to act, in reliance on the information contained in this book or for any decision based on it. If legal or other expert assistance is required, the services of a competent professional should be sought.

The author and publisher cannot warrant that the material contained herein will continue to be accurate nor that it is completely free of errors when published. Readers should verify statements before relying on them.

Purpose

This book is information only and has been prepared for general guidance for those who are interested in learning how to work as an Accountant as described in the job description of an Accountant on page 1 of this book and is current at the time of publication.

About this book

This book is a step by step guide designed to
provide practical information on how to work as
an accountant using QuickBooks online
accounting software.

"And God said, let there be light: and there was light."
Genesis 1:3

WORKING AS AN ACCOUNTANT

The accountancy profession is a very dynamic one. If you desire a future of constant growth and change, then the accounting profession will certainly provide that for you.

An Accountant can fill many different business positions and roles. The opportunities are great. You can work for yourself, work in an accounting firm, in a company in a particular industry, or the government, to name but a few.

The primary task of accountants, which extends to all the others, is to prepare and examine financial records.

Accountants make sure that records are accurate and that taxes are paid promptly and adequately. Accountants and auditors perform overviews of the financial operations of a business to help it run efficiently. They also provide the same services to individuals, helping them create plans of action for improved financial well-being.

In working as an accountant, your job will entail doing the following:

At a junior level;

- ✓ Processing customer invoices and receipts
- ✓ Collecting outstanding amounts from debtors
- ✓ Processing supplier invoices & supplier payments
- ✓ Supplier statement reconciliations
- ✓ Payroll processing and posting payroll journals
- ✓ Sorting out; the post and providing clerical support to management
- ✓ Bank reconciliation
- ✓ VAT Return preparation and submission to HMRC
- ✓ Managing petty cash
- ✓ Answering phones and ordering stationery
- ✓ Assisting with credit control
- ✓ Doing month end accounting procedures
- ✓ Yearend accounts preparation
- ✓ Preparing Tax returns & submitting them to HMRC

And at a senior level:

- ✓ Examining statements to ensure accuracy
- ✓ Ensuring that statements and records comply with laws and regulations
- ✓ Computing taxes owed, prepare tax returns, ensure prompt payment
- ✓ Inspecting account books and accounting systems to keep up to date
- ✓ Organising and maintaining financial records
- ✓ Improving businesses efficiency where money is concerned
- ✓ Making best-practice recommendations to management
- ✓ Suggesting ways to reduce costs, enhance revenues and improve profits
- ✓ Providing auditing services for businesses and individuals

Accountants are needed in all areas of the economy. Different sectors and employers all have their advantages and disadvantages – you have to decide what suits your personality and career aspirations best.

Testing your practical accounting knowledge (17 Questions & Answers)

Question 1: Under what legal entities can businesses operate in the UK?

Answer: *Sole Trader, Partnership, Company Limited by Shares (LTD), Company Limited by guarantee (Charity), Community Interest Company (CIC), Limited Liability Partnership (LLP) Designated Activity Company, Public Listed Company (PLC)*

Question 2: What is a tax year and what is a financial year?

Answer: *A tax year in the UK is from the 6th of April the current year to the following 5th April next year.*
A financial year is a 12-month period commencing from the date the business starts trading or gets registered with Companies House (UK)

Question 3: What are the three key stages of the accounting cycle?

Answer: *Analysis stage, Recording stage and Reporting stage*

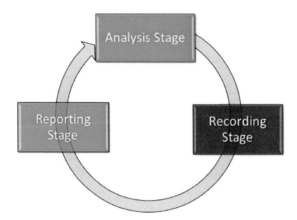

Question 4: Briefly describe what you should do at each of the three stages listed above.

Answer:
    a. *Analysis Stage*
        - *Classification of financial documents*
        - *Checking that the correct values are reflected in the financial documents*
        - *Making sure that the documents are within the financial year date to which they relate to.*

    b. *Recording stage*
        - *It is mostly about data entry*
        - *Using double-entry bookkeeping principles*

    c. *Reporting stage*
        - *Checking for any errors in the nominal accounts*
        - *Making yearend/period end adjustments*
        - *Producing yearend/period end reports and statements for filing with government agencies (Companies House & HMRC in the UK)*

Question 5: What are the key steps in the sales ledger (Accounts Receivable process)

Answer:

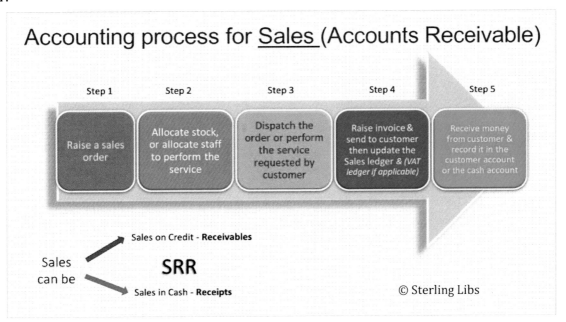

Question 6: What are the key steps in the purchase ledger (Accounts payable) process

Answer:

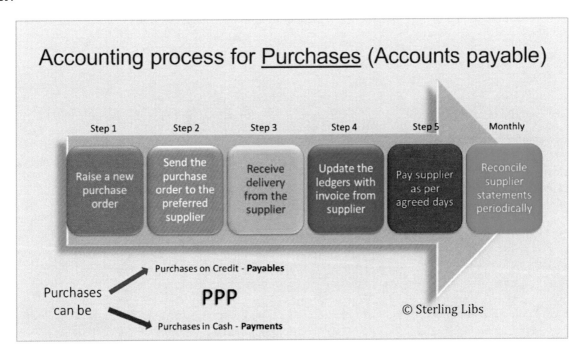

Question 7: When does a business need to register for PAYE in the UK?
Answer: *When it starts employing people/when it becomes an employer*

Question 8: When does a business have to register for VAT?

Answer: *Compulsory registration: You must register for VAT if your VAT taxable turnover is more than £85,000 (the 'threshold') in a 12-month period or if you expect to go over the threshold in a single 30-day period.*

Question 9: What is the current standard rate of VAT in the UK
Answer: *20%*

Question 10: What is the current rate of corporation tax in the UK?
Answer: *19% for tax year 2017/2018*

Question 11: What is normally done at the month end close process
Answer: *Three key steps are usually performed to manage the end-of-the-month accounting process successfully. They are:*

Description of the key steps	What to do at each stage (the tasks)
Key step 1: Checking the general ledger accounts for errors & making the necessary corrections	• *Correct the general ledger account errors including mispostings and inaccuracies.*
Key step 2: Doing Adjustments and Reconciliations	• *Financial adjustments, e.g. interest payments adjustments, prepayments, accruals and depreciation* • *Control account reconciliations: Debtors' control account, Creditors' control account, VAT control account, Bank account, Wages account etc.* • *Balance sheet reconciliation (Reconciliation of the Assets, Liabilities, Equity & Reserves)* • *Calculations of closing balances of the accounts after adjustments & reconciliations*
Key step 3: Reporting to senior management	• *Producing a profit & Loss statement and other various management reports if necessary.*

Question 12: Why is it important to do bank reconciliation?

Answer:
A bank reconciliation is used to compare your records to those of your bank, to see if there are any differences between these two sets of records for your cash transactions. The ending balance of your version of the cash records is known as the book balance, while the bank's version is called the bank balance. It is extremely common for there to be differences between the two balances, which you should track down and adjust in your own records. If you were to ignore these differences, there would eventually be substantial variances between the amount of cash that you think you have and the amount the bank says you actually have in an account. The result could be an overdrawn bank account, bounced checks, and overdraft fees. In some cases, the bank may even elect to shut down your bank account.

It is also useful to complete a bank reconciliation to see if any customer checks have bounced, or if any checks you issued were altered or even stolen and cashed without your knowledge. Thus, fraud detection is a key reason for completing a bank reconciliation. When there is an ongoing search for fraudulent transactions, it may be necessary to reconcile a bank account on a daily basis, in order to obtain early warning of a problem.

Question 13: Which government agencies do businesses in the UK need to submit accounts and returns to?

Answer:
Her Majesty's Revenue and Customs (HMRC) and Companies House.

Question 14: Which reports usually are submitted to the government agencies you have stated above?

Answer:
a) HMRC – *Tax returns, VAT Returns,*
b) Companies House - *Statutory annual accounts and annual returns*

Question 15: And who is legally responsible for submitting the reports you've stated above?

Answer: *The Director(s) of the company*

Question 16: What key competencies will help you work effectively as an accountant?

Answer:
    a. Attention to detail
    b. Analytical skills
    c. Numerical skills
    d. Communication skills and teamwork
    e. Accounting software skills
    f. Speed and accuracy

Question 17: What code of ethics are accountants expected to abide by?

Answer:
    a. Integrity
    b. Objectivity
    c. Confidentiality
    d. Professional competence and due care
    e. Adopting professional behaviour

The professional code of ethics you are required to abide by as an accountant.

Under the Code of Professional Ethics, as an accountant, you must follow these five principles:

1. **Integrity.**

You must be straightforward and honest in all professional and business relationships.

2. **Objectivity.**

You must not compromise professional or business judgment because of bias, conflict of interest or the undue influence of others.

3. **Professional competence and due care.**

You must maintain professional knowledge and skill (in practice, legislation and techniques) to ensure that a client or employer receives competent professional service.

4. **Confidentiality.**

You must not disclose confidential professional or business information or use it to your advantage unless you have explicit permission to disclose it, or a legal or professional right or duty to disclose it.

5. Professional behaviour.

You must comply with relevant laws and regulations and avoid any action that may bring disrepute to the profession.

Professional Ethics | AAT. (n.d.). Retrieved from https://www.aat.org.uk/about-aat/professional-ethics

The key skills that can help you get and keep an accounting job

Skilled people in any profession are very valuable. So let me take this opportunity to talk to you about some of the skills you should look to develop at the early formative years of your accounting career.

Identifying the skills that lead to success in accounting will not only increase your job satisfaction but also make it easier for you to build your long-term career goals.

No matter how big a company ever gets, the need for an accounts department persists. Perhaps that focus is on auditing, maybe management or tax and finance related. Chances are, you will start in one of two career paths – technical or commercial.

Accounting requires certain hard skills, such as mathematics and expertise with accounting software. Thorough knowledge of relevant laws and regulations is necessary for many positions, too.

However, accounting also requires some soft skills that you might not learn in school but will help you land and keep a job.

Staying current with technology is perhaps the most significant pressure you will continuously face in your accounting and finance career. As technology impacts on the way you do your job as an accountant, make sure you stay abreast of the changes and train and retrain to keep your skills up to date

Here is a list of six accounting skills that you should look to hone in your career as a professional accountant. Your CV/resume, cover letter, job application will be scrutinised for these skills and even during your job interviews – if you make it that far. It will serve you well to be in possession of these skills in increasing measure as you progress in your accounting career.

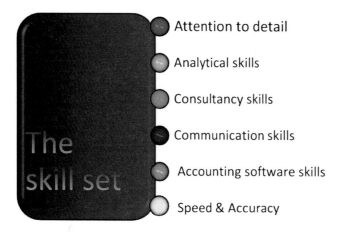

The skill set
- Attention to detail
- Analytical skills
- Consultancy skills
- Communication skills
- Accounting software skills
- Speed & Accuracy

Let me elaborate a bit more on each skill above.

Attention to detail

Attention to detail is an essential requirement for a successful accounting career. The ability to notice an error, inconsistency or discrepancy can often lead to discovering other inaccuracies. On the other hand, missing a small detail can affect the integrity of the organisation's financial records and may have dire consequences. It is therefore quite essential that you should have a detail-oriented approach to your work to ensure that financial records conform to standards, laws and regulations.

Analytical Skills

As an accountant, you must be analytical when examining documents and financial processes. The use of critical thinking skills to determine ways to make the organisation more financially efficient will be required of any good accountant. My experience in working with many businesses is that; the analytical skills help you develop ways to reduce costs, increase revenues, improve profits and eliminate waste.

You will also have to carefully evaluate financial performance and investigate financial investments at some point in your accountancy career as you keep growing and that my friend, will call for excellent analytical skills.

Hopefully, with the passage of time, you will be able to demonstrate this skill in greater measure.

Consultancy skills

The Accountant of the 21st century is more of a consultant than a person who merely deals with numbers. As a professional accountant of nowadays, you should also be a problem solver and possess sound judgement, and you shouldn't not jump to conclusions.

Good consultants study, consider the facts, ask questions, challenge the norm and then make a recommendation or a decision. They use their experience from previous assignments to solve new problems and challenges in your current assignment. They possess excellent written and oral communication skills as well as good listening skills. These are the kind of things you will be expected to do more of as the accountant of the 21st century because accounting software's are doing a lot more of what the traditional accountant of yesteryears used to do. So you need to evolve to what I would call – the Accounting consultant.

Communication skills

How are your written and verbal communication skills like?

You see, the accountant of the 21st century now interacts with a variety of people ranging from managers and directors to members of the accounting staff and various stakeholders in a business. You will meet people through the course of your work with a wide range of unique characteristics, not all of them pleasant or to your liking.
It is therefore important that train yourself to be able to clearly converse or correspond and to ask questions and discuss issues or discrepancies quite easily.
Also, accountants offer advice and make recommendations regarding the best financial business decisions. Therefore, being articulate and well presented will help a great deal here.

Accounting software skills

Gone are the days when accounting used to be done manually. Almost invariably, every business now uses some form of software to do their bookkeeping and accounts. From Excel to the more sophisticated ERP accounting software, accounting and financial analysis are now so much software based and the better you are in using any of these accounting software, the better you will be in your accounting career.

Accounting software all use the same basic principle of double entry, so if you are proficient in one, you will find it easy to learn any other accounting software relatively quickly.

I suggest therefore that you learn at least how to use one accounting software very well because that will act as a stepping stone for you learning other software should you change jobs and find that your new employer uses a different accounting software. At least know how to use one software proficiently.

Speed & Accuracy

You need to be conscious of the fact that accounting is a very dynamic profession and at times very highly pressured. If you are looking to be successful in your accounting career, you've got to develop a reputation for speed and dependability (producing accurate & trustworthy information).

Time is the currency of the 21st century. Business today is very, very dynamic. Employers are less and less patient with slow, incompetent employees because they recognise that customers will change suppliers overnight if someone else can serve them faster than the people they are currently dealing with.

So, your job, as you start developing your accountancy career is to develop a reputation for speed. Move fast on opportunities, move quickly when you see something that needs to be done. You've heard it said that whenever you want to get something done, give it to a busy man or woman.

Employees who have a reputation for moving quickly, attract more and more opportunities and possibilities to them and that is the kind of thing you want in the early years of your accountancy career development.

If you can combine your ability to determine your highest priority tasks with the commitment to getting it done quickly and accurately, you will find yourself progressing through your accounting career with flying colours and moving to the front/top of it. More and more doors and opportunities will open for you that you can't even imagine today.

One more thing – very, very important indeed.

Underlying all of the skills you will ever have is one very important and profound aspect of life you need to watch over. What am I talking about? Your attitude. That's right, has to do a lot with your quality of life and success in any career or profession.

Come to think it; you could be a genius as far as accounting is concerned and even have the most excellent and lofty practical experience there is to find. However, if you have a terrible attitude, you will realise soon or later that not many people would like to work with you or have dealings with you whatsoever. They would prefer keeping their distance from you. Is that good, you think, for your career? Not in the slightest if you ask me.

So, let me talk to you a little bit about attitude since it is such a crucial aspect of your job success as an accountant just as it is in any area of your life. Your attitude goes a long way in determining what company of people you will keep, what actions you will take, how successful you will be in your accounting career and above all, how much and how deep you will enjoy life. Something worth exploring, wouldn't you agree? Yes, of course.

Look, I can guarantee you that your current attitude is either helping you move forward or is making you lag behind in life. The good news though is this; your attitude is 100% under your control, and you can change it at any time to help support your career progression.

Your Life only gets better when you get better, and since there is no limit on how much better you can become, there is no limit on how much better your life can become. True? Well, judge for yourself.

Zig Ziglar once said; "*It's your attitude and not your aptitude that determines your altitude*".

Here then are some of the attitudes that I believe will help you make excellent progress in your accountancy career.

1. **Attitude of gratitude**

When you exude an attitude of gratitude at all times, you make people around you feel important. The truth is, everything you say or do that causes another person to feel better in any way also causes you to feel better to the same degree. Haven't you realised that when you encourage, inspire, motivate someone else, you feel motivated, inspired and encouraged yourself?

And guess what...

The converse is true when you degrade, insult and abhor someone else, you feel the same too!

The need for appreciation is a deep subconscious desire of every individual you meet. When you satisfy this need, you will by all accounts become one of the most popular people in that person's world, and what is the key to expressing gratitude and appreciation? Simple, just say 'thank you' on every occasion and mean it.

You say thanks in a whole host of different ways: by giving compliments, admiration, giving encouragement, by unconditionally accepting people for who they are, by smiling, giving a hug, a pat on the back....., all these actions communicate one message ;-well done 'buddy' I am really proud of you'. If you become a finance manager, you should do more of this with your juniors.

In fact, the best way to ensure your happiness is to assist others to experience their own. "Those who bring Sunshine to others cannot keep it from themselves" James Banie
Be a professional, happy, gregarious and friendly accountant. It will do you good.

2. A forgiving attitude
Jim Loehr & Tony Schwartz in their book; In the power of Full engagement, said: *"The richer and deeper the source of our emotional recovery, the more we refill our reserves and the more resilient we become."*

You see, people are emotional beings. People decide emotionally then justify logically. Emotion comes first. So when we are hurt, our emotions immediately take over, and for some, this leads to prolonged periods of sulking and being grumpy, and they will justify it logically by saying that they are hurt. What they seem not to understand is that a lot of their emotional energy which could otherwise be expended in some other productive venture is being put to waste on destructive tendencies. So the faster they recover from any hurt through total and sincere forgiveness, the better for them.

I know it is not easy to forgive, but I also know that it is difficult to enjoy life in an accounting career if you are hurting from the inside.

So if there is anyone who has hurt you; whoever it is, or wherever it was, please forgive them. It could be your parent(s), your spouse, your close friend, your sibling, your pastor, teacher, work mate, it could be anyone and everyone really, whoever it is, find it in your heart to forgive and release them from the pain they have caused you. It's very noble, and it is an eternal act, which has both present and eternal rewards.

Forgiveness is a choice, and we all have to make that choice time and again if our relationships and careers are to be worth our time, effort and rewards thereof.
Be a forgiving accountant. Don't be a grumpy & bitter accountant.

3. Courageous attitude
Courage is a very admirable quality. Your boldness will help you get as much as you need in life. The bold move makes you seem larger and more powerful than you are. More than that, the bold draw attention and what draws attention, draws power. We simply cannot keep our eyes off the audacious, can we? We can't wait to see their next bold move.
Everyone admires the bold; no one honours the timid, isn't that true?

Better still...

A courageous person is an upward and forward-looking person, he/she faces the future without fear but with determination, not with doubt but with faith. He/she is willing to take great chances and reach for new horizons and remake the world around them. They recognise that there is more to their life than the ordinary, they take the status quo and turn it around. It is simply magnetic and very inspiring to be around them. The good news is that you can be one of those very courageous ones as well.

The courageous individuals teach us to have our horizons limitless. Ultimately if we are to be true to our past, we also have to seize the future every day, and courage will help us make the most of our; time, abilities (effort), and opportunities that will ultimately help us make the most of our lives and accounting career.

And...

No matter how bitter the raw, how stony the accountancy road, courage enables us to persevere, not to falter or grow weary but to demand, strive and shape a better accountancy career for yourself!
Simply refuse to give up on the idea of the forward and upward move but ultimate triumph, despite the most extreme odds that you will sometimes face during your accountancy career. In some circumstances, you will need a lot of courage to do the right thing that the code of ethics demands of you.

4.   A compassionate attitude
Compassion makes you believable, it magnetises and magnifies the power of your faith and undeniably makes you very welcoming and attractive in the sight and hearts of many people. Compassion moves the heavens on your behalf and bestows upon you the invisible power of influence and force of accomplishment.

Compassion naturally leads you to be a giver; it enhances the quality of benevolence - one of the hallmark characteristics of the truly superior person.

When you give freely and generously of yourself to others or for a cause, you feel more valuable and happier inside.
Here is a principle to remember when it comes to benevolence and compassion: "The more you give of yourself to others without expectation of return, the more good things there are that will come back to you from most unexpected sources."

You will also realise that, over time, you are becoming more patient and understanding, less judgmental or demanding of others. You will feel peaceful, confident and pleasant to be around. In a nutshell, you become a better and finer person and more importantly a compassionate accountant.

Isn't that wonderful?

5.   Integrity
Your Character is the most important thing that you develop in your entire life, and one of the cornerstones of your character is your integrity.

You develop integrity, and become a completely honest person, by practising telling the truth to yourself and others in every situation.

It is imperative that your relationships and accountancy career are based on the foundation of truth, and this can be done by developing the habit of living in truth with yourself and with everyone around you. Of course, this does not mean that you will always be right 100% of the time, it, however, emphasises the fact that you endeavour to tell the truth, as you see or know it.

Others will learn to know that they can confidently rely on you and your word (and that is very important for an accountant). Though they may not like what you say on certain occasions, they will still know that you always speak the truth. This goes a very long way to earn you a great reputation in your accounting career and form a very solid foundation for your integrity. Listen to what Shakespeare once wrote, *"To thine own self be true, and then it must follow, as the night the day, thou canst not then be false to any man"*.

In this day and age with the advancement of technology, CCTV and satellite, you cannot afford to be careless about how you conduct yourself or how you treat others or do business. To be successful nowadays is largely determined by the number of people who trust you and who are willing to work with you or give you credit if you are a borrower or help you during difficult times etc. Trust is essential, and trust is earned not given, and you earn trust by being a person of integrity.

You must guard your integrity as a sacred thing, as the most important statement about you as an accountant.
As Brian Tracy once said; "Whenever you are in doubt about a course of action, simply ask yourself, Is this the right thing to do?" And then behave accordingly.

"Weakness of attitude becomes weakness of Character" – A. Einstein

6. A loving attitude

As Apostle Paul said in 1Corinthians 13:2-3 *"And though I have the gift of prophecy, and understand all mysteries, and all knowledge; and though I have all faith so that I could remove mountains,.....And though I bestow all my goods to feed the poor, and though I give my body to be burned, and have not Love, I am nothing."*

Without genuine, heartfelt love for the people in your life and the things you do, your relationships and success in life are doomed to fail.

Jesus Christ emphasised this point of love so much that He gave a new commandment: *"...Thou shalt love the Lord thy God with all thy heart, and with all thy soul and with all thy mind........., Thou shalt love thy neighbour as thyself"* Matthew 22:37-3

To love is a decision you make and should form a core part of your attitude in life and especially in your accounting career.
I think it is important to bear in mind what Jesus Christ said in the scripture above and also to embrace the Golden Rule: *"Do unto others what you would have them do unto you"*.

In closing on this aspect of attitudes of success in accountancy, I would like to say that; the way to a super attitude and hence a great accountancy career at any time of the day and at any day of the week is to trust in God with all your heart and lean not on your own understanding.

I am not being religious here, but simply stating the obvious and plain truth. If you don't believe me, try it your way or any other way and see how far you can go being successful and happy at the same time.

I hope you will forever resolve to be a grateful, forgiving, courageous, compassionate, trustworthy and loving accountant. I really do hope so.

Okay. I am done with that bit. Let's get to work, shall we?

Integrity

You must guard your integrity as a sacred thing, as the most important statement about you as an accountant.

As Brian Tracy once said; "Whenever you are in doubt about a course of action, simply ask yourself, is this the right thing to do?" And then behave accordingly.

TASK 1: SETTING UP & GETTING STARTED

"A journey of a thousand miles begins with a single step" **Laozi**

Introduction to QuickBooks Online

QuickBooks is an accounting software package developed and marketed by Intuit. QuickBooks products are geared mainly toward small and medium-sized businesses and offer on-premises accounting applications as well as cloud-based versions that accept business payments, manage and pay bills, and payroll functions.

There are three versions of QuickBooks Online. A plan can be chosen to suit the requirements of the business. Each offering provides features relevant to the selected plan. Further details on the features available under each product version can be found at https://quickbooks.intuit.com/pricing/

Task 1a: Setting up the business in QuickBooks Online

The details you have been given about the business to set up in QuickBooks Online are as follows:

- **Company/Business name:** *Horizon Tristar Ltd*
- **Business address:** *77 Lee Road, London, SE3 9DE*
- **Financial year:** *Set to the 1st November last year*
- **Home currency:** *Depending on where you are doing this work experience from (country), Use the currency of that country as the home currency in QuickBooks Online (We will be using the British Pound in this tutorial)*
- **VAT information:** *Registered for VAT on the standard VAT scheme and the registration number is 843277159*
- **Director/Manager:** *Mr Terry Smith*
- **Opening balances** to be entered in QuickBooks online as of 1st January this year.

Let's get started.

Look at the links below and depending on which part of the world you are in, use the appropriate link to get started.

If you are based in the **United Kingdom (UK),** use/click on - https://quickbooks.intuit.com/uk/

If you are based in the **United States (US)**, use/click on - https://quickbooks.intuit.com

If you are based in the **European Union (EU)**, use/click on - https://quickbooks.intuit.com/eu/

If you are based in **Australia,** use/click on - https://quickbooks.intuit.com/au/

For all the **Rest of the World**, use/click on - https://quickbooks.intuit.com/global/

For this work experience, I have opted to use the UK site, https://quickbooks.intuit.com/uk/ because I live in the UK. However, the software functionally is the same regardless of which part of the world you are based in. So, follow through with me.

Once you visit any of the sites above, the landing pages are quite similar, and there will be an offer for a free 30 day trial in almost all the sites - See figures 1 & 2 below.

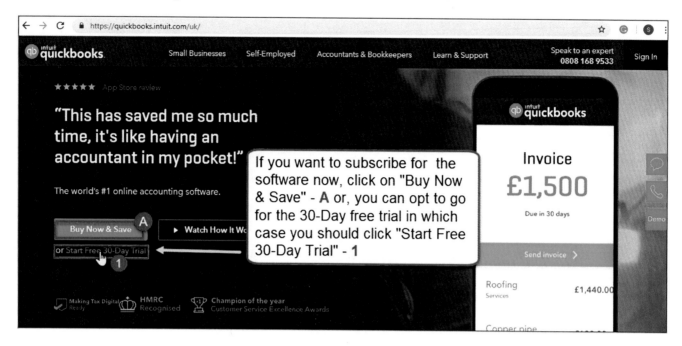

Fig. 1

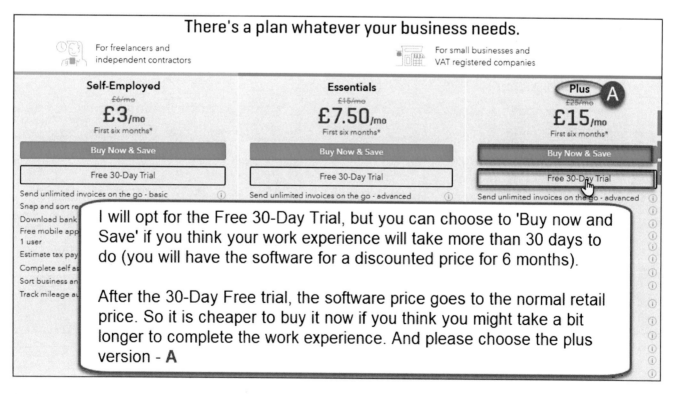

Fig. 2

Fig. 3

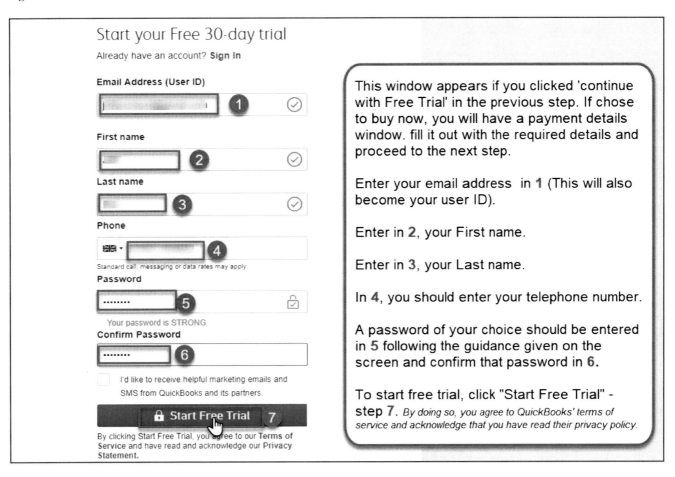

Fig. 4

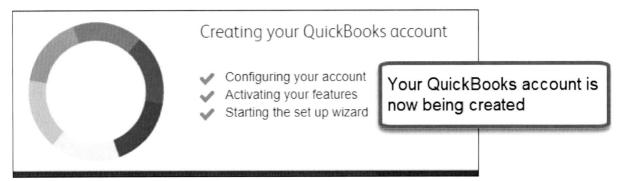

Fig. 5

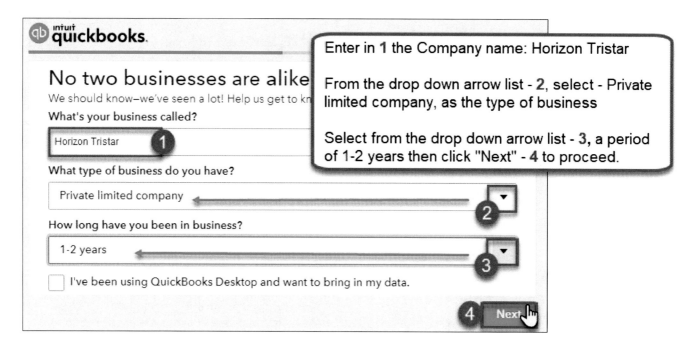

Fig. 6

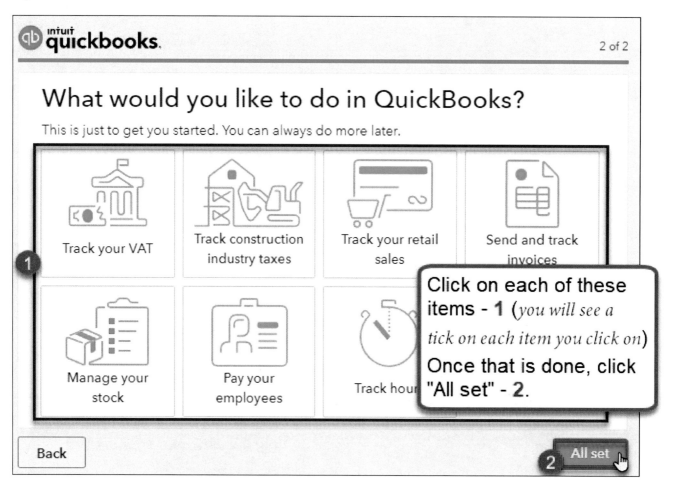

Fig. 7

After you click "All set" as illustrated in the figure above, the home page appears. The Home page displays a summary of key information. A new file set up would display as in figure 8 (on the next page) with no transactions.

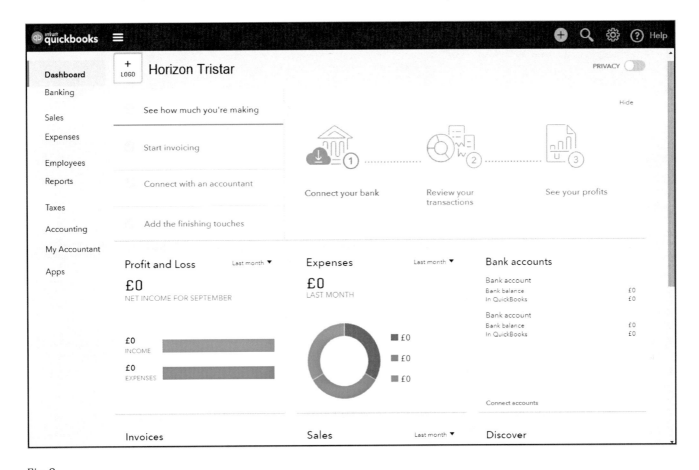

Fig. 8

To sign out of your QuickBooks online screen, see details on the figure below.

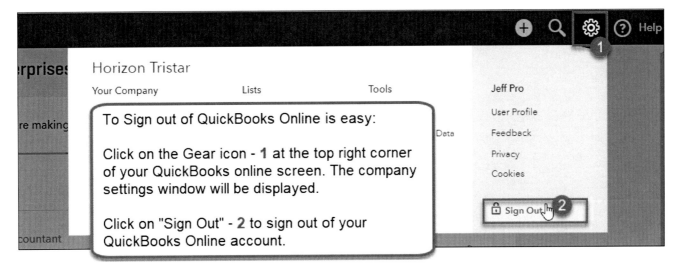

Fig. 9

> *This space is for notes*

To sign back into your QuickBooks online account, follow the steps as illustrated in the figure below.

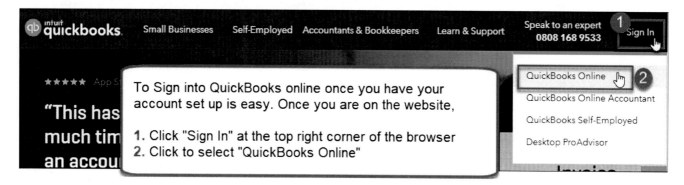

Fig.10

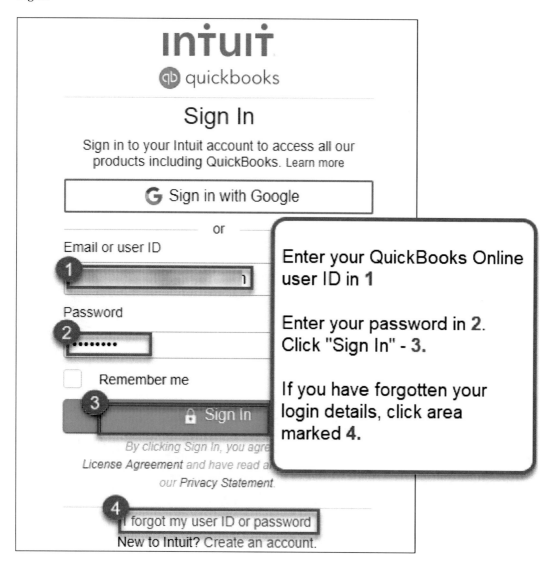

Fig. 11

Task 1a(i). Understanding the general layout of QuickBooks Online

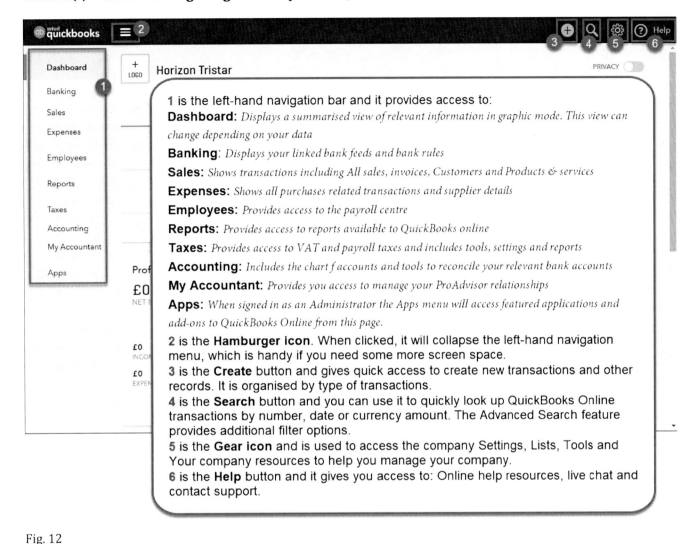

Fig. 12

Let's move on and set up the company's financial year date.

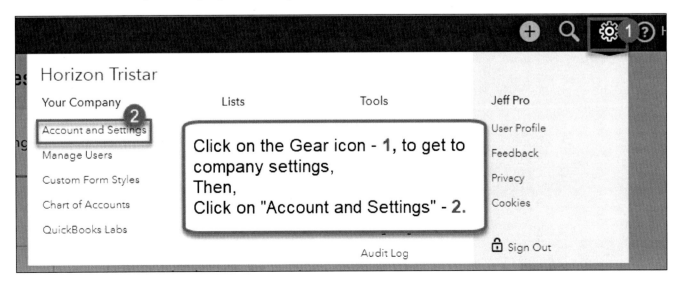

Fig. 13

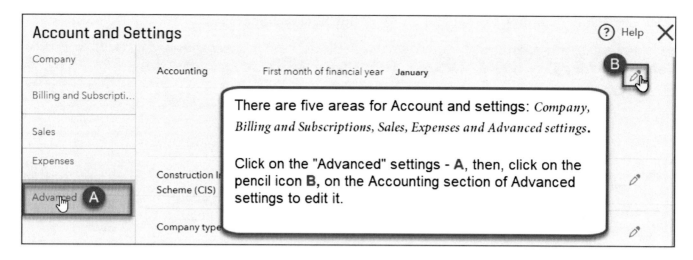

Fig. 14

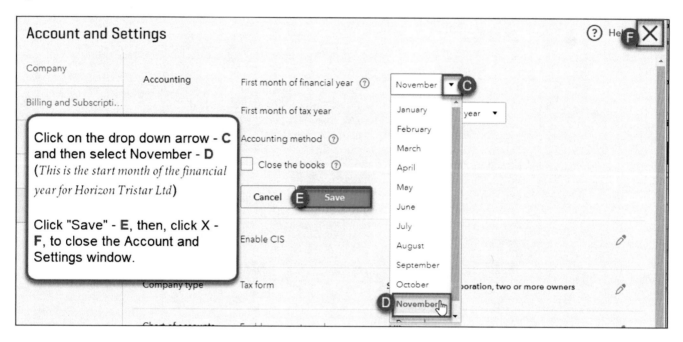

Fig. 15

Multicurrency

Trade nowadays is quite international, and that means having to deal with different currencies as a business buys and sells internationally. We are therefore going to set the multicurrency option in QuickBooks Online for Horizon Tristar Ltd.

To do so, go to the company settings – see figure 16 on the next page – see figure 16 on the next page

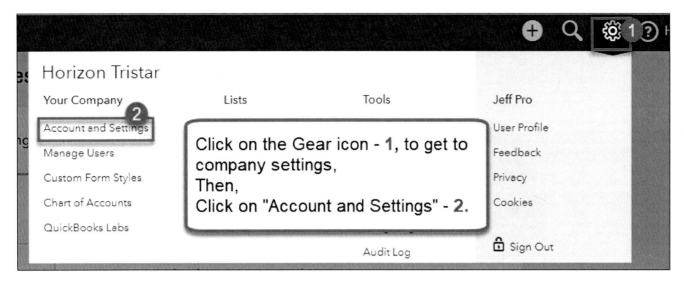

Fig. 16

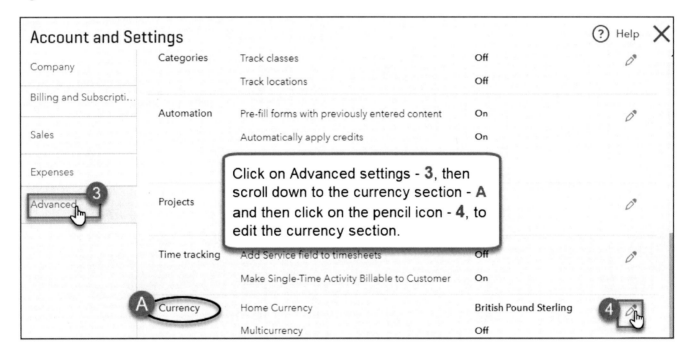

Fig. 17

This space is for notes

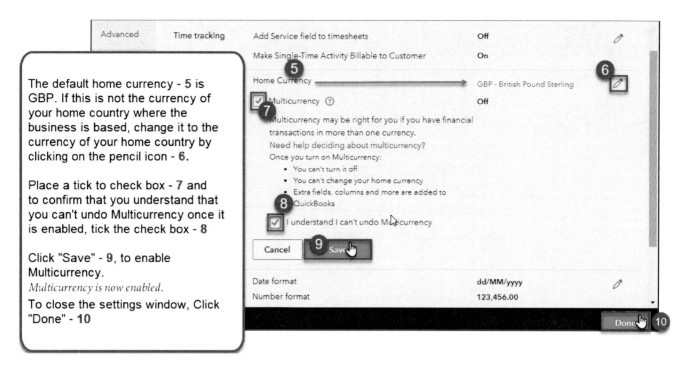

The default home currency - **5** is GBP. If this is not the currency of your home country where the business is based, change it to the currency of your home country by clicking on the pencil icon - **6**.

Place a tick to check box - **7** and to confirm that you understand that you can't undo Multicurrency once it is enabled, tick the check box - **8**

Click "Save" - **9**, to enable Multicurrency.
Multicurrency is now enabled.
To close the settings window, Click "Done" - **10**

Fig. 18

The Multicurrency section of the set up is now done. Let's move next to looking at the VAT codes in QuickBooks Online.

Task 1a(ii). Understanding QuickBooks Online VAT Codes

Horizon Tristar Ltd is registered for VAT and therefore has to charge VAT at the standard rate on all its taxable goods and services.

To understand more about VAT rates, visit HMRC website on http://www.hmrc.gov.uk/vat/start/ to find out what rate of VAT applies in any particular set of circumstances.

To understand the VAT codes in QuickBooks Online, we have to first set up VAT in QuickBooks.

To do so, **Click on Taxes on the left navigation bar > then click on Set up VAT**

Fig. 19

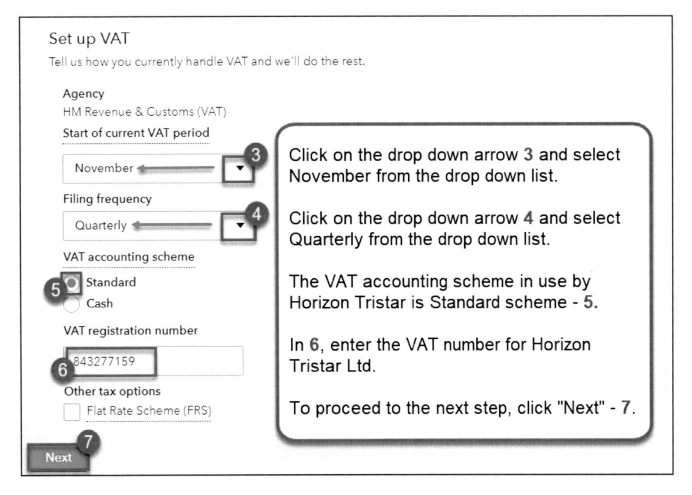

Fig. 20

Fig. 21

This space is for notes

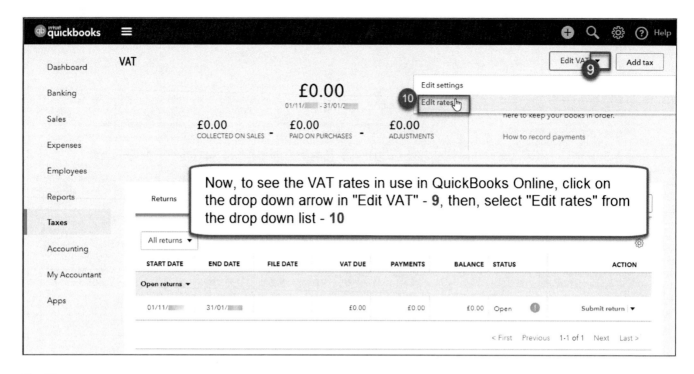

Fig. 22

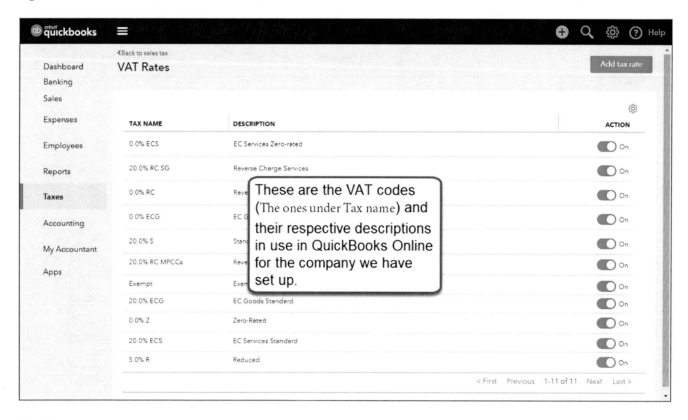

Fig. 23

The VAT setup is now complete. Let's move on to QuickBooks chart of accounts next.

Task 1a(iii). Understanding QuickBooks Online chart of accounts

Chart of Accounts is the complete list of all the company's accounts and balances. In QuickBooks, it represents and organises the company's assets, liabilities, income, and expense.

QuickBooks Online automatically creates your Chart of Accounts based on the type of company/business you choose when creating your company file.

Let's have a look at the chart of accounts for the company we created – Horizon Tristar Ltd.

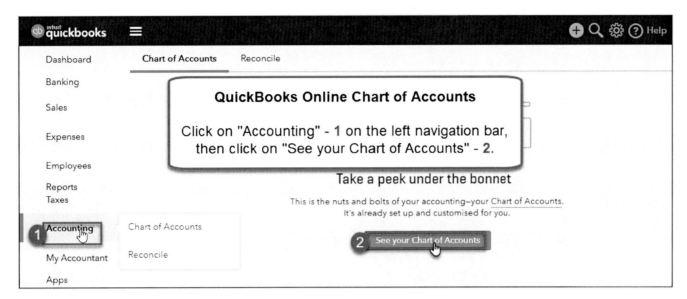

Fig. 24

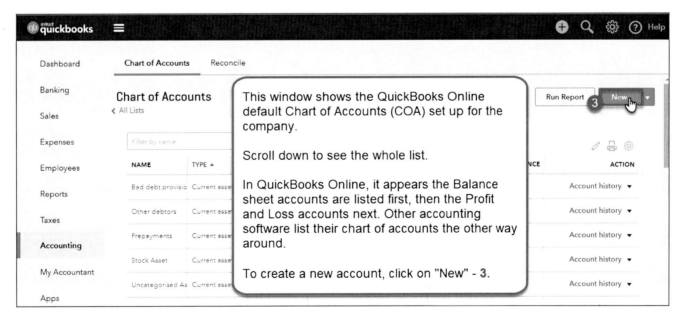

Fig. 25

Here are some new accounts you need to create:

- ✓ The Company Current Bank Account
- ✓ Petty Cash Account
- ✓ The bank Deposit Account
- ✓ Income/Sales account for Office furniture, Office equipment and Consumables

The Company Current Bank Account

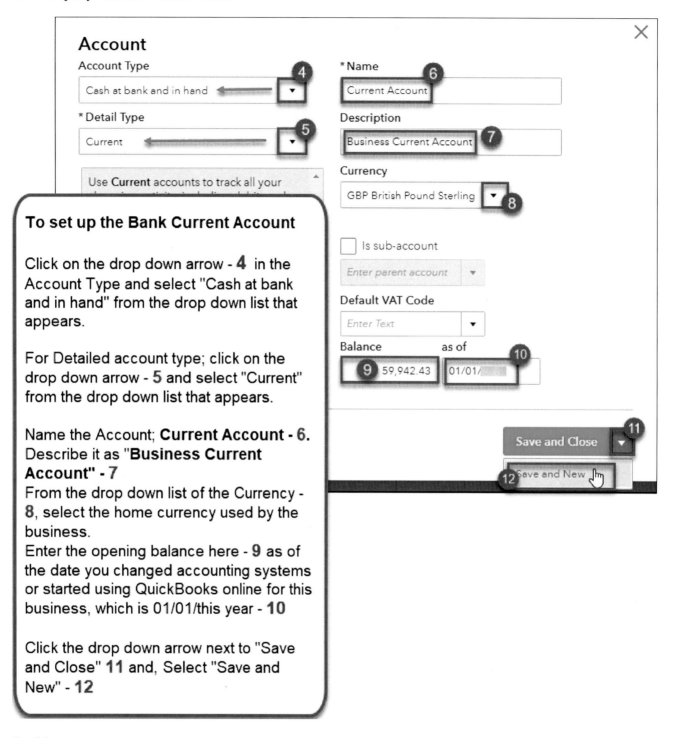

Account

Account Type

Cash at bank and in hand ← **4**

*Detail Type

Current ← **5**

Use **Current** accounts to track all your

*Name

Current Account **6**

Description

Business Current Account **7**

Currency

GBP British Pound Sterling **8**

☐ Is sub-account

Enter parent account

Default VAT Code

Enter Text

Balance   **as of**

9 59,942.43   01/01/ **10**

Save and Close **11**

12 Save and New

To set up the Bank Current Account

Click on the drop down arrow - **4** in the Account Type and select "Cash at bank and in hand" from the drop down list that appears.

For Detailed account type; click on the drop down arrow - **5** and select "Current" from the drop down list that appears.

Name the Account; **Current Account - 6.** Describe it as "**Business Current Account**" - **7**
From the drop down list of the Currency - **8**, select the home currency used by the business.
Enter the opening balance here - **9** as of the date you changed accounting systems or started using QuickBooks online for this business, which is 01/01/this year - **10**

Click the drop down arrow next to "Save and Close" **11** and, Select "Save and New" - **12**

Fig. 26

Next is Petty Cash Account.

Petty Cash Account

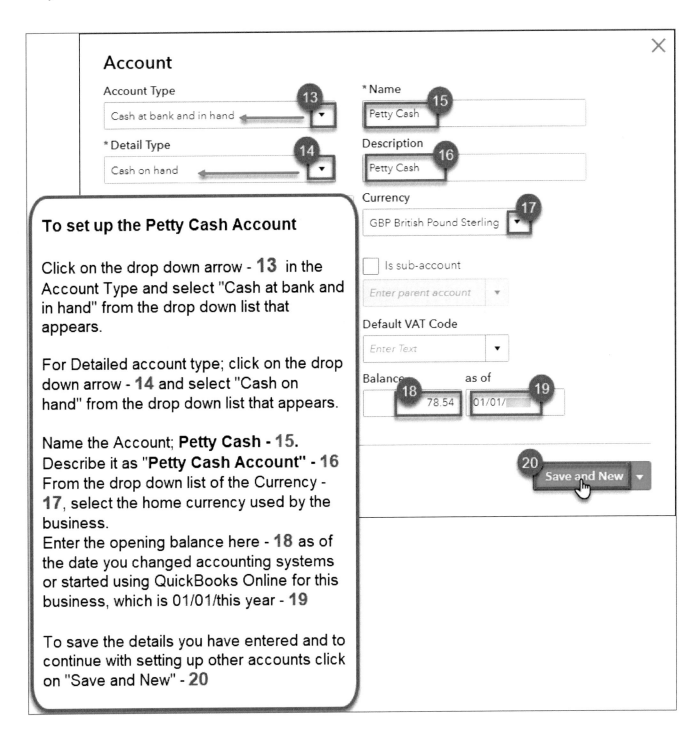

Fig. 27

This space is for notes

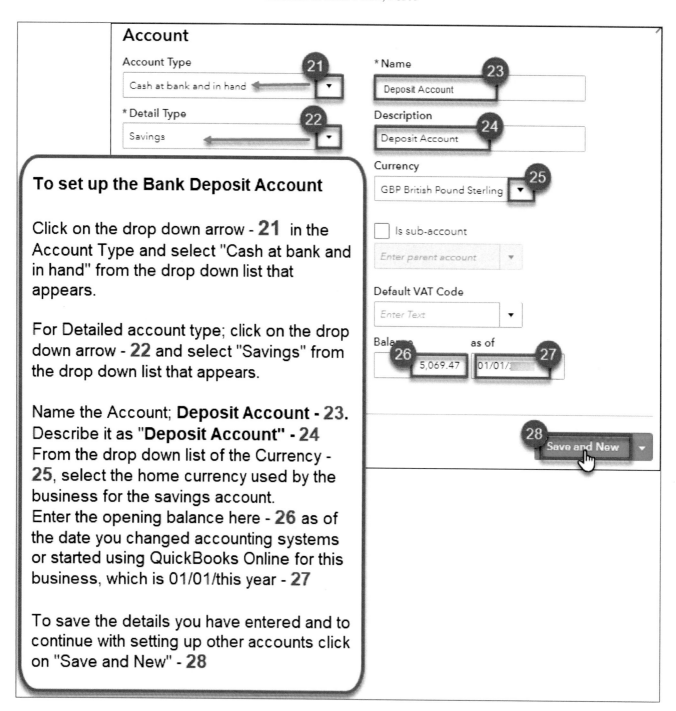

Account

Account Type   **21**   * Name   **23**

Cash at bank and in hand   ◄————   ▼   Deposit Account

* Detail Type   **22**   Description   **24**

Savings   ◄————   ▼   Deposit Account

To set up the Bank Deposit Account

Click on the drop down arrow - **21** in the
Account Type and select "Cash at bank and
in hand" from the drop down list that
appears.

For Detailed account type; click on the drop
down arrow - **22** and select "Savings" from
the drop down list that appears.

Name the Account; **Deposit Account - 23**.
Describe it as "**Deposit Account**" - **24**
From the drop down list of the Currency -
25, select the home currency used by the
business for the savings account.
Enter the opening balance here - **26** as of
the date you changed accounting systems
or started using QuickBooks Online for this
business, which is 01/01/this year - **27**

To save the details you have entered and to
continue with setting up other accounts click
on "Save and New" - **28**

Currency   **25**

GBP British Pound Sterling   ▼

☐ Is sub-account

Enter parent account   ▼

Default VAT Code

Enter Text   ▼

Balance   as of
26   **27**
5,069.47   01/01/

28
Save and New   ▼

Fig. 28

Current Account, Petty Cash Account and Bank Deposit Account done. If you needed to create a credit card account and Savings account, you would follow the same steps as above making sure you keep Account type as Cash at bank and in hand and changing all the other entries as required.

Let's move on to creating new accounts for income.

This space is for notes

Income Accounts:

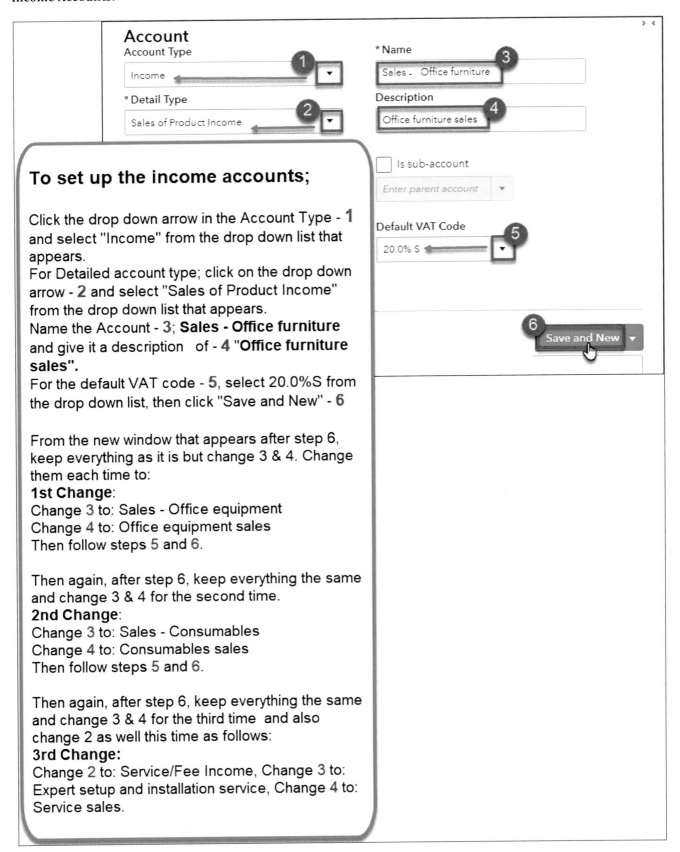

Fig. 29

Task 1b: Setting up Customers & Suppliers

Task 1b(i): Setting up Customers and corresponding opening balances

You can add Customers in QuickBooks online in two ways:

1. Add them directly as shown in the figure below
   or
2. Upload them using a csv template that has the customer details you want to add to QuickBooks Online.

The direct way of adding a Customer to QuickBooks Online is as illustrated in the figure below.

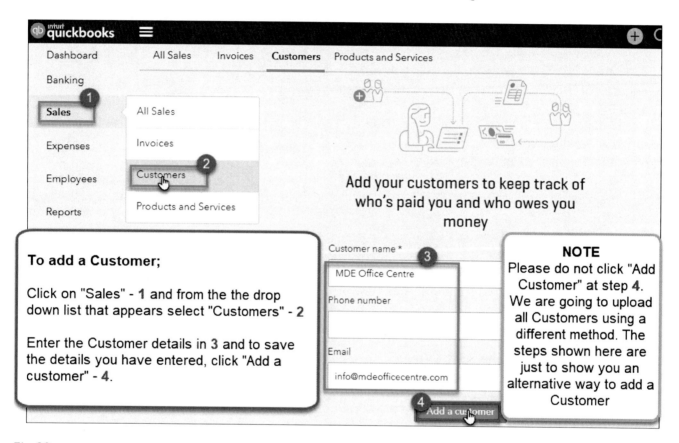

Fig. 30

Let's now look at an alternative way to add a customer to QuickBooks Online – the second option in our tutorial.

The second option is much faster and enables you to add more details about the customer at once. So, we will be using the second method, but I will also show you how to use the first method.

This space is for notes

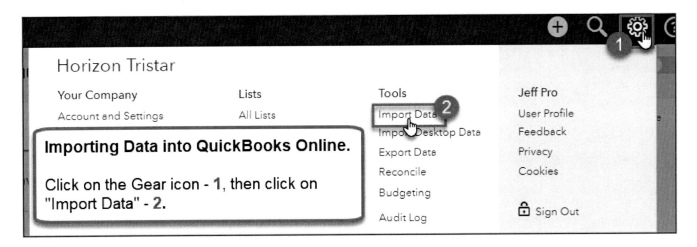

Fig. 31

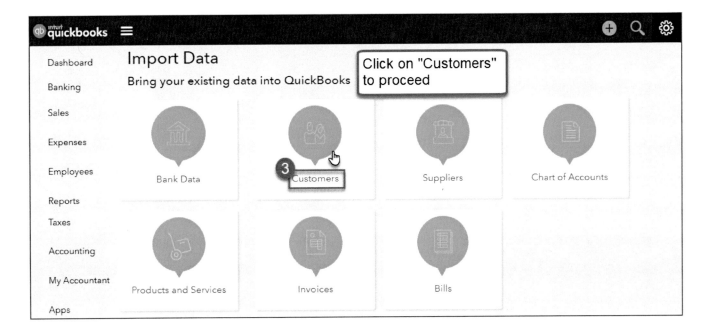

Fig.32

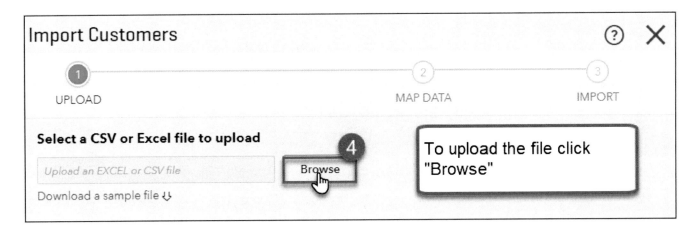

Fig. 33

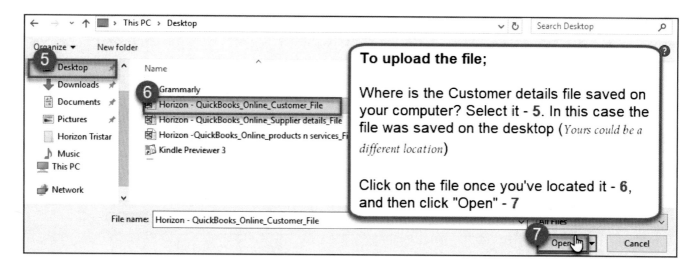

Fig. 34

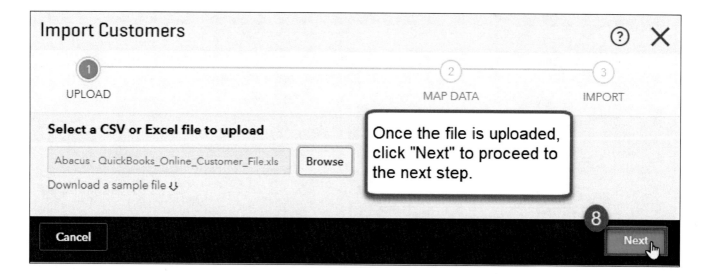

Fig. 35

This space is for notes

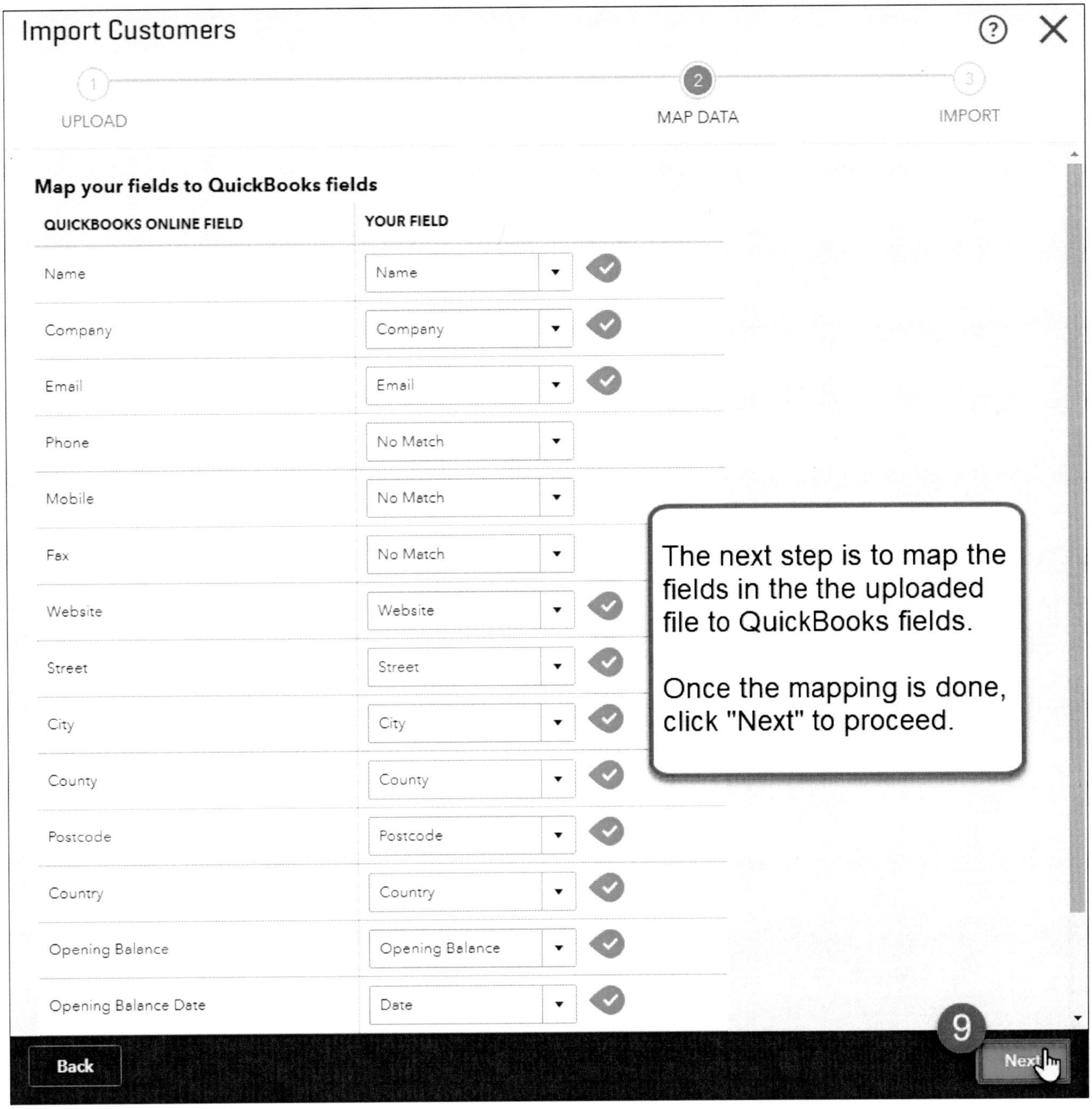

Fig. 36

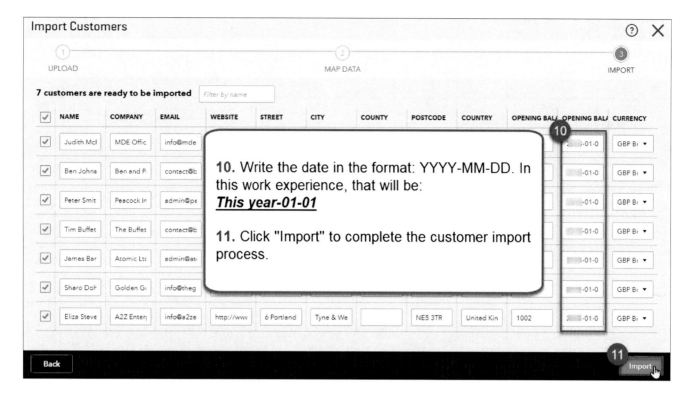

Fig. 37

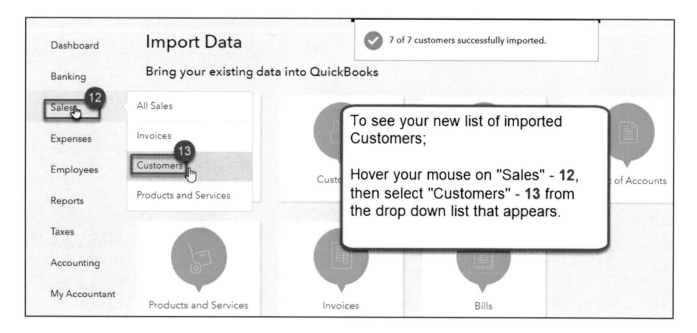

Fig. 38

This space is for notes

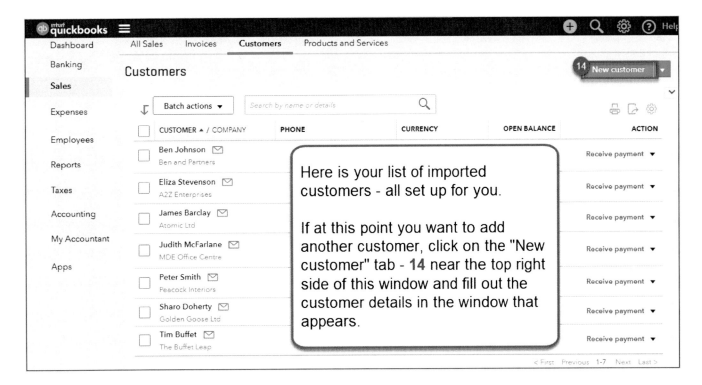

Fig. 39

Please note that when you import Customers to QuickBooks Online the way we have just done, QuickBooks puts the contact persons for each of the Customers you set up as the display names for those respective Customers. It does not pick up the Business names and puts them as display names. So, we will need to edit the Customers details so that the display names reflect the Company/Business name instead of the Customers contact persons name.

Editing Customer details:

The display name for the customers at this point is the Customer contact person. We need to change the display name to the Company name to make it easier later to invoice the customers through the create button.

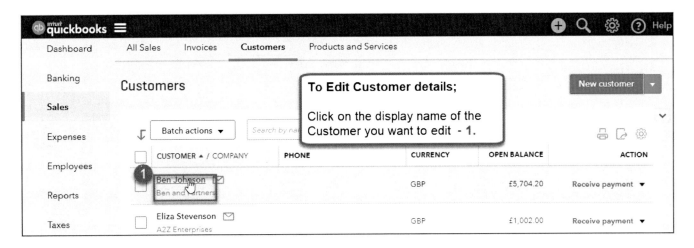

Fig. 40

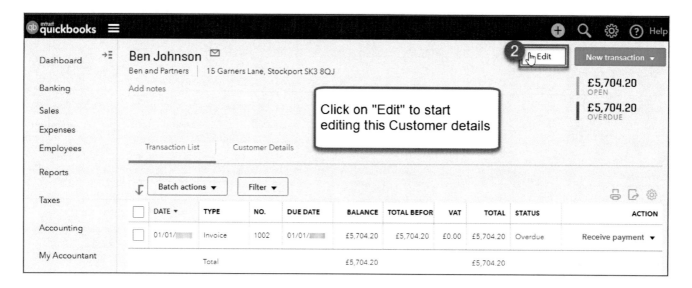

Fig. 41

Customer information

Title	First name	Middle name	Last name	Suffix
	Ben		Johnson	

Email

contact@benandpartners.co.uk

Company

Ben and Partners

Phone	Mobile	Fax

* Display name as

Ben and Partners ◄——————— **3** ▼

Other

Website

http://www.benandpartners.co.uk

☐ Is sub-customer

Change the display name from the contact name to the Company name - **3**.

Edit any of the details for this Customer as required and click "Save" - **4**

Steps 5 & 6, for now, are for illustration purposes only. Do not do them.
If you want to stop dealing with this Customer, you can do so by making their account inactive. For that, click "Make inactive" - **5**.
If you have just realised at this point that you didn't actually need to edit this Customer details, just click "Cancel" - **6**.

6 Cancel | **5** Make inactive | Privacy | **4** Save

Fig. 42

Please go ahead and edit the display names for the rest of the other Customers. Do not proceed to the next task before editing the display names for all the Customers.

Task 1b(ii): Setting up Suppliers and corresponding opening balances

You can add Suppliers in QuickBooks online in two ways:

i.   Add them directly, or,
ii. Upload them using a csv template that has the Suppliers details you want to add to QuickBooks Online.

The direct way of adding a Supplier to QuickBooks Online is as illustrated in the figure below.

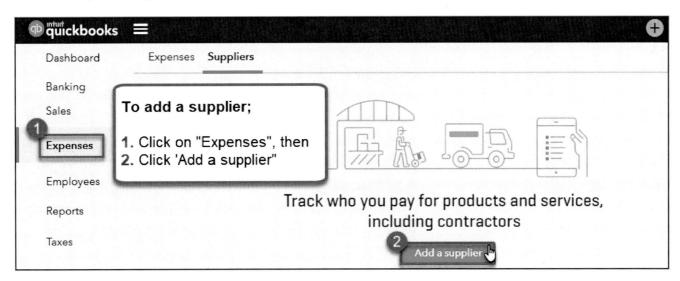

Fig. 43

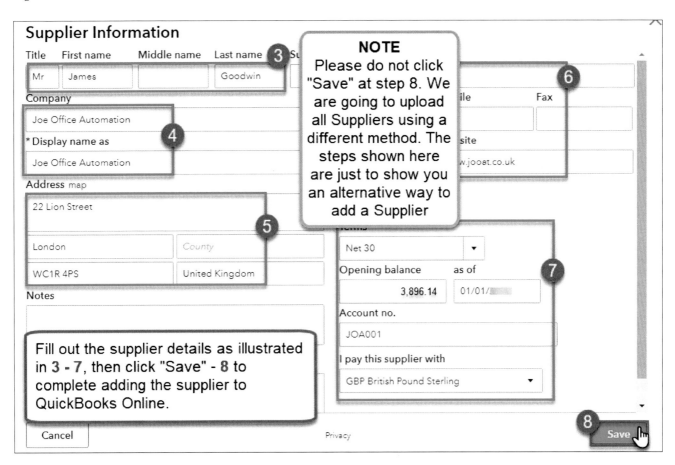

Fig. 44

The second option is much faster and enables you to add more suppliers at once. So, let's do it.

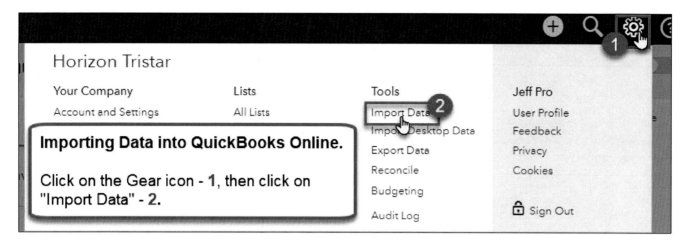

Fig. 45

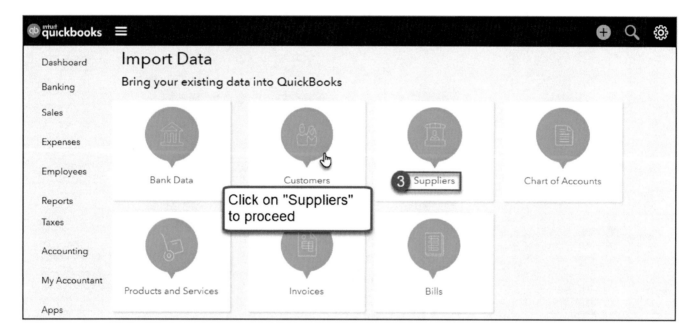

Fig. 46

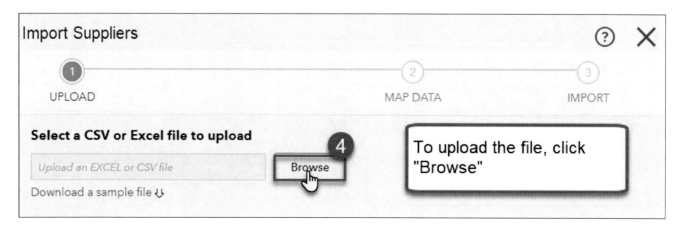

Fig. 47

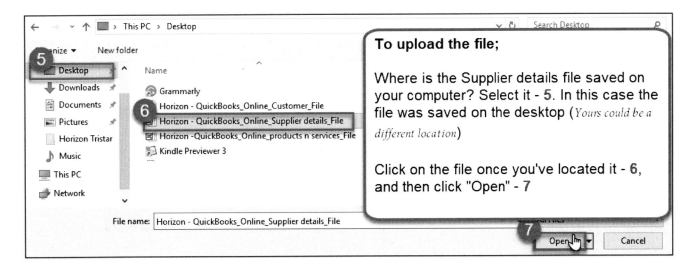

Fig. 48

Fig. 49

This space is for notes

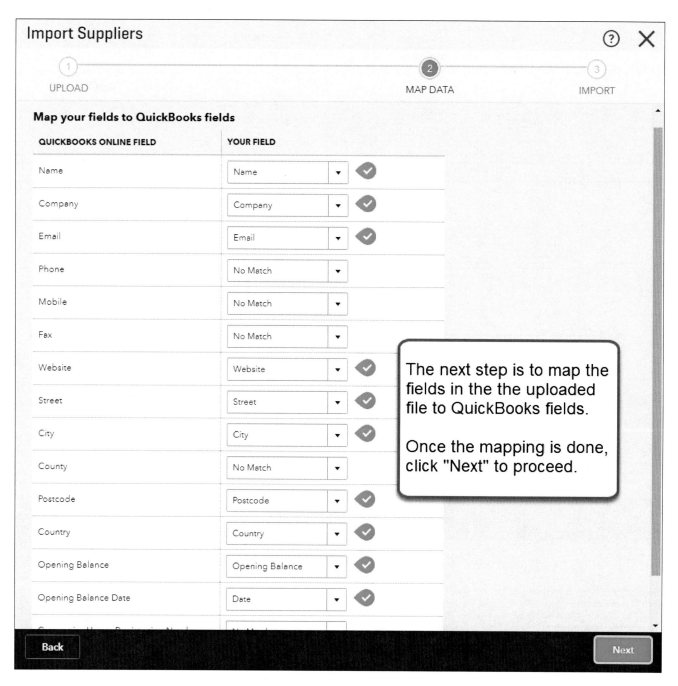

Fig. 50

This space is for your notes

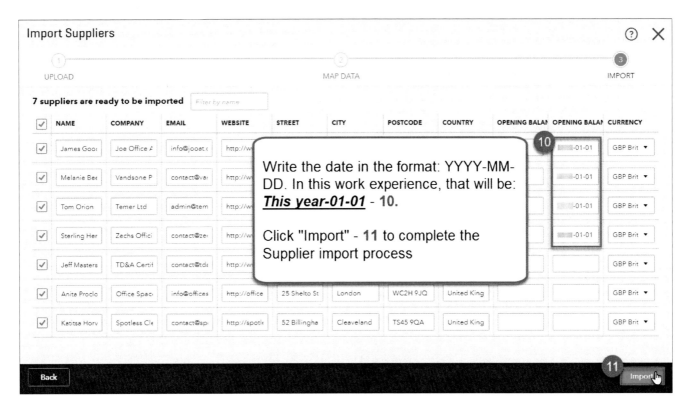

Fig. 51

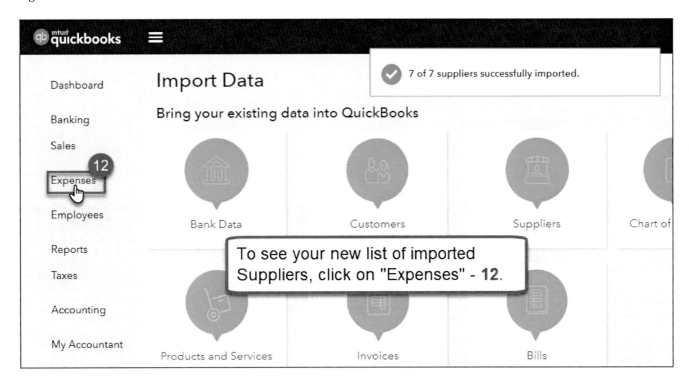

Fig. 52

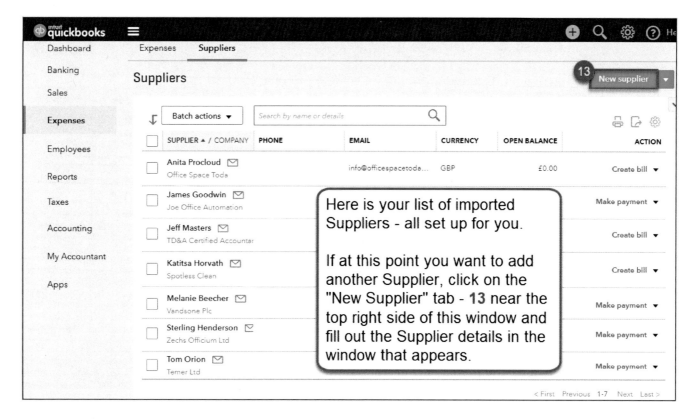

Fig. 53

Please note that when you import Suppliers to QuickBooks Online the way we have just done, QuickBooks puts the contact persons for each of the Suppliers you set up as the display names for those respective Suppliers. It does not pick up the Suppliers business or Company names. So, we will need to edit the supplier details so that the display names reflect the Suppliers Company/Business name instead of the Suppliers contact persons name.

Editing Supplier details:

The display name for the customers at this point is the Supplier contact person. We need to change the display name to the Company name to make it easier later to record invoices/bills from the Suppliers through the create button.

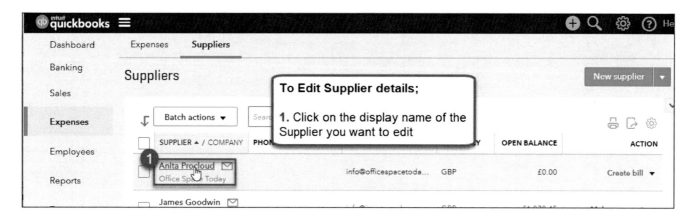

Fig. 54

Fig. 55

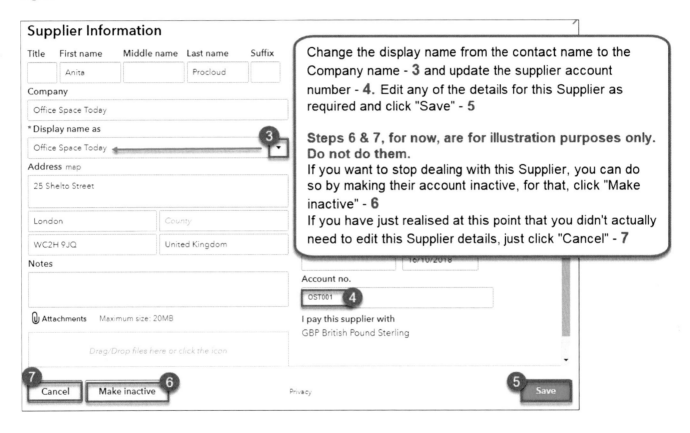

Fig. 56

Please go ahead and edit the display names for the rest of the other Suppliers. Do not proceed to the next task before editing the display names for all the Suppliers.

Task 1c: Setting up products & services

You can get to add a product or service in QuickBooks Online in two ways;

You can do so by clicking the Gear icon, then selecting products and services, then clicking on "Add a product or service" - see below

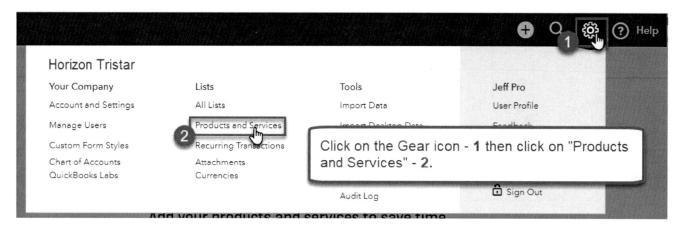

Fig. 57

Or,

You can also get to add a product or service by clicking on Sales, Products and Services, then click on "Add a product or service – see below.

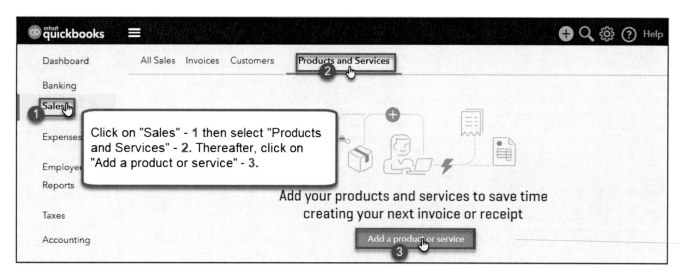

Fig. 58

This space is for notes

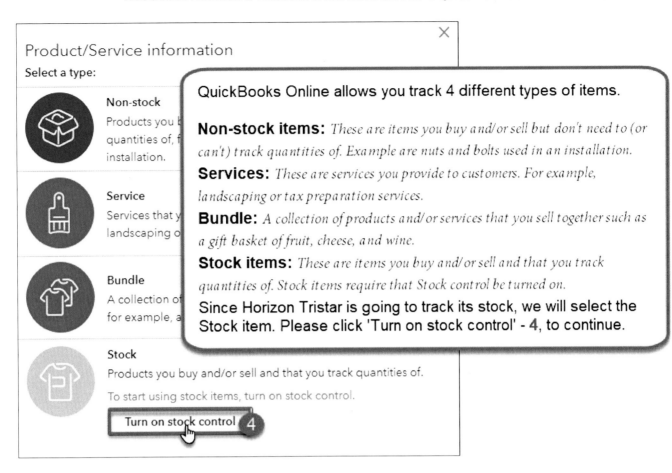

Fig. 59

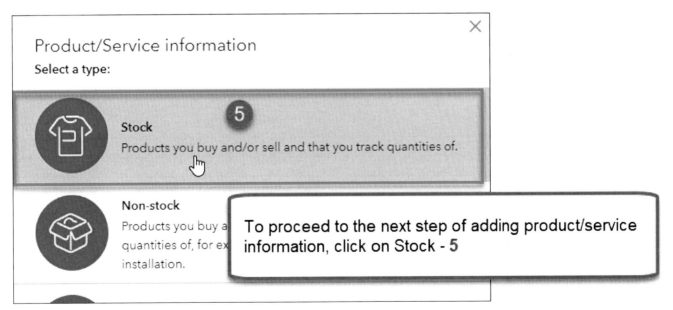

Fig. 60

This space is for notes

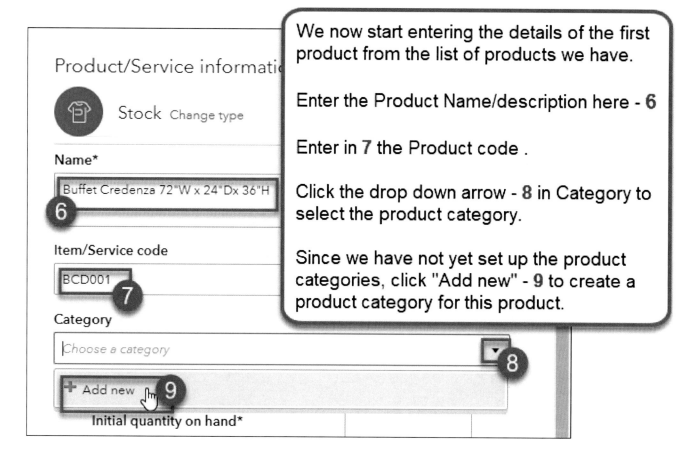

We now start entering the details of the first product from the list of products we have.

Enter the Product Name/description here - 6

Enter in 7 the Product code .

Click the drop down arrow - 8 in Category to select the product category.

Since we have not yet set up the product categories, click "Add new" - 9 to create a product category for this product.

Fig. 61

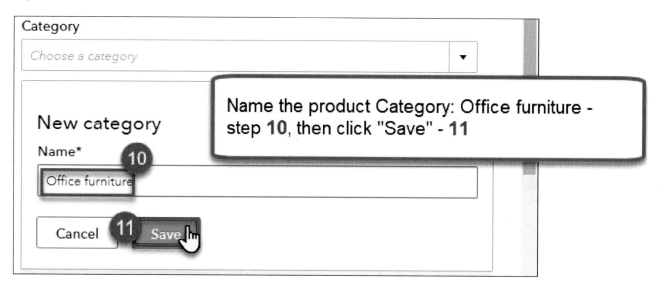

Name the product Category: Office furniture - step 10, then click "Save" - 11

Fig. 62

This space is for notes

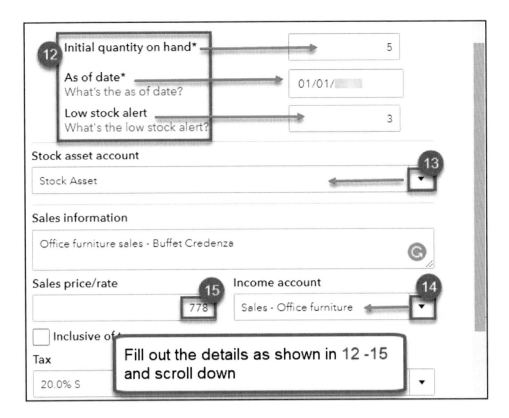

Fig. 63

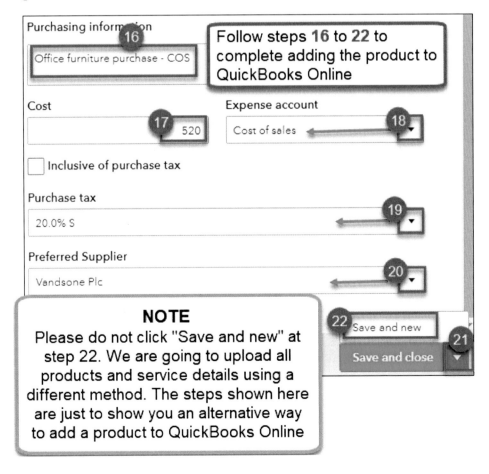

Fig. 64

The alternative way to add products and services to QuickBooks Online is by uploading a CSV or excel file that has all the products and services already added. Let me show you how to do it.

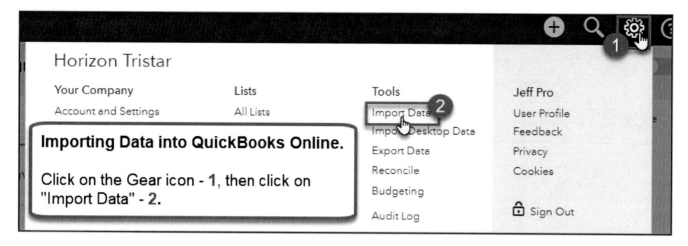

Fig. 65

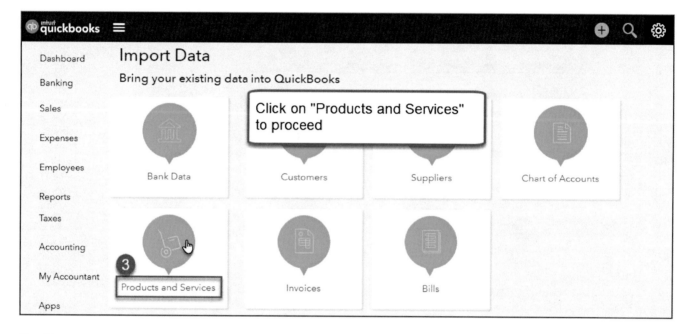

Fig. 66

This space is for notes

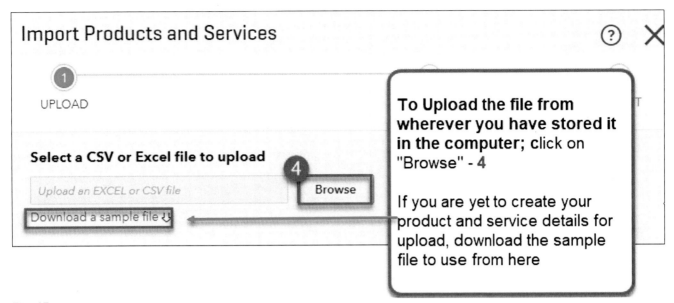

Fig. 67

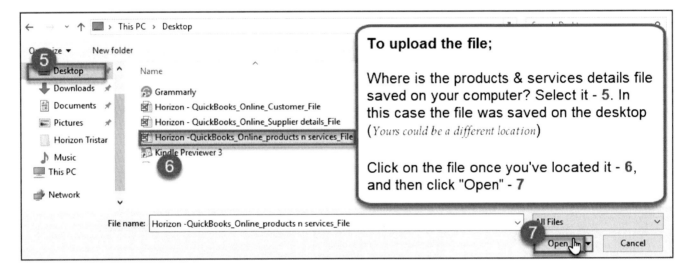

Fig. 68

Fig. 69

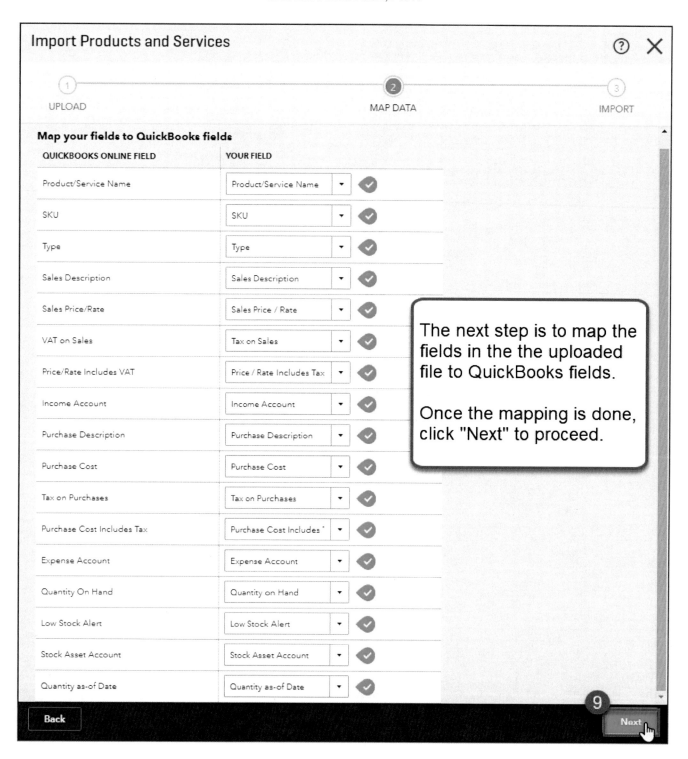

Fig. 70

This space is for notes

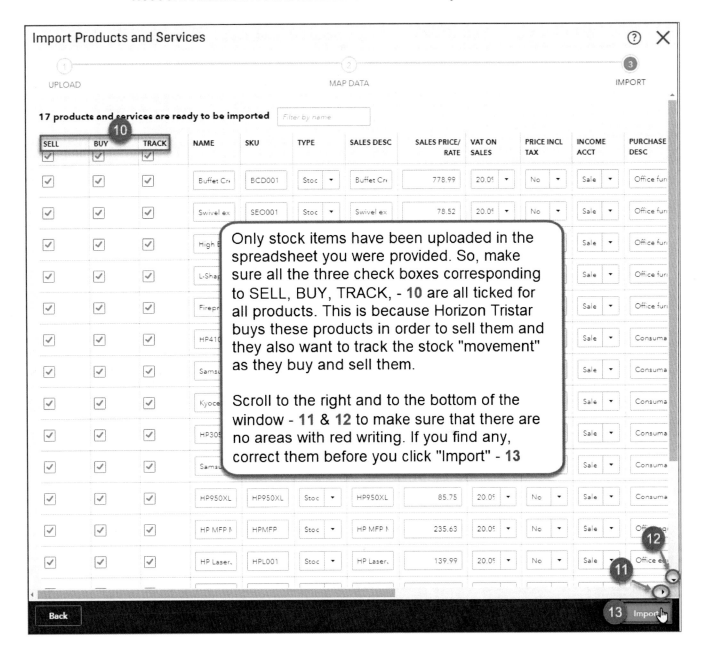

Fig. 71

This space is for notes

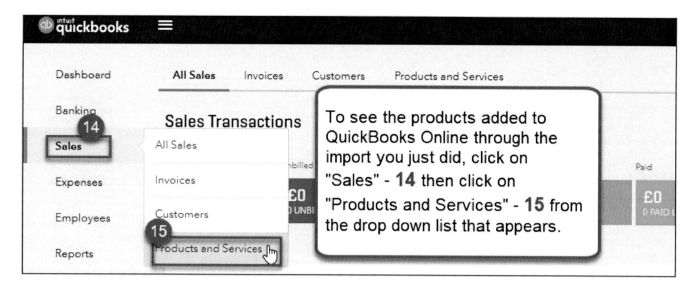

To see the products added to QuickBooks Online through the import you just did, click on "Sales" - **14** then click on "Products and Services" - **15** from the drop down list that appears.

Fig. 72

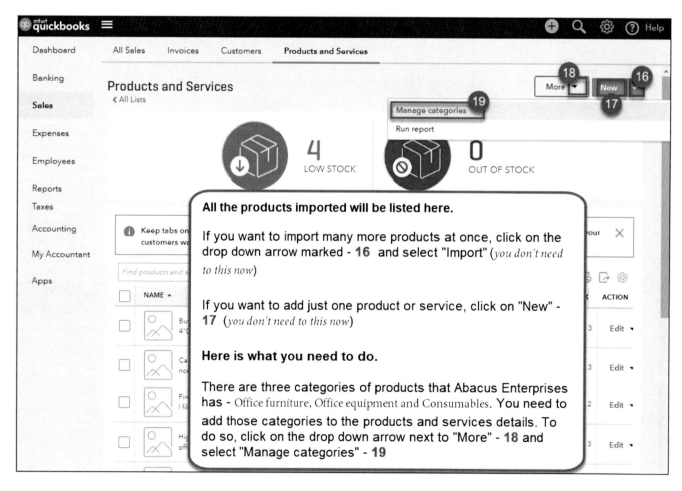

All the products imported will be listed here.

If you want to import many more products at once, click on the drop down arrow marked - **16** and select "Import" (*you don't need to this now*)

If you want to add just one product or service, click on "New" - **17** (*you don't need to this now*)

Here is what you need to do.

There are three categories of products that Abacus Enterprises has - Office furniture, Office equipment and Consumables. You need to add those categories to the products and services details. To do so, click on the drop down arrow next to "More" - **18** and select "Manage categories" - **19**

Fig. 73

Fig. 74

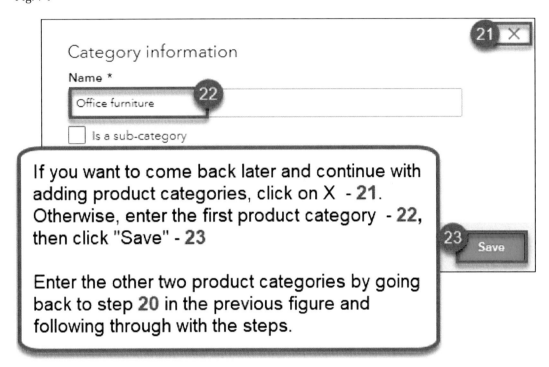

Category information

Name *

Office furniture 22

☐ Is a sub-category

If you want to come back later and continue with adding product categories, click on X - **21**. Otherwise, enter the first product category - **22**, then click "Save" - **23**

Enter the other two product categories by going back to step **20** in the previous figure and following through with the steps.

Fig. 75

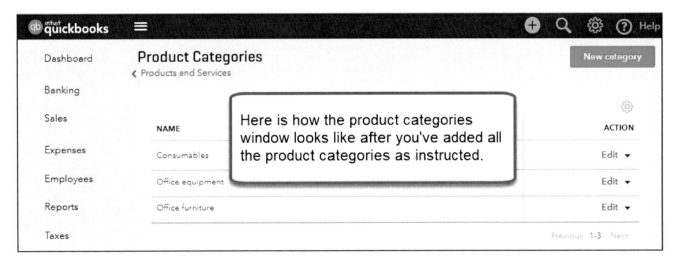

Here is how the product categories window looks like after you've added all the product categories as instructed.

Fig. 76

Task 1d: Setting up the fixed assets register

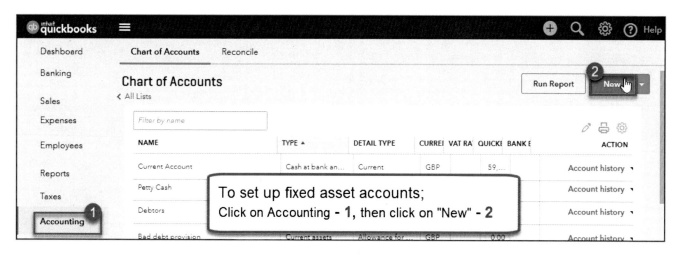

Fig. 77

Using the list of the Fixed assets you have been given, here is how to set up the fixed asset accounts for them. I will do the first one with you; then you can carry on with the rest.

Fixed assets are any assets that cannot be easily converted to cash. They are typically tangible, physical things that have an economic life of longer than a year. These include buildings, vehicles, furniture and office equipment. Fixed assets normally don't include intangible things like royalties and brand names.

Fixed assets are also known as non-current and long-term assets. They may also be referred to as property, plant and equipment. They are assets intended to be used within the business, not sold or converted to cash.

This space is for notes

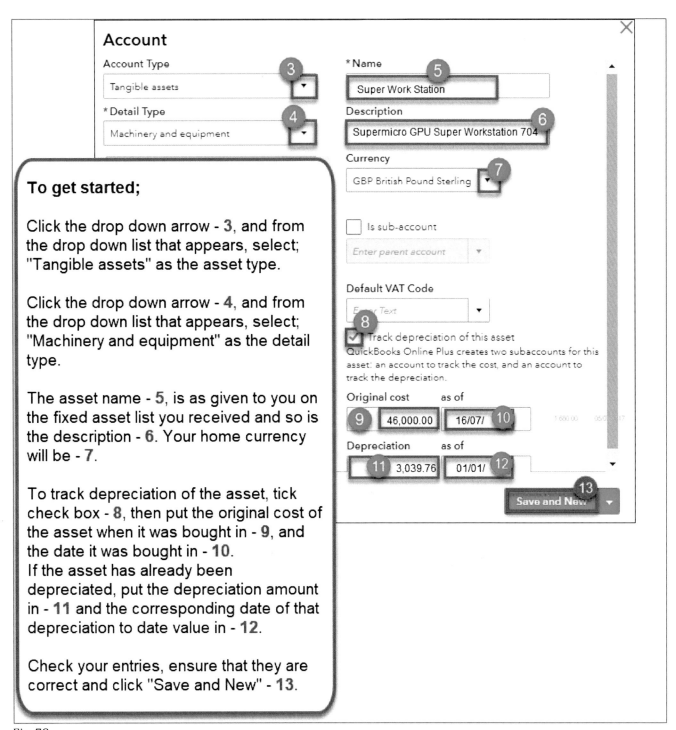

Account

Account Type
Tangible assets ③ ▼

*Detail Type
Machinery and equipment ④ ▼

*Name ⑤
Super Work Station

Description ⑥
Supermicro GPU Super Workstation 704

Currency ⑦
GBP British Pound Sterling ▼

☐ Is sub-account
Enter parent account ▼

Default VAT Code
Enter Text ▼

⑧ ☑ Track depreciation of this asset
QuickBooks Online Plus creates two subaccounts for this asset: an account to track the cost, and an account to track the depreciation.

Original cost   as of
⑨ 46,000.00   16/07/ ⑩

Depreciation   as of
⑪ 3,039.76   01/01/ ⑫

⑬ **Save and New** ▼

To get started;

Click the drop down arrow - **3**, and from the drop down list that appears, select; "Tangible assets" as the asset type.

Click the drop down arrow - **4**, and from the drop down list that appears, select; "Machinery and equipment" as the detail type.

The asset name - **5**, is as given to you on the fixed asset list you received and so is the description - **6**. Your home currency will be - **7**.

To track depreciation of the asset, tick check box - **8**, then put the original cost of the asset when it was bought in - **9**, and the date it was bought in - **10**.
If the asset has already been depreciated, put the depreciation amount in - **11** and the corresponding date of that depreciation to date value in - **12**.

Check your entries, ensure that they are correct and click "Save and New" - **13**.

Fig. 78

This space is for notes

Task 1e: Setting up opening balances from the Trial balance

Overview of this task

The opening balance is the balance that is brought forward from the end of one accounting period to the beginning of a new accounting period or from one accounting system to a new accounting system.

The funds in a company's/business accounts at the start of a new financial period are called the opening balances. The opening balance is the first entry in a company's accounts, either when they are first starting up or at the start of a new financial year or when changing accounting systems.

In the case of a new company, the opening balances usually are just two: one is the cash on hand, and the other is the capital contributed by the company's founders or loan from investors.

Opening balances are entered into the accounting system using the double entry accounting principles.
The best way to gather your opening balances is to prepare an opening trial balance. This is done by listing all your nominal accounts and the value (balance) on each account.

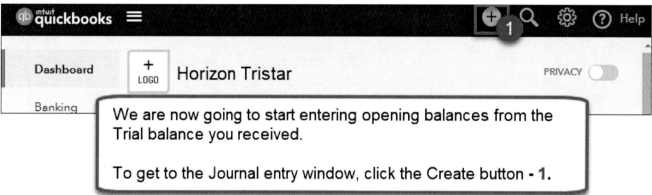

Fig. 79

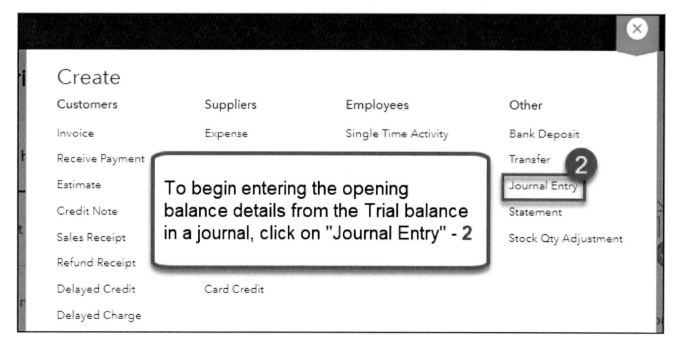

Fig. 80

In the set-up steps earlier on did record opening balances for the items in the trial balance up until Creditors Control Account, we will continue from Sales tax Control Account (Credit balance of 22,182.53 in the Trial balance) and then enter the rest of the balances as shown in the Trial balance.

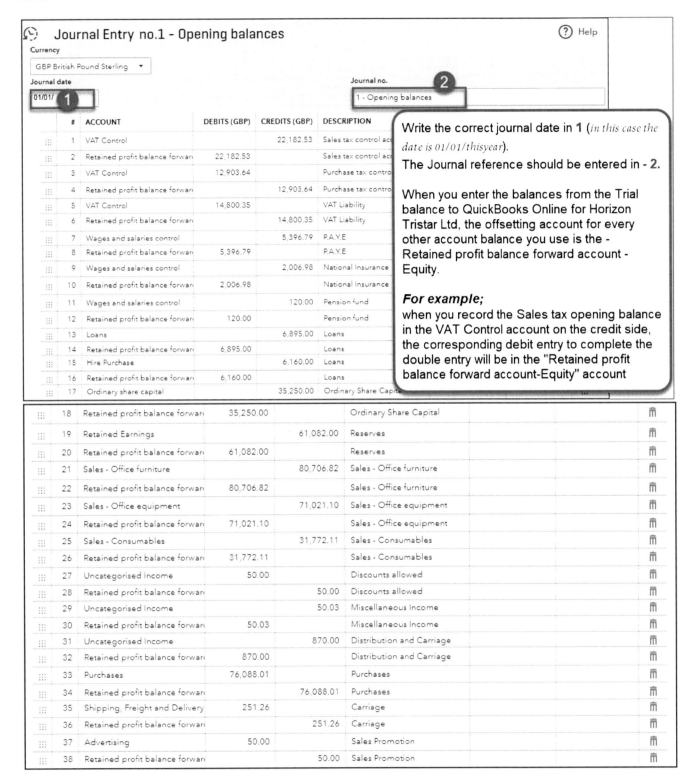

⠿	39	Advertising	465.00		Advertising			🏛
⠿	40	Retained profit balance forward		465.00	Advertising			🏛
⠿	41	Advertising	115.00		Gifts and Samples			🏛
⠿	42	Retained profit balance forward		115.00	Gifts and Samples			🏛
⠿	43	Advertising	1,050.00		P.R. (Literature & Brochures)			🏛
⠿	44	Retained profit balance forward		1,050.00	P.R. (Literature & Brochures)			🏛
⠿	45	Gross Wages	32,472.11		Gross wages			🏛
⠿	46	Retained profit balance forward		32,472.11	Gross wages			🏛
⠿	47	Employer's NI contributions	3,327.24		Employers NI			🏛
⠿	48	Retained profit balance forward		3,327.24	Employers NI			🏛
⠿	49	SSP	107.60		Statutory Sick Pay reclaimed			🏛
⠿	50	Retained profit balance forward		107.60	Statutory Sick Pay reclaimed			🏛
⠿	51	SMP	255.00		Statutory Maternity Pay			🏛
⠿	52	Retained profit balance forward		255.00	Statutory Maternity Pay			🏛
⠿	53	Rent	12,720.00		Rent			🏛
⠿	54	Retained profit balance forward		12,720.00	Rent			🏛
⠿	55	Light and heat	1,052.00		Electricity			🏛
⠿	56	Retained profit balance forward		1,052.00	Electricity			🏛
⠿	57	Motor running expenses	620.95		Fuel and Oil			🏛
⠿	58	Retained profit balance forward		620.95	Fuel and Oil			🏛
⠿	59	Motor running expenses	492.15		Repairs & Servicing			🏛
⠿	60	Retained profit balance forward		492.15	Repairs & Servicing			🏛
⠿	61	Motor running expenses	67.50		Miscellaneous Motor Expen			🏛
⠿	62	Retained profit balance forward		67.50	Miscellaneous Motor Expen			🏛
⠿	63	Motor running expenses	90.27		Scale Charges			🏛
⠿	64	Retained profit balance forward		90.27	Scale Charges			🏛
⠿	65	Travelling expenses	201.00		Travelling Expenses			🏛
⠿	66	Retained profit balance forward		201.00	Travelling Expenses			🏛
⠿	67	Travelling expenses	150.00		Car hire			🏛
⠿	68	Retained profit balance forward		150.00	Car hire			🏛
⠿	69	Travelling expenses	720.00		Hotels			🏛
⠿	70	Retained profit balance forward		720.00	Hotels			🏛
⠿	71	Entertaining	149.50		U.K. Etertainment			🏛
⠿	72	Retained profit balance forward		149.50	U.K. Etertainment			🏛
⠿	73	Printing, postage and stationer	54.10		Printing			🏛
⠿	74	Retained profit balance forward		54.10	Printing			🏛
⠿	75	Printing, postage and stationer	102.50		Postage and Carriage			🏛
⠿	76	Retained profit balance forward		102.50	Postage and Carriage			🏛
⠿	77	Telephone	178.72		Telephone			🏛
⠿	78	Retained profit balance forward		178.72	Telephone			🏛

Fig. 81

This space is for notes

58

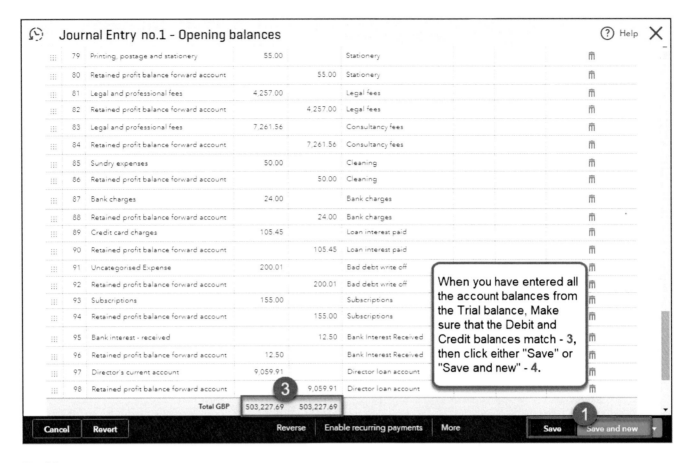

Fig. 82

This space is for notes

What is Opening balance

The opening balance is the balance that is brought forward from the end of one accounting period to the beginning of a new accounting period or from one accounting system to a new accounting system.

TASK 2: HOW TO DO BUDGETING IN QUICKBOOKS ONLINE

In the context of business management, the purpose of budgeting includes the following three aspects:
- A forecast of income and expenditure (and thereby profitability)
- A tool for decision making
- A means to monitor business performance

A carefully constructed budget allows a business to continually track where they are financially. This allows for strategic, long-term planning for everything from current operating costs to potential expansion. Knowing where the budget stands opens up the ability to hire new staffers, invest in new product lines and set earning goals in line with the organisations' corporate financial objectives.

Let's get going with producing Horizon Tristar's budget.

To create, access, edit, or delete budgets in QuickBooks Online, you must have Administrator Access Rights (All Access Rights).

Your budget will start with the first month of the fiscal year you have set up in QuickBooks Online (For Horizon Tristar Ltd it is November of last year). Therefore, you should check that the Fiscal Year setting is accurate before continuing with the Budget set up process.

Here is what you need to do to check Fiscal Year settings:

1. Select the **Gear icon** at the top, then choose **Account and Settings** (or **Company Settings**).
2. Select **Advanced**.
3. Check if the first month of fiscal year is ***November***. If not, select the pencil icon in the Accounting section and set it to November last year.
4. Select **Save**.

With that done, let's proceed.

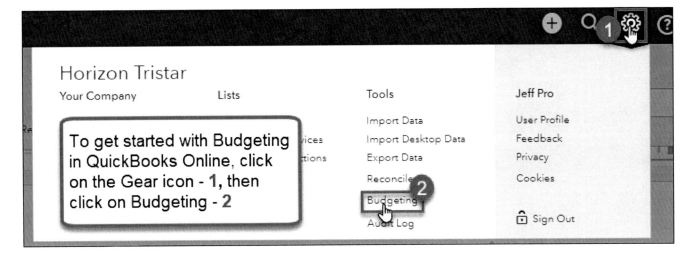

Fig. 83

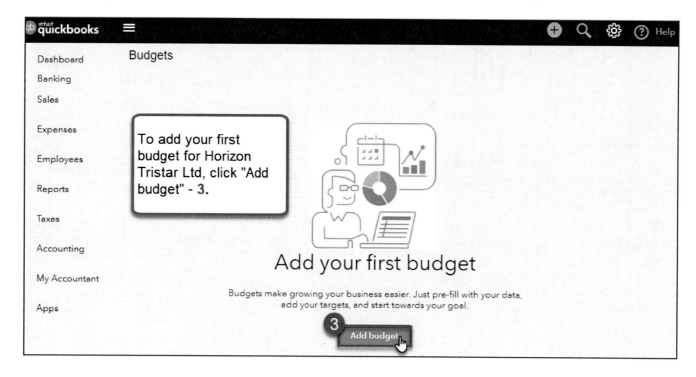

Fig. 84

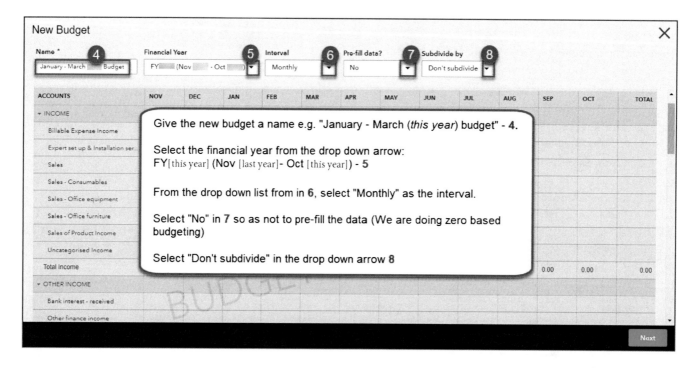

Fig. 85

This space is for notes

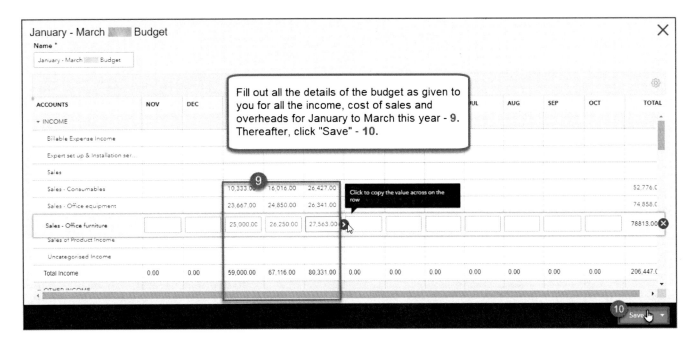

Fig. 86

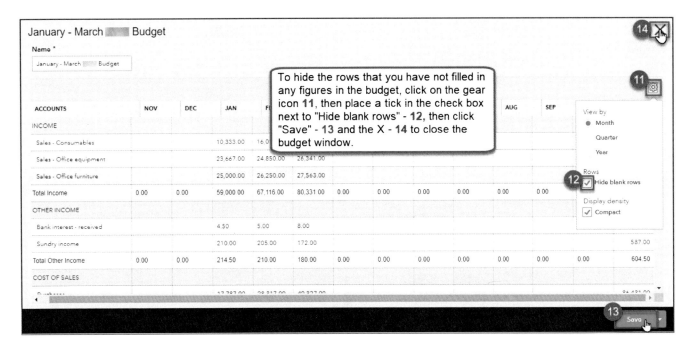

Fig. 87

This space is for notes

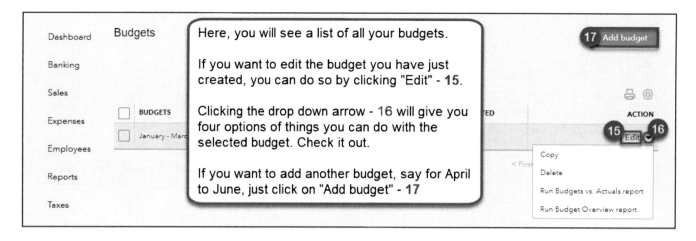

Fig. 88

That's it, you have managed to set up Horizon Tristar's budget for January to March this year. You will have the opportunity in March to compare the budget figures you have just entered to the actual figures that will reflect the actual performance of the business and with that, do some variance analysis.

We will now move on to the next task – Doing Accounts payable tasks.

This space is for notes

TASK 3: DOING THE ACCOUNTS PAYABLE TASKS

How to analyse a financial document before recording it.

Let's do this task by analysing one of the invoices received by Horizon Tristar Ltd.

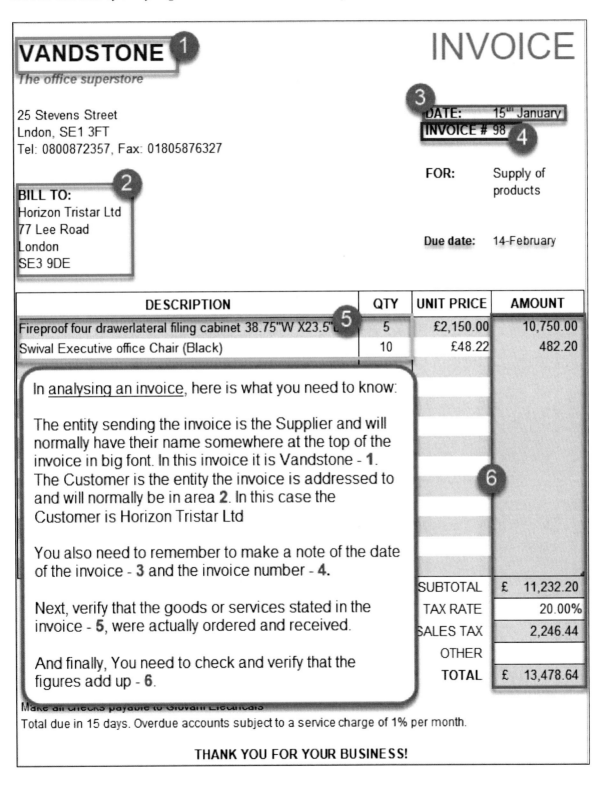

VANDSTONE ①
The office superstore

25 Stevens Street
Lndon, SE1 3FT
Tel: 0800872357, Fax: 01805876327

BILL TO: ②
Horizon Tristar Ltd
77 Lee Road
London
SE3 9DE

INVOICE

③
DATE: 15ᵀᴴ January
INVOICE # 98 ④

FOR: Supply of products

Due date: 14-February

DESCRIPTION	QTY	UNIT PRICE	AMOUNT
Fireproof four drawerlateral filing cabinet 38.75"W X23.5" ⑤	5	£2,150.00	10,750.00
Swival Executive office Chair (Black)	10	£48.22	482.20

⑥

In <u>analysing an invoice</u>, here is what you need to know:

The entity sending the invoice is the Supplier and will normally have their name somewhere at the top of the invoice in big font. In this invoice it is Vandstone - **1**.
The Customer is the entity the invoice is addressed to and will normally be in area **2**. In this case the Customer is Horizon Tristar Ltd

You also need to remember to make a note of the date of the invoice - **3** and the invoice number - **4**.

Next, verify that the goods or services stated in the invoice - **5**, were actually ordered and received.

And finally, You need to check and verify that the figures add up - **6**.

SUBTOTAL	£	11,232.20
TAX RATE		20.00%
SALES TAX		2,246.44
OTHER		
TOTAL	£	13,478.64

Make all checks payable to Giovani Electricals
Total due in 15 days. Overdue accounts subject to a service charge of 1% per month.

THANK YOU FOR YOUR BUSINESS!

Fig. 89

Here are further details on the analysis of an invoice for your consideration.

Features of a valid invoice	
Address details	Invoices must be addressed to the business or department within the organisation. The name of an individual may also appear as long as this is an authorised signatory
Status of document	The document must be an invoice rather than a delivery note, order acknowledgement or statement. Some invoices from smaller entities may not contain all of the details for VAT purposes. If the word 'invoice' appears on the document, then it should be treated as an invoice.
Accurate	The Gross value in the invoice should be arithmetically correct [Subtotal plus Tax (if any)].
VAT invoice	Invoices that charge VAT must contain all of the following details in addition to those given above: • *The entity's VAT number;* • *The entity's trading name and address;* • *Description of goods or services;* • *Invoice number;* • *Invoice date;* • *Time of supply - 'tax point' if different from the invoice date;* • *Analysis of VAT charged, including value and rate used*

Task 3a: A brief overview of the Accounts payable process:

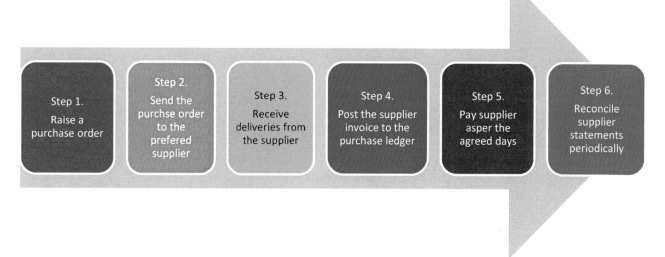

Step 1.
Raise a purchase order

Step 2.
Send the purchse order to the prefered supplier

Step 3.
Receive deliveries from the supplier

Step 4.
Post the supplier invoice to the purchase ledger

Step 5.
Pay supplier asper the agreed days

Step 6.
Reconcile supplier statements periodically

Fig. 90

A Note

When a company orders and receives goods (or services) in advance of paying for them, we say that the company is purchasing the goods *on account* or *on credit*. The supplier (or vendor) of the goods on credit is also referred to as a creditor. If the company receiving the goods does not sign a promissory note, the vendor's bill or invoice will be recorded by the company in its liability account Accounts Payable (or Trade Payables).

Accounts Payable will normally have a credit balance. Hence, when a Supplier/vendor invoice is recorded, Accounts Payable will be credited and another account must be debited (as required by double-entry accounting). When an account payable is paid, Accounts Payable will be debited and Cash will be credited. Therefore, the credit balance in Accounts Payable should be equal to the amount of vendor invoices that have been recorded but have not yet been paid.

Under the *accrual method of accounting*, the company receiving goods or services on credit must report the liability no later than the date they were received. The same date is used to record the debit entry to an expense or asset account as appropriate. Hence, accountants say that under the accrual method of accounting expenses are reported when they are *incurred* (not when they are paid).

Let's spend some time exploring the steps mentioned in the figure above, shall we?

To begin with, it is essential to know that a business can buy goods & services both in cash and on credit. When it buys on credit, it creates – a payable (which means something purchased on credit and payment will be due at a later date). When it buys in cash, that's different; it has made a cash payment.

Let's look at those steps in the figure above.

Step 1: Raising a purchase order

First, let's define a purchase order, shall we?

Of course, here is what it is:

A purchase order is a legally binding document between a supplier and a buyer. It details the items the buyer agrees to purchase at a certain price point. It also outlines the delivery/shipping date and terms of payment for the buyer.

Purchase orders are often used when a buyer wants to purchase supplies or inventory on account; this means that the supplier delivers or ships the purchased items before payment, with the purchase order serving as its risk protection.

How should you go about raising a purchase order?

First, a purchase requisition for the details of what needs to be purchased should be raised by the person or department that needs the goods or services. The request should then be sent to the appropriate budget holder(s) for approval.

When the Budget Holder approves the requisition, it should then be sent to the purchasing department, and a Purchase Order will be raised. The order will typically have:
- Purchase Order (PO) number
- Delivery/Shipping date
- Billing address
- Delivery/Shipping address
- Requested terms

- A list of products/services with quantities and price

Step 2: Placing the order with the preferred supplier.

The Purchase Order can then be faxed or emailed to the supplier if necessary.

Suppliers should not be asked/requested to supply goods until the purchase order has been generated. The purchase order number should be given to the supplier who should in turn quote this number on their invoice.

Step 3: Receiving delivery of goods/services from a supplier

When the supplier delivers the goods, you should then raise a Goods Received Note (GRN). A GRN is a record of goods received at the point of receipt. You should raise the GRN after inspecting delivery for proof of order receipt. It's used by stores, procurement and finance to raise any issues, update your stock records and it should be matched against the original purchase order and supplier invoice, to allow payment to be made.

GRNs play an essential part in the accounts payable process by confirming that items have been received as expected, in accordance with the original purchase order, and that the items can, therefore, be invoiced by the supplier and subsequently paid for by the buyer.

Step 4: Post the invoice from supplier to the purchase ledger

The "Tax Invoice" received from the supplier should now be posted to the accounting software.

An invoice is a document that a business issues to its customers, asking the customers to pay for the goods or services that the business has supplied to them. Invoices can be issued either before or after the goods or services are supplied.

If the business issuing the invoices is registered for VAT, the invoices must comply with specific requirements as laid down by HMRC.

Many accounting software these days are used to raise purchase orders, and they seamlessly allow you to update the records with the supplier invoices received and thus easily record the supplier invoices.

Step 5: Pay the supplier as per the agreed days

Just as you expect others to pay you on time, it's just as important that you pay your bills on time.

A supplier invoice should ideally not be paid without a matching purchase order (except for utility bills like gas, electricity, telephone – which generally might be paid by direct debit/standing order). This ensures both that the organisation does not pay for unauthorised purchases and that authorised purchases will be paid in a timely fashion.

Suppose that today is the end of the month, and you have to pay for 200 invoices from 50 suppliers. You can process each payment individually by going into the supplier accounts - select the invoices, generate the payment list, write out the cheques, get the manager to authorise, send the cheques to the suppliers together with remittance advise notes.

This process will probably take you hours to complete manually.

There could be a better way.

If your purchase ledger system has a Batch Payments to Suppliers facility, all this is going to take you is the best part of 10 minutes. Just display a list of the 200 invoices on the screen, scan through them to note down the ones you don't want to pay, press the Select All button to highlight the lot, double-click on the two or more invoices you want to deselect, then press the button.

Here is how you go about it in detail; typically, the process will involve several stages, with the opportunity to review and correct at each stage. Below is a step by step example of how you might want to handle a batch payment run:

1. *Print a report of invoices due for payment and send this report to the manager requesting authorisation to pay.*
2. *Manager returns report indicating invoices approved or refused.*
3. *Display the list of all invoices due for payment on the Accounts software on-screen, press select to highlight all invoices and then deselect any invoices that have not been authorised for payment.*
4. *Print off resultant remittance advice note(s) in the draft to check for errors. Any necessary corrections should be done. Use the software to recalculate payments and reprint remittances.*
5. *Check and reprint until satisfied and then finalise the payment. Many Accounts packages allocate reference numbers to each payment. [Note - Payment transactions are now committed and cannot be changed]*
6. *The software prints final remittance advice and outputs BACS file, output onto an external disk.*
7. *Load file from external disk into your banks BACS system and complete the process.*

Batch Payments to Suppliers is one of the biggest time-savers in any accounts package, and it is handy if you process many payments at one time. However, if you only issue a dozen or so payments, you might as well keep doing them manually.

Send suppliers remittance advice slips

A remittance advice note is a note sent from a customer to his supplier, informing the supplier that he/she has paid the invoice. The advice may contain elements such as a text note, the invoice number and the invoice amount, among others.

Remittance advice notes are not required, but they are seen as a courtesy since they make it easier for the supplier to match invoices with payments.

Remittance advice note could be compared to a receipt from a cash register, in that they serve as a record of received payment.

At its simplest, a remittance advice note can be a letter or a note that outlines the invoice number and the payment amount sent or enclosed (such as when attached to a cheque).

Send your suppliers' remittance advice notes. It's a courteous business practice.

Step 6: Supplier statement reconciliation

Most organisations have to reconcile supplier accounts as part of their audit processes, which is an arduous task.

In principle, the process for reconciling supplier accounts is very straightforward. The supplier's credit control department sends a statement of account, which contains the unpaid invoices on their sales ledger, to the buyer's accounts payable department. The accounts payable team at the buyer's organisation compare the statement to their accounts payable in the creditors' ledger should be immediately debited. However, the money might not arrive at the supplier's account for a few days (especially if you are paying by cheque). In the meantime, the supplier will be showing that amount still owing, and the supplier thus will send you a statement showing unpaid invoices.

When you receive a supplier's statement, you should try to reconcile it to the supplier's account in your creditors' ledger. The term 'reconcile' means that you try to explain the difference between the two figures.

Any differences that you cannot explain are probably caused by errors – either yours or the suppliers.

To reconcile a supplier's statement to the balance on an account, you must go through the entries on each, marking off the ones which match. Any entries which don't match, whether on the statement or the account, need to be investigated and explained.

The first stage in the reconciliation is to 'tick off' all the items in common between the account and the statement. These items cannot be contributing to the difference. Whatever is left unticked should be "investigated."

Generally, to reconcile the supplier's statement, adjust for any payments made on or before the reconciliation date. For the ledger account, add any invoices issued by the supplier on or before the reconciliation date, but not yet entered into the supplier's account.

Supplier statement reconciliation is an opportunity for accounts payable to spot any discrepancies before suppliers request for payment of unpaid invoices is processed and to make sure the invoice process is complete.

The key to identifying discrepancies is to determine which invoices or credit notes on the supplier statement that are not on the accounts payable ledger or vice versa.

Task 3b: How to raise a purchase order & purchase invoice

In the previous task, we saw that the first task in the accounts payable process was to raise a purchase order for the goods or services needed. Let's go ahead and do just that with the details of the requisition sent by email from the store manager.

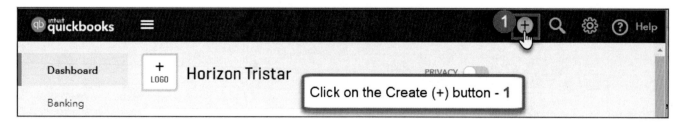

Fig. 91

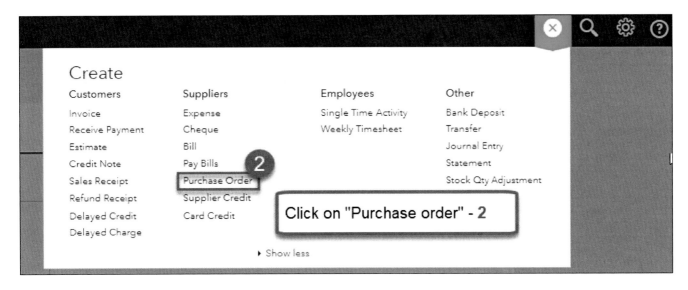

Fig. 92

Fig. 93

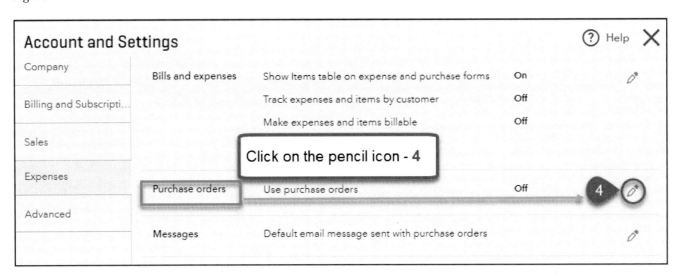

Fig. 94

This space is for notes

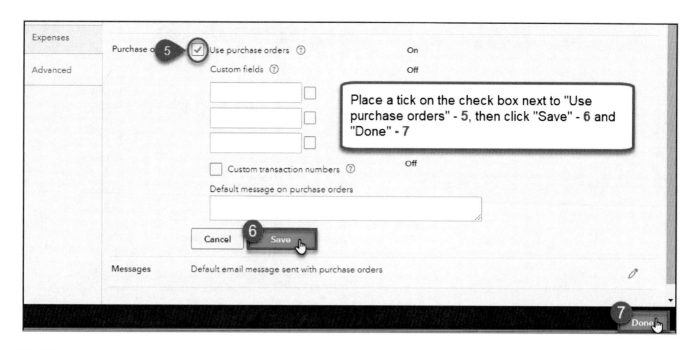

Place a tick on the check box next to "Use purchase orders" - **5**, then click "Save" - **6** and "Done" - **7**

Fig. 95

You are now ready to create a purchase order.

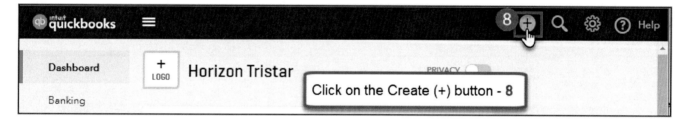

Click on the Create (+) button - **8**

Fig. 96

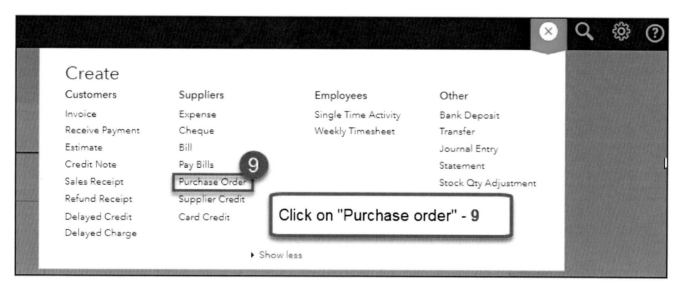

Click on "Purchase order" - **9**

Fig. 97

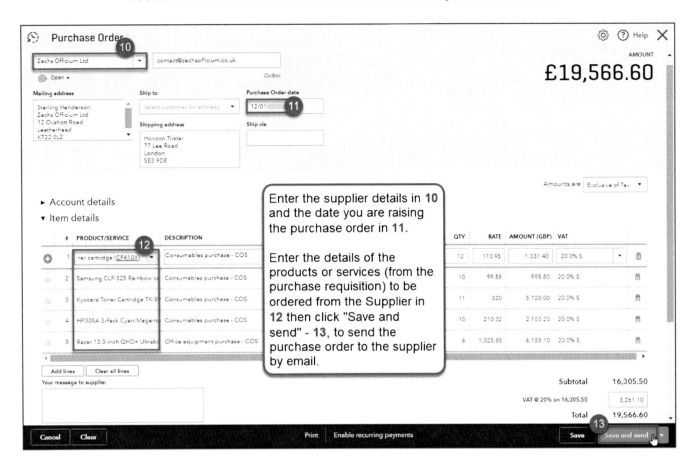

Enter the supplier details in **10** and the date you are raising the purchase order in **11**.

Enter the details of the products or services (from the purchase requisition) to be ordered from the Supplier in **12** then click "Save and send" - **13**, to send the purchase order to the supplier by email.

Fig. 98

This space is for notes

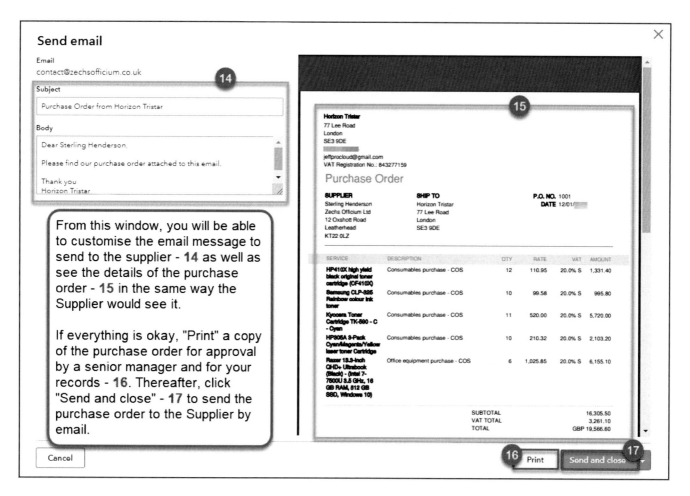

Fig. 99

It's now your turn.

There are still two more purchase orders to raise – one to Vandstone plc and the other to Joe Office Automation. **Follow steps 8 to 13 in figure 98** to raise those purchase orders using the details of the purchase requisition you received for Vandstone plc and Joe Office Automation.

Your final purchase order, ready to be sent to the Supplier (Vandstone Plc), should look like figure 100.

This space is for notes

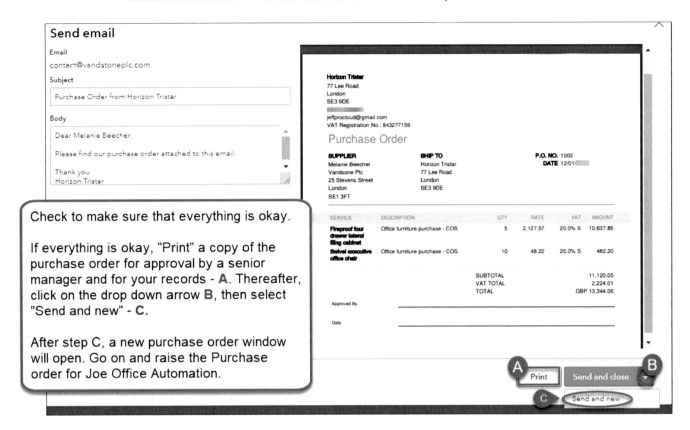

Fig. 100

From the new purchase order window that appears, enter the details from the purchase requisition for the product to be ordered from Joe Office Automation. The purchase order you raise, ready to be emailed to Joe Office Automation, should look similar to the figure below.

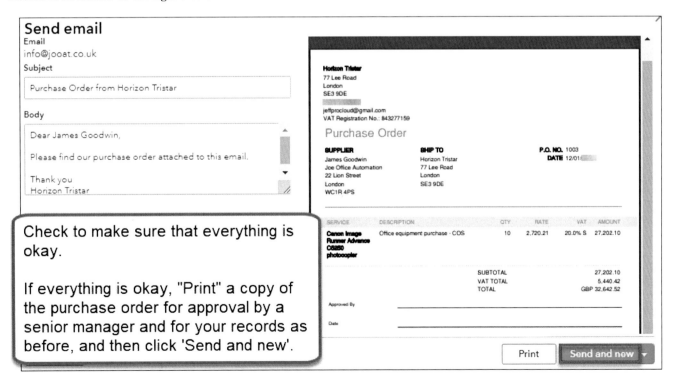

Fig. 101

Let's now check to make sure that we have raised all the purchase orders.

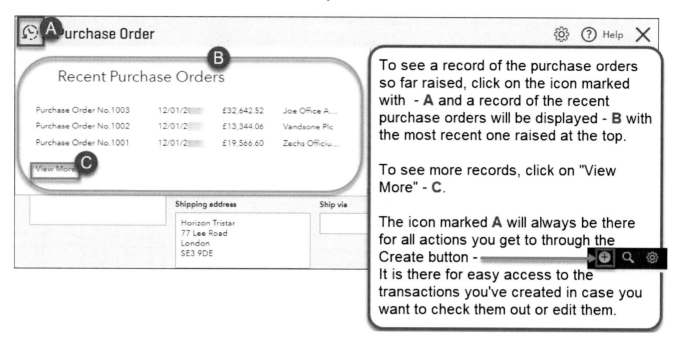

Fig. 102

What if you want to delete a purchase order you created in error, how do you go about doing it?

Let me show you.

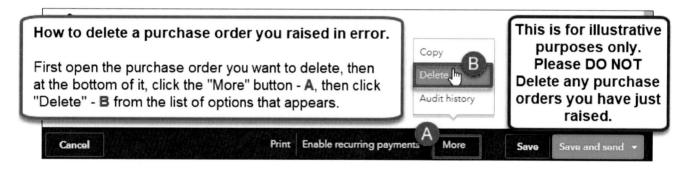

Fig. 103

Zechs Officium Ltd, Vandstone plc and Joe Office Automation were delighted to receive "purchase orders" from Horizon Tristar Ltd and promptly delivered the products to Horizon Tristar on the 15th and 17th January.

What you need to do now is to post the invoices sent by those suppliers into QuickBooks Online.

This space is for notes

Task 3c: Processing Purchase invoices

There are two ways you can enter/process purchase invoices in QuickBooks Online.

Product Invoices

1ˢᵗ option is to:

Click on the create button - [icon], then select Bill from the options under supplier and then process the Supplier invoice by entering the details from the invoice received from the Supplier.

2ⁿᵈ option (the one we will use) is as shown below:

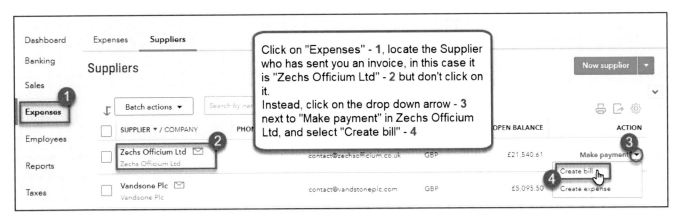

Fig. 104

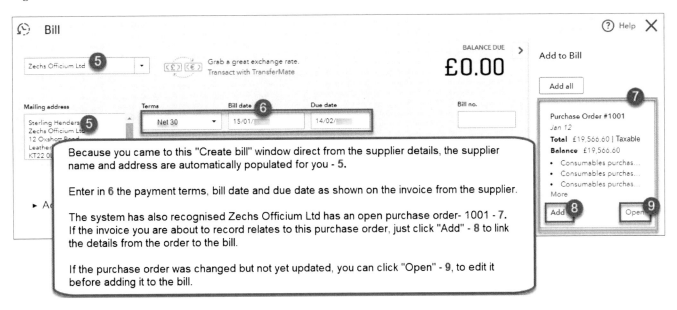

Fig. 105

This space is for notes

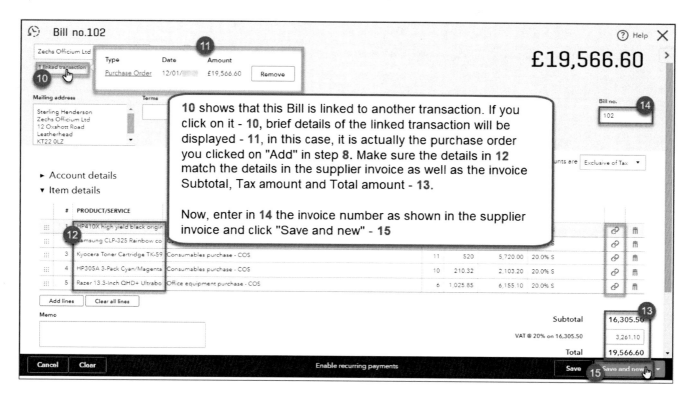

Fig. 106

Now it's your turn.

You have two more bills to process; one from Vandstone plc and the other from Joe Office Automation.

Here is what to do, from the new bill window that appears after step 13 in the figure above, **enter the supplier name – Vandstone plc** in the supplier name box. **After that, follow steps 6 to 8 above** in figure 105 and your bill, ready to be posted, should look like what is shown in the figure below.

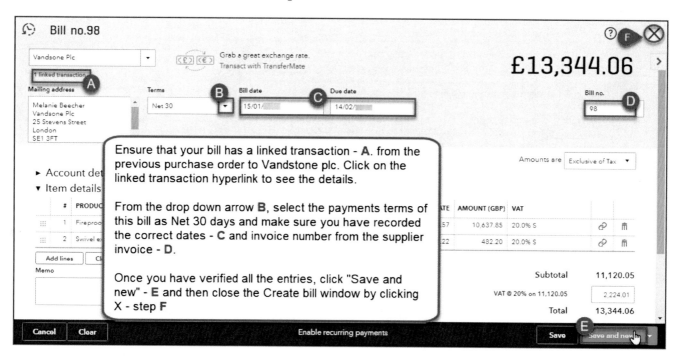

Fig. 107

Vandstone plc invoice is done.

Let's do the Joe office automation invoice together because it appears not all the products ordered from them were delivered – only seven of the ten items ordered were delivered, and as such we have to keep the purchase order open till all the items are delivered.

Let's do it.

We are going to process this invoice a bit differently, – from the purchase order window.

Click on the create button- ⊕ Q ⚙, then **select Purchase order** from the options under Supplier then follow the steps as illustrated in the figure below.

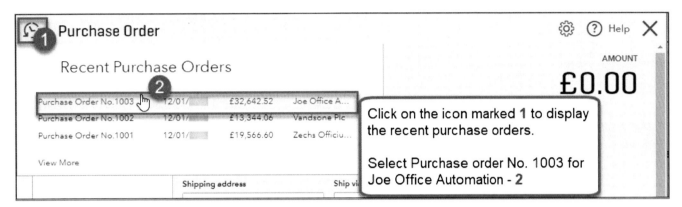

Fig. 108

Fig. 109

This space is for notes

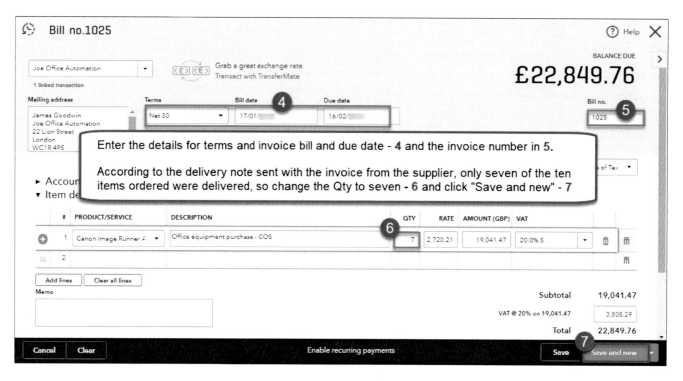

Fig. 110

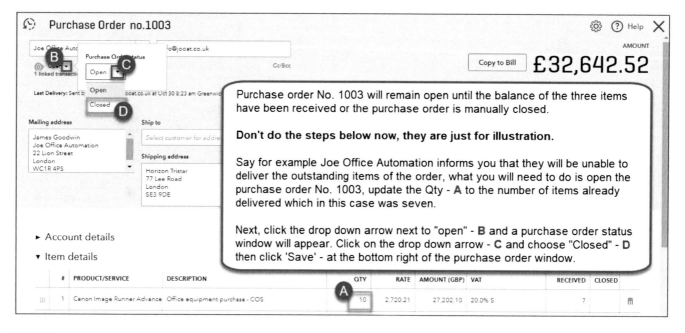

Fig. 111

Recording an advance payment made to a supplier

Horizon Tristar Ltd made a payment of £1,984.32 inclusive of Tax (VAT) to Bimpressive.com Ltd, a new supplier.

Here is how to record that payment in QuickBooks Online.

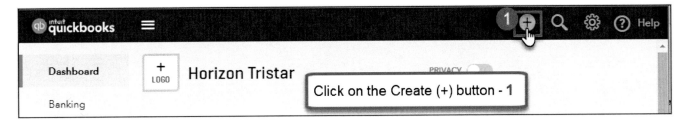

Fig. 112

Fig. 113

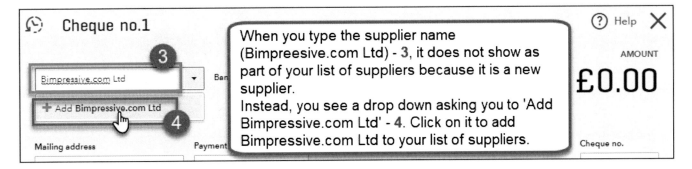

Fig. 114

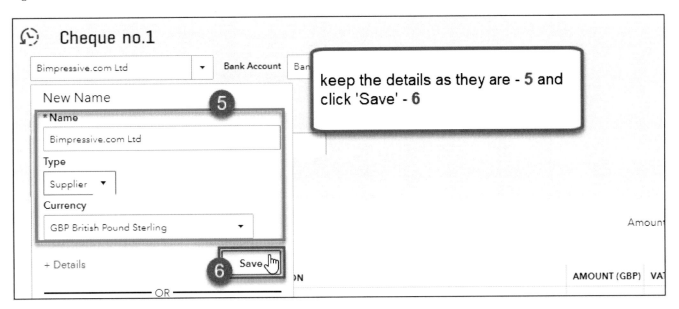

Fig. 115

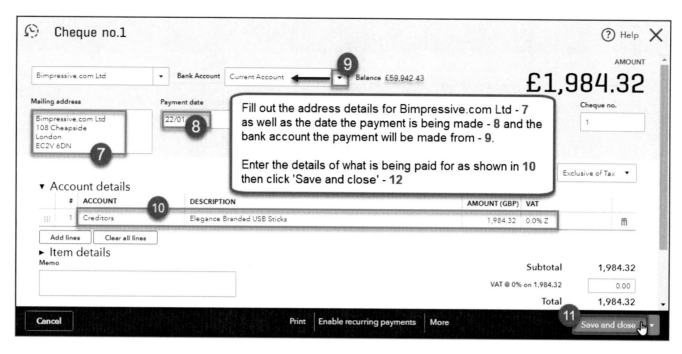

Fig. 116

Service Invoices

Processing supplier service invoices in QuickBooks Online is similar to processing supplier product invoices.

Click on the create button - [icons], **then select Bill** from the options under supplier and then process the Supplier invoice by entering the details from the invoice received from the supplier.

For **TD&A Certified Accountants Invoice**, enter TD&A Certified Accountants in the supplier name box and fill out the other details like the invoice number, terms, invoice date and enter the rest of the entries as shown in the figure below:

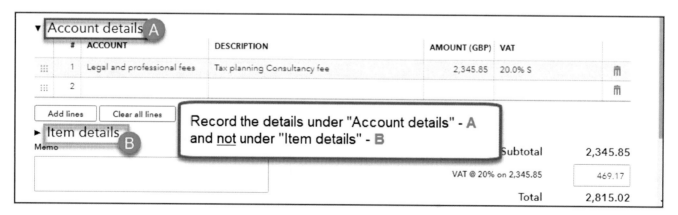

Fig. 117

For the **Office space Today invoice**, here is how the entry details should look like after you have entered the terms, invoice date and invoice number:

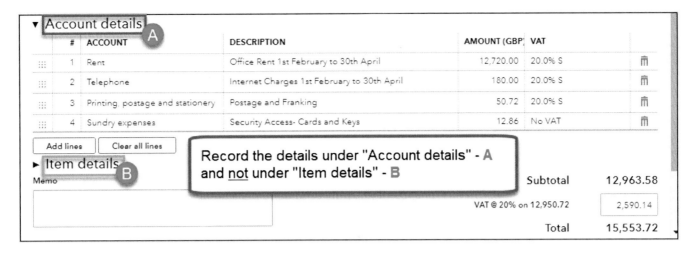

Fig. 118

For the **Spotless Clean invoice**, here is how the entry details should look like after you have entered the terms, invoice date and invoice number:

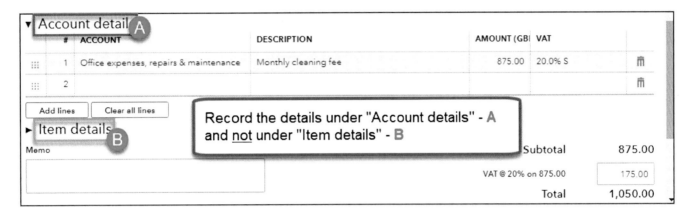

Fig. 119

For the **Bimpressive.com Ltd invoice**, here is how the entry details should look like after you have entered the terms, invoice date and invoice number:

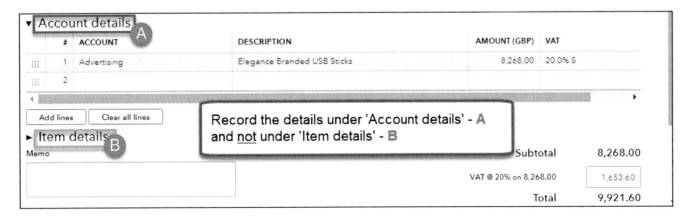

Fig. 120

Because the Bimpressive.com Ltd invoice was partly paid in advance, you now need to allocate that payment to the invoice you have just processed.

To do so, here is what you need to do.

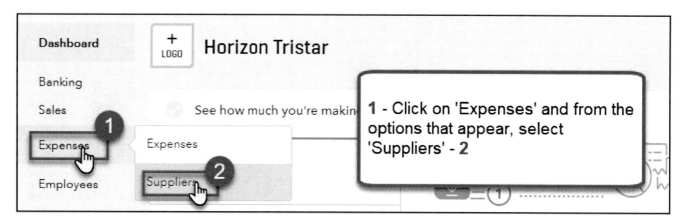

Fig. 121

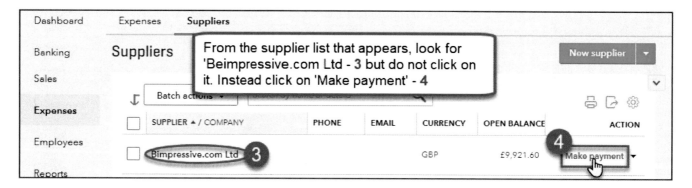

Fig. 122

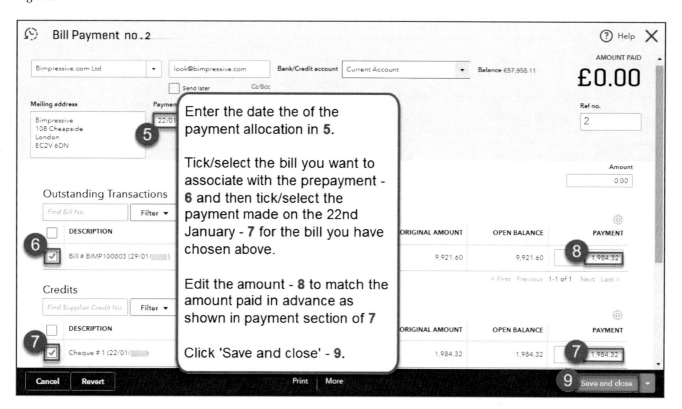

Fig. 123

Task 3d: How to process a purchase credit note

The store manager found out that two (2) of the HP305A 3 Pack Cyan/Magenta/Yellow original toner Cartridge (CF370AM) that were ordered from Zechs Officium Ltd and delivered on the 15th January were damaged. The supplier was informed, and he immediately issued a credit note and so you are now going to post that credit note into QuickBooks Online.

Here is how to do it.

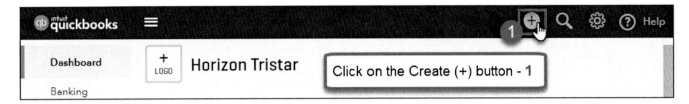

Fig. 124

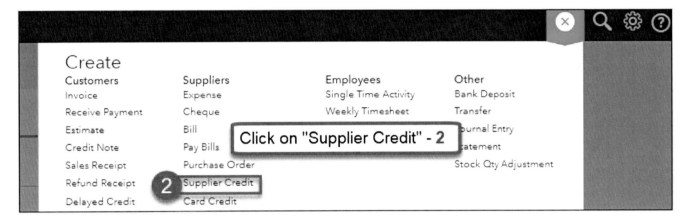

Fig.125

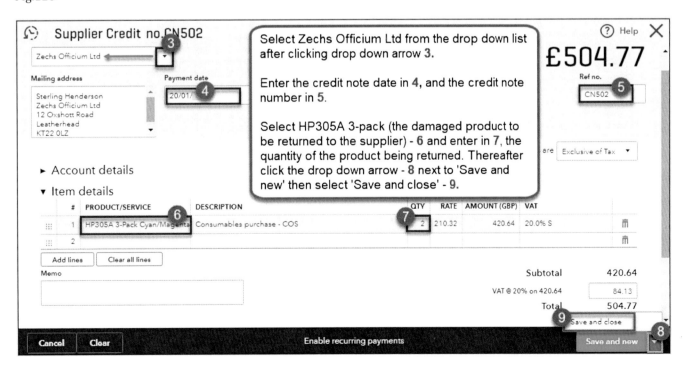

Fig. 126

Task 3e: How to record supplier payments & expense receipts

Overview of this task

There are three ways you can pay your suppliers:
1. Pay the outstanding invoice in full (full payment)
2. Pay part of the outstanding invoice (part payment)
3. Make a payment on account (payment made to reduce the overall outstanding on the account)

It is important to:
- Have a management policy on prompt payment of bills. Ensure that all staff are aware of it, especially but not only those in finance and purchasing.
- Agree on terms of payment at the start of all contracts.
- Monitor your payment system regularly for timely payment of invoices.
- Have a good system for clearing disputes quickly.
- Foster good relationships with suppliers by informing them of your payment procedures and who is responsible.

Key points to note when making payments are:

i. First check that there is enough money to make payment (perform a bank reconciliation)
ii. Get creditors ageing report
iii. Decide which suppliers to pay based on
iv. Credit terms with the supplier
v. Get approval from the manager
vi. Write the cheques or do BACS transfer
vii. Print remittance advice slip and send to the supplier

3e(i). Processing supplier payments

Here is how to make multiple payments at once – Batch payments or what is popularly known as payment runs.

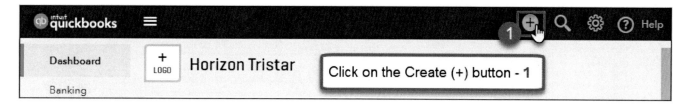

Fig. 127

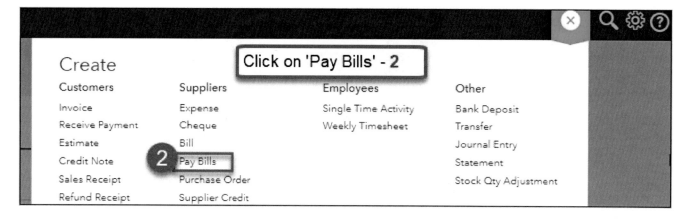

Fig. 128

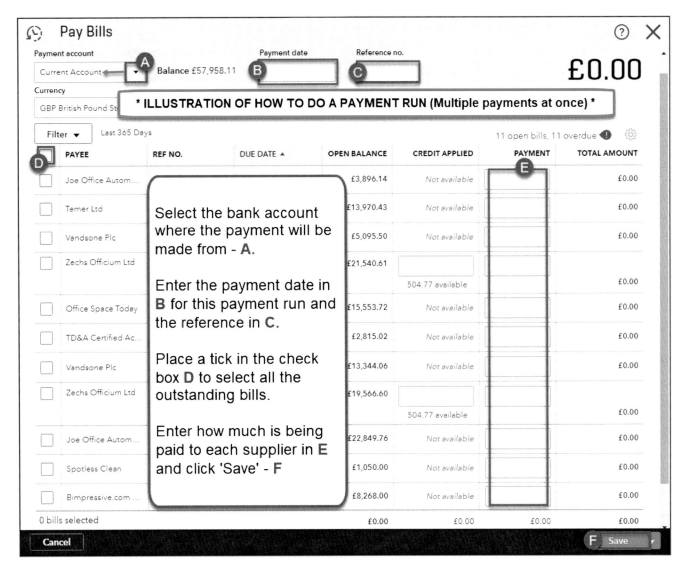

Fig. 129

Because the payments that Horizon Tristar Ltd is making to its suppliers are made on different dates, you can't do a payment run. Instead, you have to make payments one at a time.

This space is for notes

Now, from the Pay Bills window that is still open on your screen, record the payment that has been made to Temer Ltd.

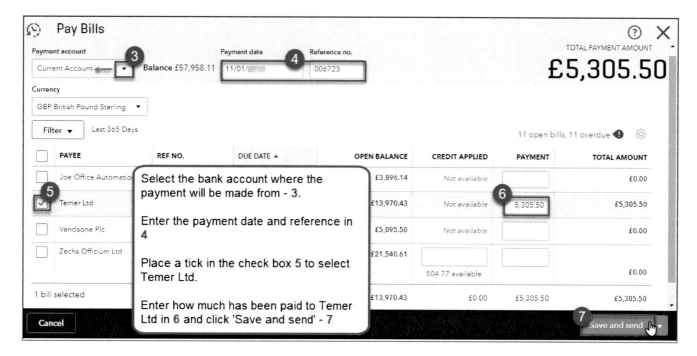

Fig. 130

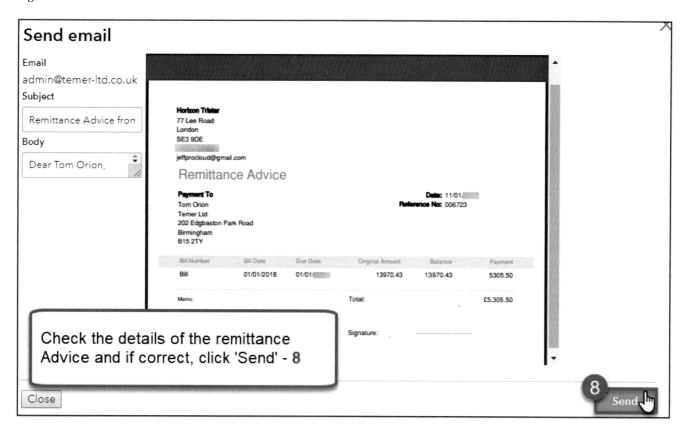

Fig. 131

From the Bill payment window still open on your computer screen, record payment to Joe Office Automation as illustrated in the figure below.

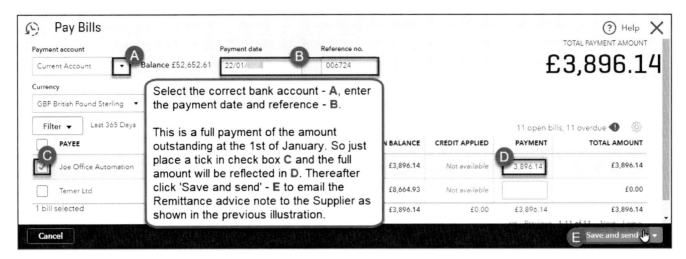

Fig. 132

The next payment to Office Space today has been made by the Director – Terry Smith using his own funds, and as such, this transaction will need to be recorded via the Director Account and not the Current bank account.

Proceed by first setting up another Director account as a bank account, and this will be the account where all the Director transactions with Horizon Tristar will be recorded. There is already a Director account in the default chart of accounts in QuickBooks Online for limited companies. However, this account can not be used to pay supplier invoices (because it is a liability account) and hence why we need to set up a separate bank account and call it Director account. When the Director any transactions with the company like just happened with payment of the supplier invoice, use this account to record such transactions. I will give more details about Director account later.

Right, let me show you how to set up the Director 'bank' account and how to process the payment of the rent invoice by the Director – Terry Smith.

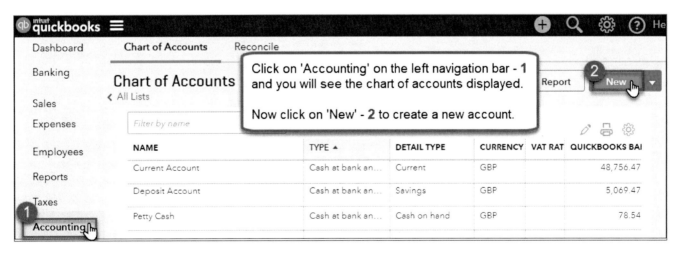

Fig. 133

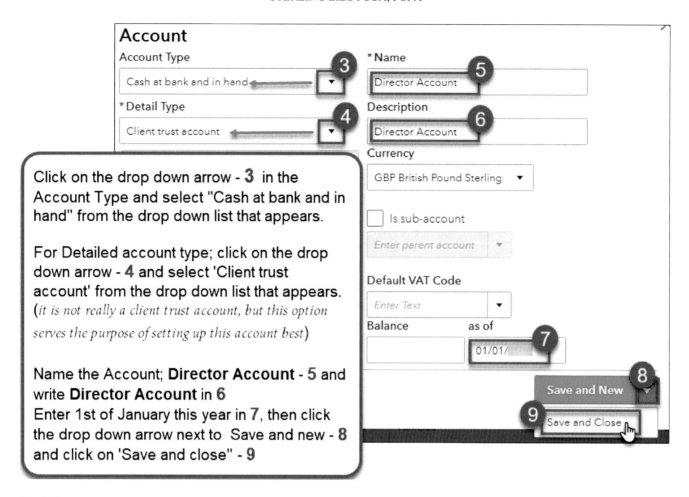

Fig. 134

Now you are ready to pay the invoice from Office space today using the Director account. Horray! Let's do it.

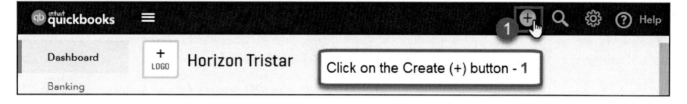

Fig. 135

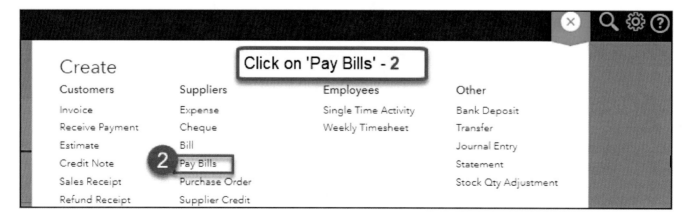

Fig. 136

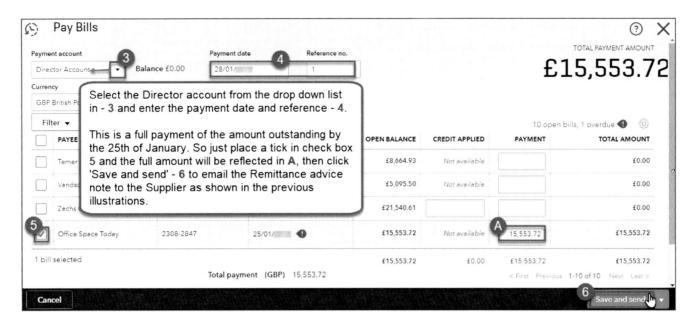

Fig. 137

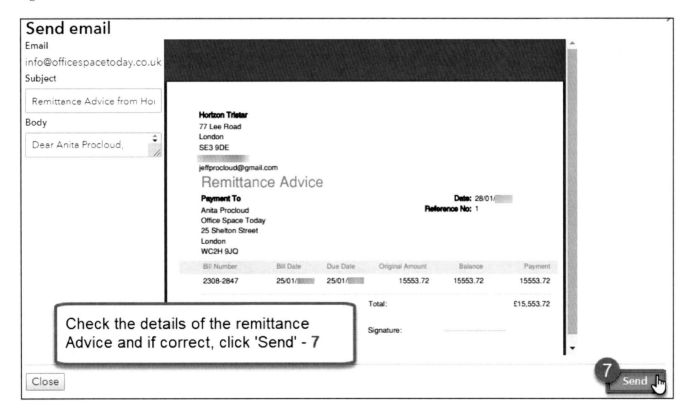

Fig. 138

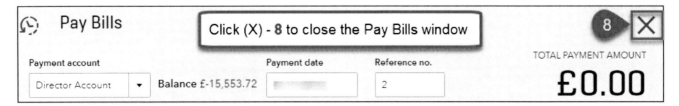

Fig. 139

Just one more thing to do. There is a balance in the default Director account that you now need to transfer to the Director bank account you have just created because this is now the Director account that will be used for all transactions between the Director and the business (Horizon Tristar Ltd).

To make the transfer, here is what you should do.

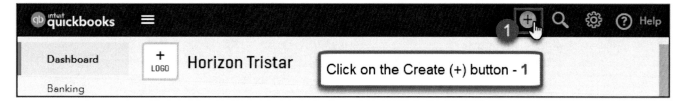

Fig. 140

Fig. 141

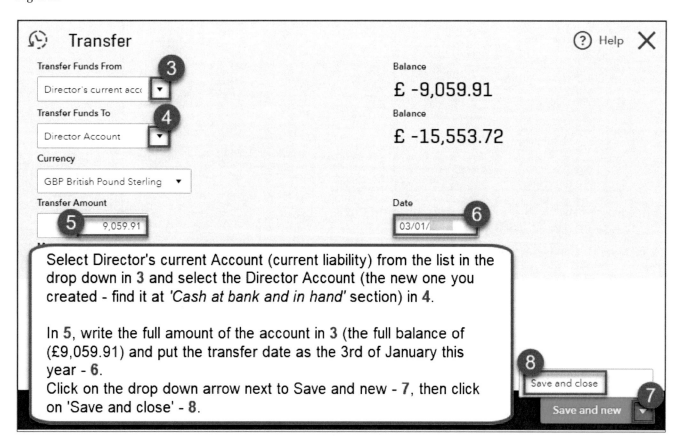

Fig. 142

If you now check the Director's current Account (Current liability), you will notice that the balance is 0.00 because you have moved all the amount that was in that account to the new Director account ('Bank account'). The previous debit balance in the Director's current account (the current liability account) meant that the Director – Terry Smith owed the company money – the £9,059.91.

However, when Terry Smith paid the rent invoice from Office Space Today Ltd using his own money, he in effect lent the company money – the £15,553.72.

The net position after these two transactions is that the company now owes Terry Smith £6,493.81 and if you check the Director account ('bank account') now, that is the amount you will see. Go on, check it out.

A brief overview of Director loan account

The Director current account (DCA) (also known simply as the Directors account) is a notional balance between a company and its Directors. It is not a real bank account and is not represented by real monies.

It records:

- Monies drawn by the director as salary or dividends (if not attributed to salary/dividend at the time of drawing), expenses etc.
- Other drawings by the director – e.g. personal bills paid by the company
- Net amounts of salary and dividend due
- Expense re-reimbursements due.

Task 3e(ii). Recording small expense receipts

First, begin by analysing all the receipts.

The first receipt from Sainsbury's, the Wasabi receipts and the receipt from Boots have not been recorded yet due to insufficient analytical information: We know the date of the transaction and what was bought in each receipt, but we do not know whether these were business transactions or not. The best thing to do is to keep these receipts aside and not record them until all the analytical information is received.

The other Sainsbury's receipt is a transaction for the purchase of fuel (diesel) using the company credit card, the Clintons and Specsavers receipt are transactions using company debit card receipt.
These receipts have all the relevant analytical information for them to be recorded. We know the cards being used for payment, the Items bought, the date of the transactions.

To record these transactions into QuickBooks online, here is what you should do:

Set up the company credit card account in QuickBooks Online because some of the expenses have been paid by Credit card and you don't have that set up yet in QuickBooks Online.

This space is for notes

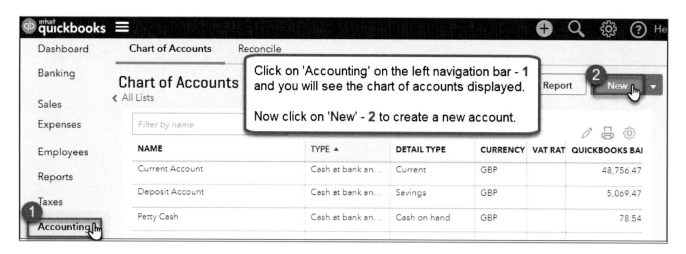

Fig. 143

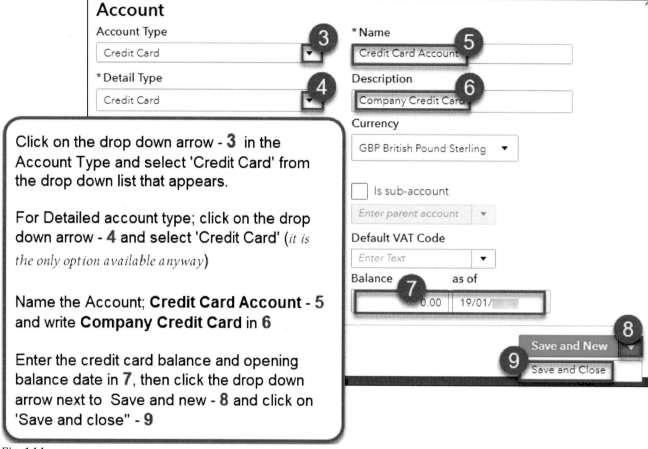

Fig. 144

Next,

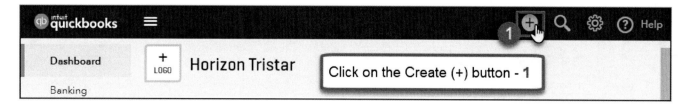

Fig. 145

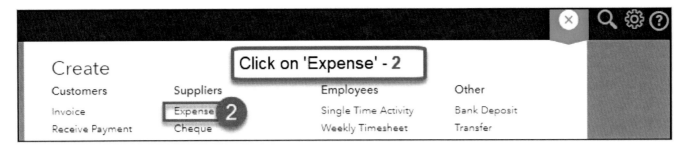

Fig. 146

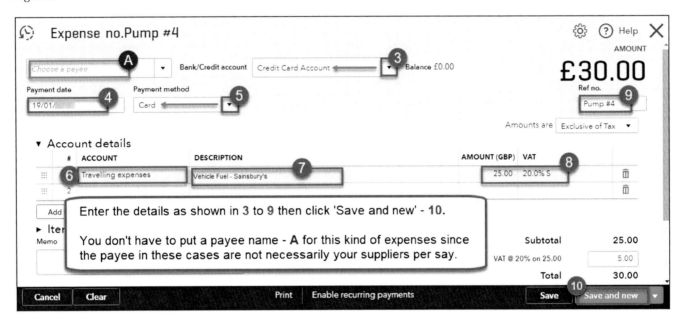

Fig. 147

For how to record the transaction from Clintons, see below.

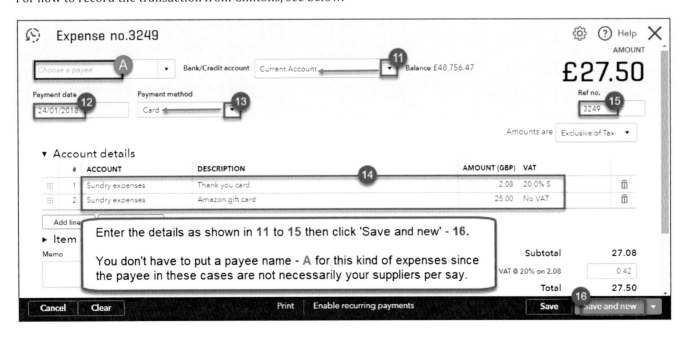

Fig. 148

And finally, the transaction from Specsavers is recorded as shown in figure 149.

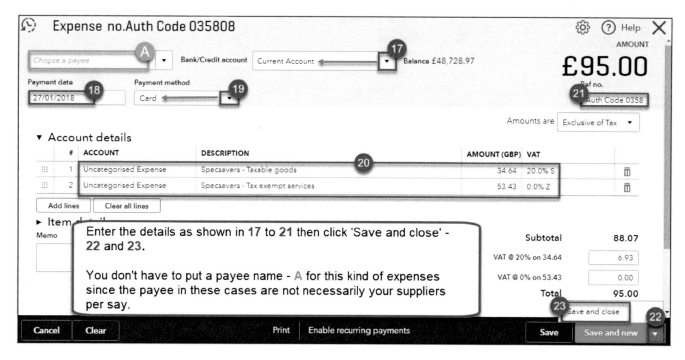

Fig. 149

Task 3f: Petty Cash management

The objective of the petty cash management is to ensure that control is kept over the petty cash tin and that all cash payments are recorded correctly and entered to the accounting system.

Businesses generally keep small amounts of cash to meet small miscellaneous payments such as entertainment expenses and stationery costs. Such payments are generally handled by a petty cash imprest system whereby an amount of 'Float' is fixed (say £250). This is the maximum amount of cash that can be held at any time, and each time cash level runs low, the petty cash imprest is injected with cash by drawing a cheque.

When you give cash to an employee, have the person sign a slip of paper (Petty cash voucher) to keep a record of who, when and what the money was used for. The voucher should be authorised by the financial accountant or designated signatory.

For security reasons, the petty cash fund should be locked at all times when it is not in use. Access to petty cash tin is restricted and money cannot be taken out of it without approval.

Any money taken from the petty cash tin should be replaced with a petty cash voucher. At all times, the amounts on the Petty cash vouchers and the cash you have left in the tin/box should add up to the amounts you've float (which in the case of Horizon Tristar Ltd is £250).

Whenever a voucher is completed, it is good practice for the custodian to immediately update the petty cash book by adding the amount, type, and date of the expenditure and updating the running cash balance. For example, if you got some refreshments for the office, e.g. some sweets and you need to be reimbursed the amount you spent, you would need to fill out a petty cash voucher with the details of the purchase.

Petty cash tin illustrative picture.

Fig.

There was £178 transferred from the Current account to the petty cash account. To record that transaction, do the following.

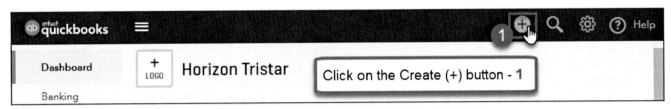

Fig. 150

Fig. 151

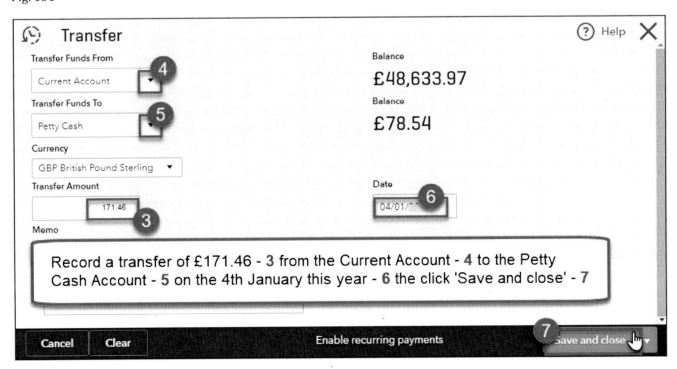

Fig. 152

Now it is time to record the transactions in the petty cash Vouchers.

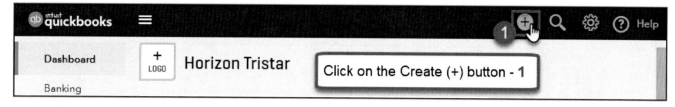

Fig. 153

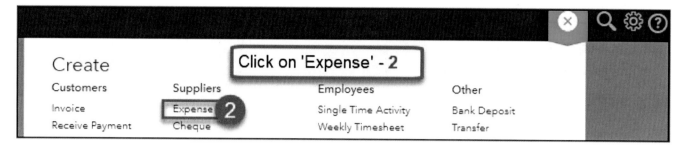

Fig. 154

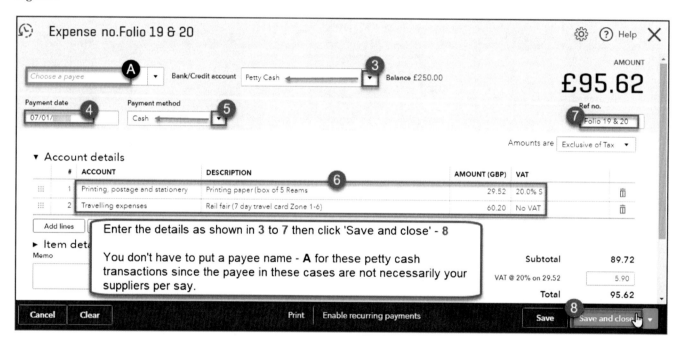

Fig. 155

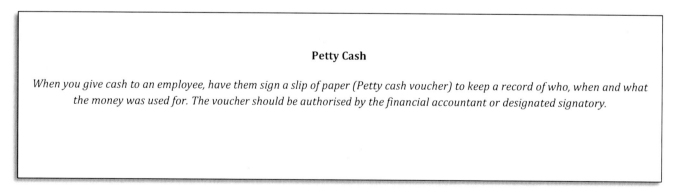

Petty Cash

When you give cash to an employee, have them sign a slip of paper (Petty cash voucher) to keep a record of who, when and what the money was used for. The voucher should be authorised by the financial accountant or designated signatory.

TASK 4: DEALING WITH LEASES & RECURRING ENTRIES

Horizon Tristar Ltd purchased a BMW 3 series for £30,000 inclusive of 20% VAT on 2nd January this year for the Sales manager from BMW dealer 1. A cash deposit of £10,200 inclusive of VAT was paid, and the balance is to be paid on finance: £654 gross (inclusive of finance cost -interest of £54) per month starting 1st of next month for 33 months.

So, step 1 is to record the deposit of £10,200 that was made by Horizon Tristar Ltd to BMW Dealer 1. Click on the plus button - then select 'Cheque' under suppliers then fill out the details as follows.

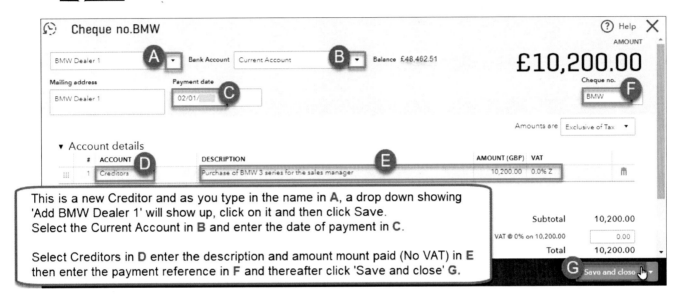

Fig. 156

The next thing is to record the bill of £30,000 from BMW Dealer 1. Click on the plus button - then select 'Bill' under suppliers then fill out the details as follows.

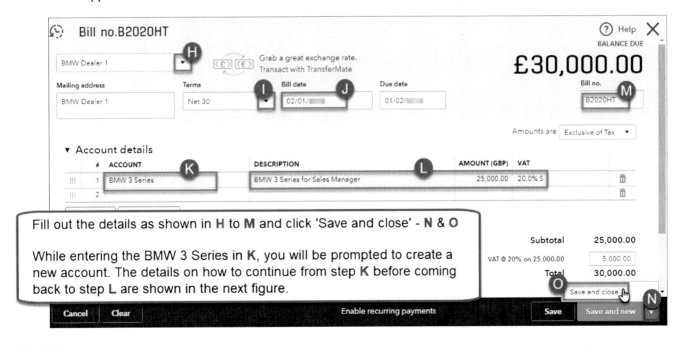

Fig. 157

The next figure shows the details of how to finish step K in figure 157 in the previous page.

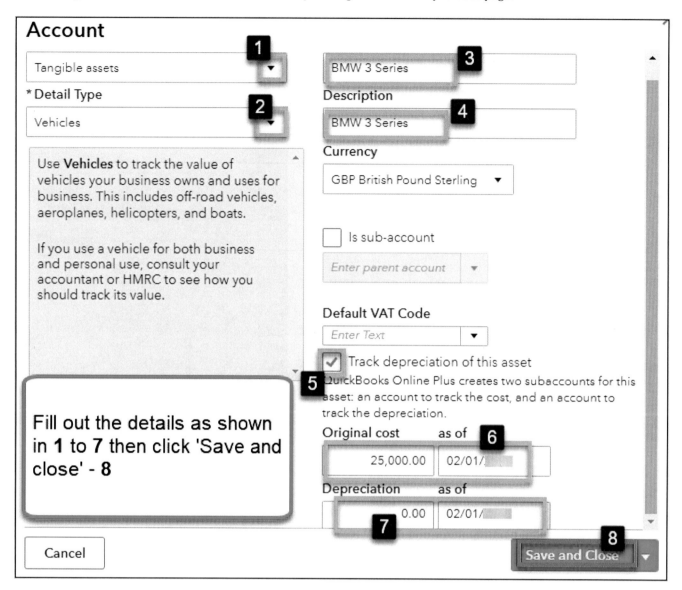

Fig. 158

Now, allocate the deposit payment of £10,200 made to BMW Dealer 1 to the invoice.

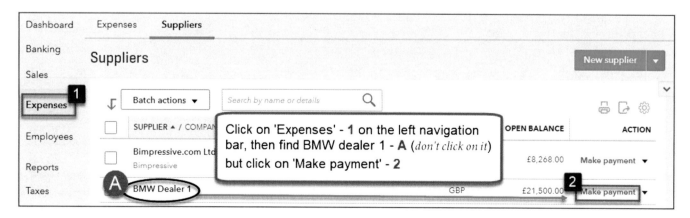

Fig. 159

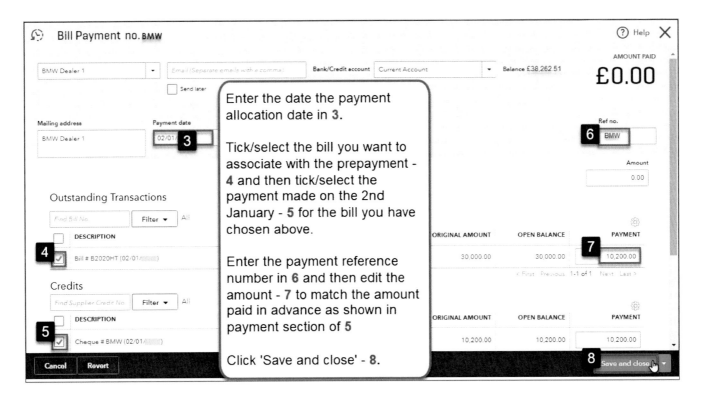

Fig. 160

How to set up and process standing orders and direct debits

In this task, you are required to set up recurring entry templates for the standing orders and direct debit mandates that have been set up in the bank. Refer to the updated list of the standing orders and direct debts you have been given to proceed.

Here is how to go about it.

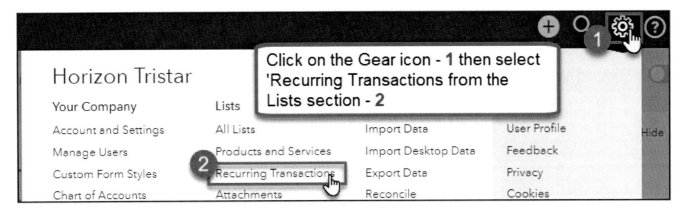

Fig. 161

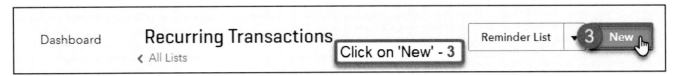

Fig. 162

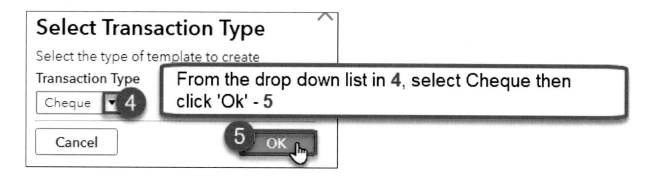

Fig. 163

Follow through and set up the hire purchase payment and interest recurring entries as follows:

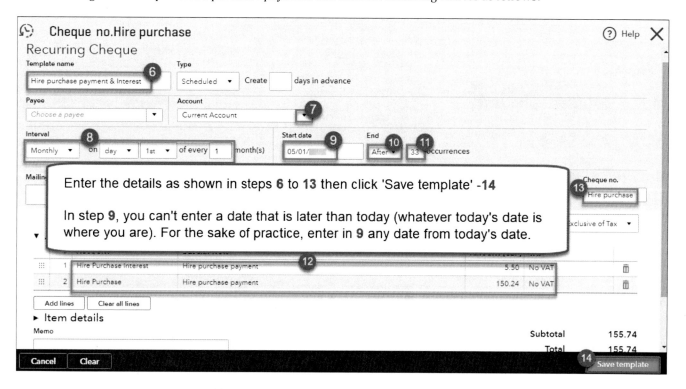

Fig. 164

This space is for notes

It's now your turn. Go ahead and enter the recurring entry details for the Loan payment and interest.

When you are done, here is how it should look like just before you click 'Save template'

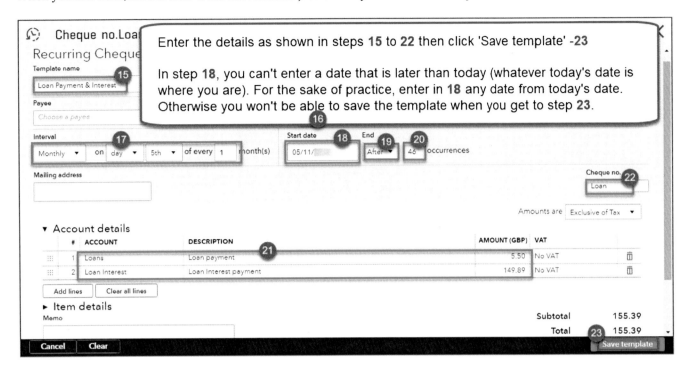

Fig. 165

And finally, here is how the recurring entry for the finance lease payments and interest should look like.

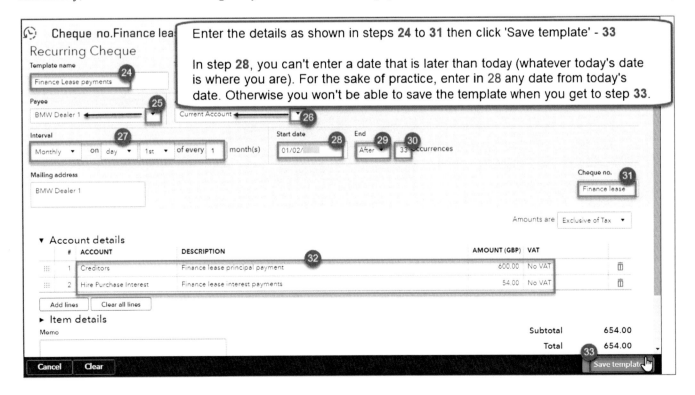

Fig. 166

Difference between a standing order & Direct Debit

A **standing order** is a regular payment that you can set up to pay other people, organisations or transfer to your other bank accounts. You can amend or cancel the standing order as and when you like.

A **Direct Debit** can only be set up by the organisation to which you're making the payment. Normally, you sign a mandate that gives the company permission to take funds from your account in an agreed way – like a monthly gym membership or your mobile phone bill. It normally confirms who's receiving the payment, the account to be debited, the amount and the dates of the payment. You're protected under the Direct Debit Guarantee scheme so that any amount debited in error is refunded immediately.

Source: https://www.barclays.co.uk/help/payments/payment-information/difference-order-debits/

TASK 5: POSTING PAYROLL JOURNALS AND DOING AD-HOC ADMINISTRATIVE DUTIES

Posting payroll Journals

On the 31st January, the payroll was processed and below is the payroll report for you to post not the accounts using a payroll journal.

Date :	31st January			Horizon Tristar Ltd					Page :	1 of 1					
Time :	15:19:26			Payment Summary History Part 1 - By Date											

| | | Employee Reference From : 1 | | | Payment Period : All | | | | Processing Date From : 06/01/▓▓ | | | | | | |
| | | Employee Reference To : 9999999 | | | | | | | Processing Date To : 05/02/▓▓ | | | | | | |

	Process Date:	31/01/▓	Tax Week:	43	Tax Month:	10										
E'ee Ref	Employee Name	Gross Pay pre Sacrifice	Gross Pay post Sacrifice	Taxable Gross	P.A.Y.E.	Employee NIC	Employer NIC	Employee Pension	Employer Pension*	Student Loan	SSP	SMP	SPP	SAP	ShPP	Net Pay
1	Z TOMILSON	2,333.33	2,333.33	2,333.33	274.80	198.24	227.98	0.00	0.00	0.00	0.00	0.00	0.00	0.00	0.00	1860.29
2	K PRICHARD	2,083.33	2,083.33	2,083.33	224.80	168.48	193.75	0.00	0.00	0.00	0.00	0.00	0.00	0.00	0.00	1690.05
3	A WILLIAMS	2,083.33	2,083.33	2,083.33	224.80	168.48	193.75	50.00	80.00	0.00	0.00	0.00	0.00	0.00	0.00	1640.05
4	J JONES	2,250.00	2,250.00	2,250.00	0.00	188.64	216.94	50.00	80.00	0.00	0.00	0.00	0.00	0.00	0.00	2011.36
5	C MCFARLANE	1,092.00	1,092.00	1,092.00	218.40	49.44	56.86	0.00	0.00	0.00	0.00	0.00	0.00	0.00	0.00	824.16
	Process Date Total	9,841.99	9,841.99	9,841.99	942.80	773.28	889.28	100.00	160.00	0.00	0.00	0.00	0.00	0.00	0.00	8025.91
	Report Total	9,841.99	9,841.99	9,841.99	942.80	773.28	889.28	100.00	160.00	0.00	0.00	0.00	0.00	0.00	0.00	8025.91

For salary sacrifice pension schemes this is the employer contribution including the amount sacrificed by the employee.

Fig. 167

Here is what to do to post the payroll journal from the above payroll report:

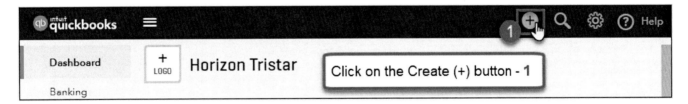

Fig. 168

Fig. 169

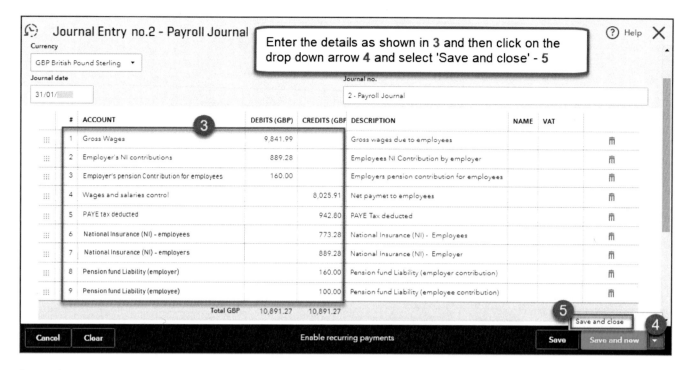

Fig. 170

Payroll Accounting Process

Payroll Accounting is the method of accounting for payroll. Payroll is the aggregate expenditure on wages and salaries incurred by a business in an accounting period. It can also refer to a listing of employees giving details of their pay.

Payroll includes the gross pay due to the employee and employer taxes. The gross pay is divided into net pay actually received by the employee and deductions made from the gross pay for employee taxes and other deductions such as pension contributions, healthcare contributions, and union subscriptions.

In payroll accounting it is important to distinguish between **employee** taxes which are deducted from the employees' gross pay and are therefore paid by the employee, and **employer** taxes which are in addition to the gross pay and paid by the employers.
Both payroll taxes are usually collected by the employer and paid over to the relevant tax authority.

Ad-hoc administrative duties

Here are some common administrative duties that you will from time to time be called upon to do in your role as an Accounts payable/Purchase Ledger Clerk.
.

1. Sorting incoming post

The objective here is to make sure that incoming mail is dealt with in a secure and controlled way. Here is how to go about doing this duty;
      a.   When mail is received, open envelopes addressed to the company
      b.   Envelopes addressed to individual people within the company and marked as 'private and confidential' should be passed to them.
      c.   Once mail is opened it should be date stamped and distributed to the relevant people.
      d.   If a courier arrives with a parcel, it should be checked for obvious damages and signed for.

e. The parcel should then be passed onto the relevant person.
f. If it is not addressed to anyone specific, it should be opened, and the contents checked to the delivery note attached to the parcel.
g. If the contents do not agree to the delivery note or are damaged in any way, contact the sender and advise them.
h. If the contents are as stated on the delivery note, the goods should be distributed, and the delivery note passed to the Financial Accountant.

2. Sorting out outgoing post

The objective here is to make sure that outgoing mail is dealt with in a secure and controlled way. Here is how to do it.

a. All outgoing mail should be put in envelopes, and any enclosures checked to ensure that they are included.
b. Relevant information, such as PRIVATE AND CONFIDENTIAL, should be written clearly on the envelope.
c. The correct postage should be applied. Make sure that you have an up to date postage rate list.
d. All parcels should clearly show the receiver on the front and the sender (our company) on the back.
e. If you need to send a parcel by courier, ensure that the contents are securely wrapped.
f. Make sure that you know the value of the contents of the parcel and its approximate weight.
g. Contact the courier company and ask them to collect the parcel. Ask them for the cost of the service.
h. You will need to give the value and weight so that they can calculate the cost of the delivery.
i. Complete a purchase order form with the courier, parcel details and cost, and give this to the Financial Accountant.

3. Answering the customer telephone queries

The objective here is to ensure that all telephone answering is done consistently, to always delight the customer. Here is how to do it:

a. Ensure that someone is available to answer the telephone at all times.
b. Keep a telephone message pad beside every telephone for taking messages.
c. Always keep an up to date list of people who are out of the office, in meetings or not taking calls.
d. When answering the telephone smile before you answer and use the script agreed by the team members.
e. Don't interrogate the caller, and if the person that they would like to speak to is unavailable, then see if you can help.
f. If a call needs returning, remind the person returning the call to make sure that it is returned.

This space is for notes

"The greatest thing anyone can do for God and for man is to pray"

S. D. Gordon

TASK 6: DOING THE ACCOUNTS RECEIVABLE TASKS

A brief over overview of the Accounts Receivable process – the key steps

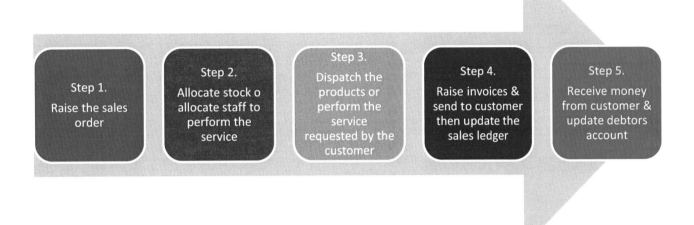

Fig. 171

You see, when a business is involved in selling its products or services, it can do so by selling on credit (this results in what is called Receivables) or selling in cash (this results in what is called technically called in accounting receipts) or you can sell in both ways (and most businesses do it both ways).

Accounting for the sales made on credit is carried out in a series of tasks/procedures called the Accounts receivable process as illustrated in figure 2.

What does 'on credit' mean? Well, it means when you sell a service or item to a customer and are not paid immediately - you are extending credit to them.

So, the accounts receivable process does not apply to sales where you are paid immediately. Sales, where you are paid promptly, are called cash sales or receipts, and their accounting process is a bit different and quite straightforward.

Now, let's look at the **Accounts receivable process** – as illustrated in figure 2 above and understand the steps involved in the process in a bit more detail.

Step 1. Send quotation for your goods/service(s) to the customer

What's a quotation/quote? Well, a quotation or quote in accounting is a formal document which explains a business's pricing for a product or service and gives the customer a precise cost for the product/service.

When a customer asks you for a quote, it means they're seriously considering doing business with you. All your sales and marketing efforts have paid off! You've shown that your service has value, and you're one step away from closing the deal.

Quotations usually are given to customers by sales staff, but the quotation stage is a significant and integral part of the accounts receivable process/function because once accepted by the customer, it has legal status in many countries. So, you usually can't charge more (raise an invoice for a different value - higher) for the product/work than you've quoted.

Step 2: Receive & process customer orders

Once the customer is happy with the quotation, they usually send an order – purchase order (ask for a written one, not verbal and make a note of the purchase order number from the customer) for the goods/services your company has quoted for them.

Your task then is to process that purchase order from the customer by raising a sales order.

A sales order is an internal document of your company, your company itself generates it.

Your sales order should record the customer's originating purchase order which is an external document. Rather than using the customer's purchase order document, an internal sales order form allows the internal audit control of completeness to be monitored as a sequential sales order number can be used by your company for its sales order documents.

The customer's Purchase Order (PO) is the originating document which triggers the creation of the sales order, and a sales order, being an internal document, can, therefore, contain many customer purchase orders under it.

If your business is in a manufacturing environment, a sales order can be converted into a work order to show that work is about to begin to manufacture, build or engineer the products the customer wants.

Many computerised accounting software systems now have the function of sales order processing built in, and hopefully, these should not be a tough task for you.

Step 3&4: Deliver the goods/services to the customer and raise the invoice

Having converted the order from the customer to accounts receivable, you will have to deliver the goods or perform the service(s) as per the request from the customer.

Bear in mind that the invoice you raise for the product or service delivered to your customer is a legal, financial document of which you have to keep records by law.

Therefore, when raising a Sales Invoice, the following should be noted:

- Your business name and address details should be in the invoice

- A unique invoice reference/number that will relate to this invoice only.
- A date for the invoice (which will generally be the date on which the invoice is created/raised)
- The prices and goods/service described in the invoice should be those agreed with the customer (via the quotation step discussed above)
- Invoices should be sent out as soon as possible following the supply of goods/services and no later than "X" number of days after the supply (These depends on what your company policy is)

- Additions and calculations in the invoice should always be checked before invoices are dispatched to customers.
- A total amount for the invoice.
- The payment terms for the invoice (i.e., how long the customer has to pay)
- If you are a registered Limited company, you must include Your Company Number and your full registered company address on the invoice.

Addressing a sales invoice

Correctly addressing invoices is crucial. If an error is made, it may be impossible to collect the outstanding debt from the customer.

The following steps should be taken:

✓ Find out who exactly will be making the payment from the customer's side.
✓ Invoices should be addressed as follows:

for the attention of:

ABC PLC/LTD

Company's full address

✓ Customer Purchase Order Number - so they know which purchase order the invoice relates to if they are using an order management system.
✓ Details on how to pay, including bank account details for BACs/ online payments.
✓ If you are VAT registered you must also include: The amount of VAT on each line of the invoice and the VAT rate charged OR the total amount of VAT charged on the invoice, and the rate, if VAT applies to all items on the invoice and don't forget to include your VAT number on the invoice.

Step 5: Maintaining invoices & payments

This is the core of your accounts receivable procedures. There is no point in selling to customers on credit and failing to collect the outstanding amounts later.

Here are the steps to follow from the time you give the customer their invoice:-

If you are using a Manual Receivables System (MRS)

a. Print a copy of the invoices and place it into your *Receivables file in sequential order - either by date or invoice number.
b. Make a cover page on which to list the unpaid invoices. Draw up columns to display i) the date, ii) the customer name, iii) the invoice number, iv) the amount, v) paid date. Keep this cover page in the front of the folder.
a. When payment is received, either by cash, cheque or internet banking, write the date it was paid into the 'paid date' column of the Receivables cover page. You can also make a note (hand-written or stamped) of the date paid on the invoice itself.
b. Remove the invoice from the Receivables file and place it into a *Sales Invoice file (an archive for all the paid invoices).

*You could instead have one folder with two sections i) Unpaid Invoices, ii) Paid Invoices, this is just one method. You can change it to suit your requirements, and indeed, design a whole different system, as long as what you do helps you keep a handle on those unpaid invoices.

If you are using Computerised Bookkeeping System (CBS)

If you are using bookkeeping software that has a receivables option, it is easy to check what is due, because when you run a receivables report it will only list the invoices that have not been paid - as long as all the payments received have been entered into the program!

Therefore, you do not need to keep a separate receivables folder. You can just place all invoices directly into the Sales Invoices folder because you will use the bookkeeping program for the accounts receivable procedures.

Customer/Debtor credit notes

On the other hand, if a customer returns goods to you for full or partial credit, you should issue the customer with a credit note. The amount shown on the credit note should be equal to the amount of error or overcharge identified. All credit notes are to be raised by the Accounts Receivable team.

Invoices raised to correct an undercharge should refer to the original invoice number.

Task 6a: How to raise sales orders, sales invoices and sales credit notes

As seen from the first step in the Accounts Receivable overview, a Sales order is generated when the seller converts the sales quote approved by the customer into a Sales Order (SO).

Suffice it to say that a sales order (SO) is an internal document generated by the seller, indicating that the customer is now ready to purchase products and services. It is a confirmation document that authorises the sale of listed items for the given amount. The document gives a clear understanding of what the customer has decided to buy. SO is often considered a legal contract that makes it mandatory for the seller to sell products at the agreed upon price. The seller generates SO when the sales quote sent to the customer is approved.

The generation of SO implies confirmation of sale and no additional charges resulting from increased labour or transportation cost will be included in the document. So once the SO is created, the seller will have to sell the products at the agreed upon price quoted with no further cost to be incurred by the buyer. In case, the sellers want to make any changes in SO document; it is necessary to take prior consent from the buyer.

While a Sales Order confirms a sale, an invoice indicates that the customer is legally bound to pay for the products that have been delivered to him. Sales order authorises the products & services that customer wants to buy from the seller. On the other hand, the invoice is the bill for the products that the customer has purchased from the seller.

Here are the steps from quotation/estimate to invoice

Fig. 172

Let's do that in QuickBooks Online, shall we?

To begin the process, click on the create (+) button as illustrated in the figure below.

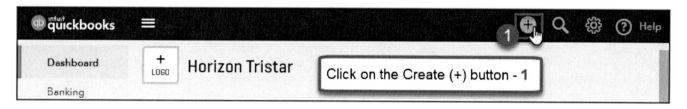

Fig. 173

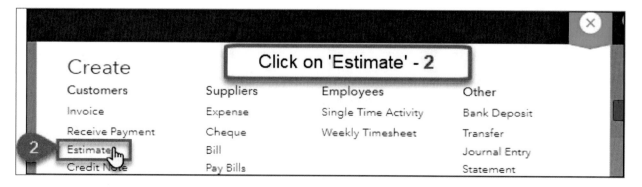

Fig. 174

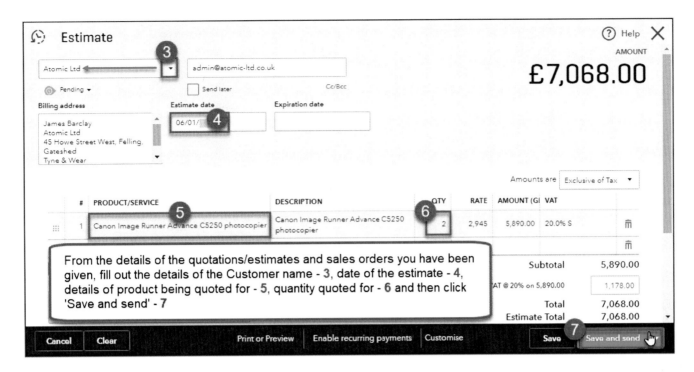

Fig. 175

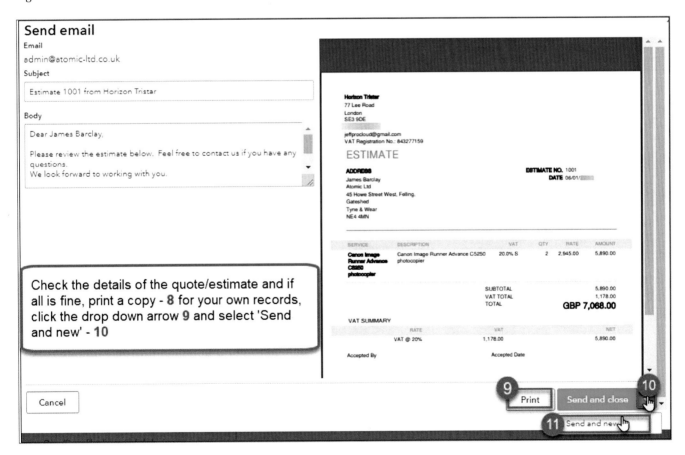

Fig. 176

After step 11 as illustrated in the figure above, fill out the details of the quotation/estimate for Golden Goose Ltd – see figure 177.

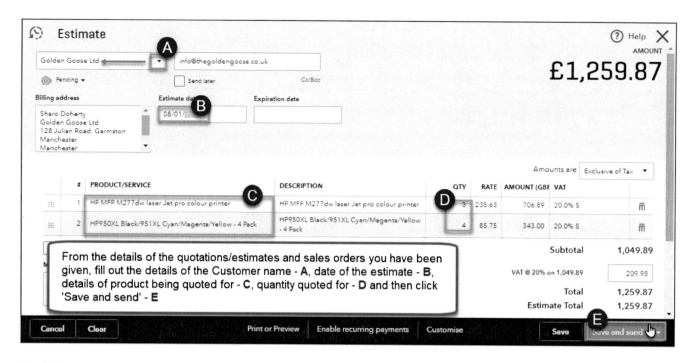

Fig. 177

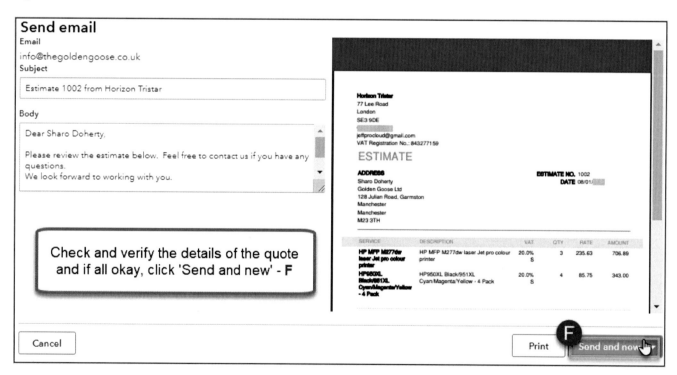

Fig. 178

And for A2Z Enterprises, here is how the quotation/estimate should look like on your screen.

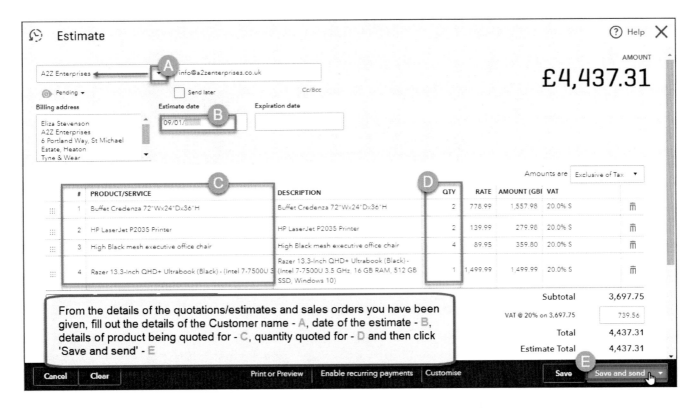

Fig. 179

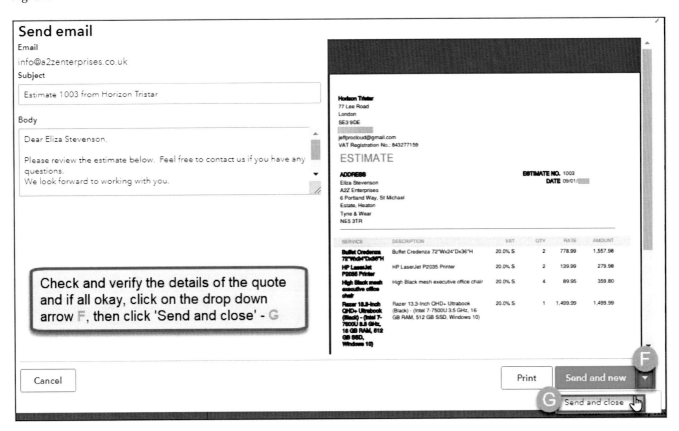

Fig. 180

Processing a customer sales invoice from sales orders.

Let's raise the first invoice Atomic Ltd. Click on the Create (+) button, then click on Invoice

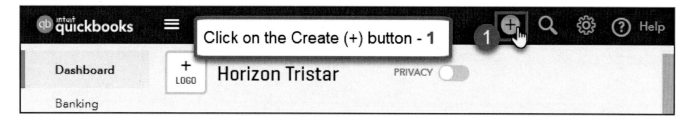

Fig. 181

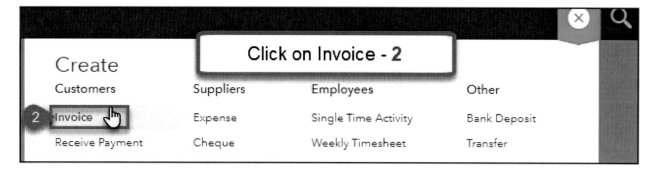

Fig. 182

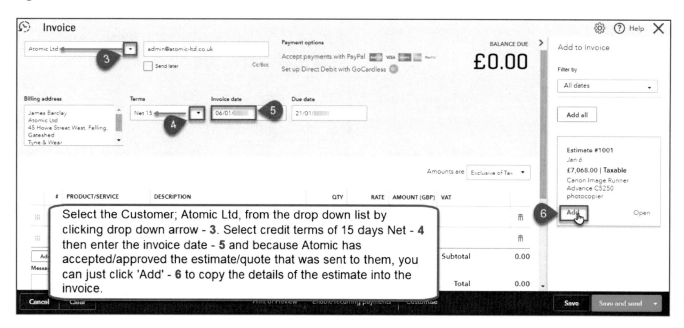

Fig. 183

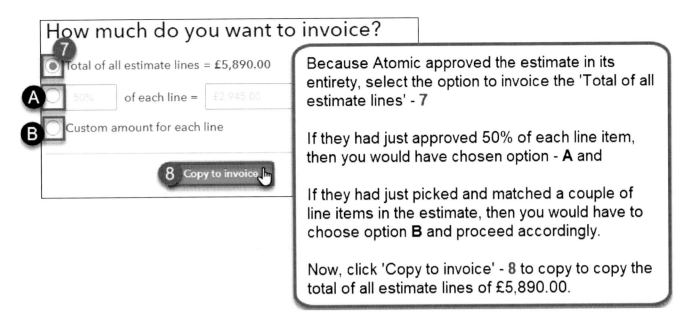

Fig. 184

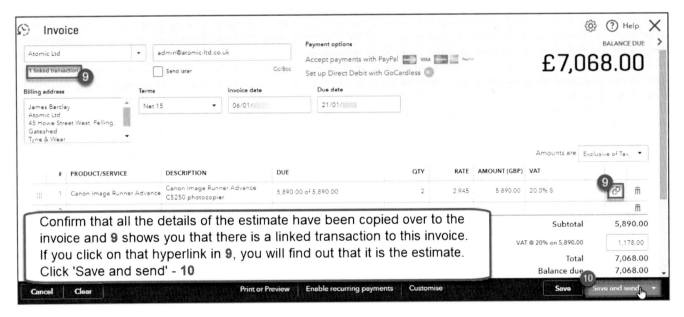

Fig. 185

This space is for notes

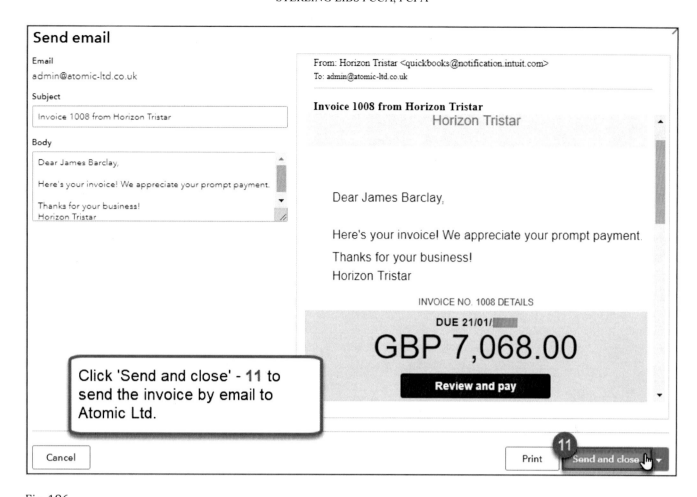

Fig. 186

For the Invoice for Golden Goose Ltd, see below.

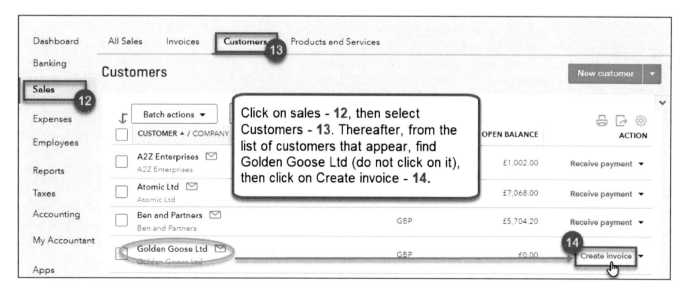

Fig. 187

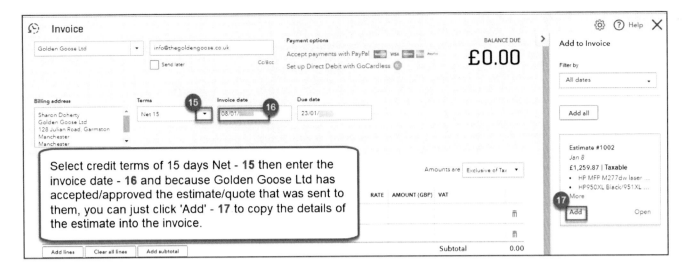

Select credit terms of 15 days Net - **15** then enter the invoice date - **16** and because Golden Goose Ltd has accepted/approved the estimate/quote that was sent to them, you can just click 'Add' - **17** to copy the details of the estimate into the invoice.

Fig. 188

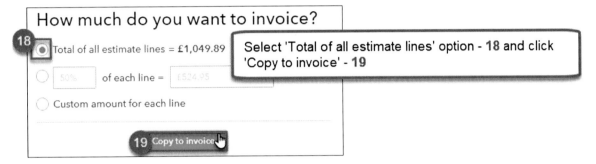

Select 'Total of all estimate lines' option - **18** and click 'Copy to invoice' - **19**

Fig. 189

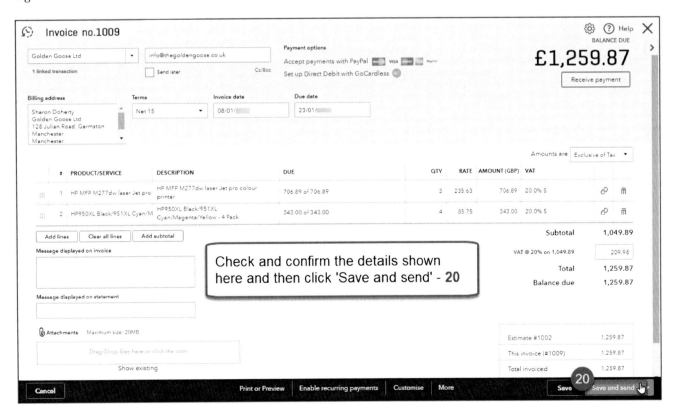

Check and confirm the details shown here and then click 'Save and send' - **20**

Fig. 190

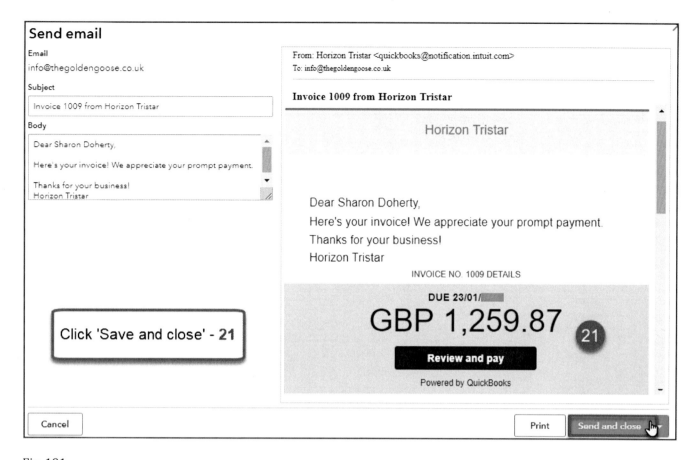

Fig. 191

Invoice for A2Z Enterprises

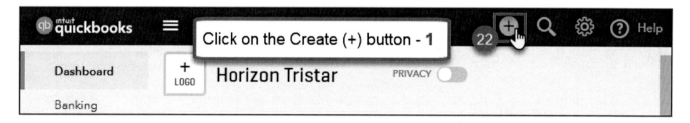

Fig. 192

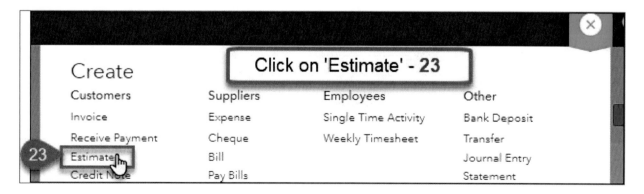

Fig. 193

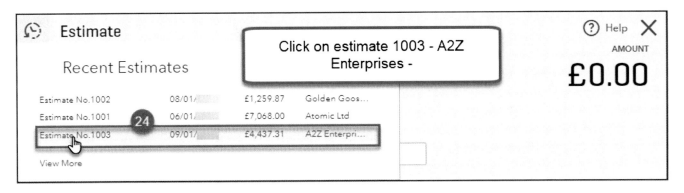

Fig. 194

Fig. 195

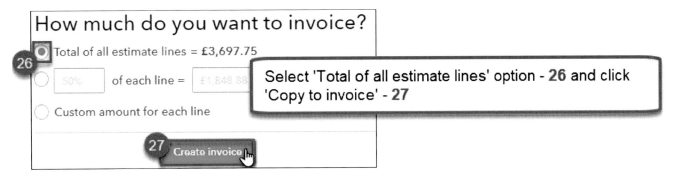

Fig. 196

This space is for notes

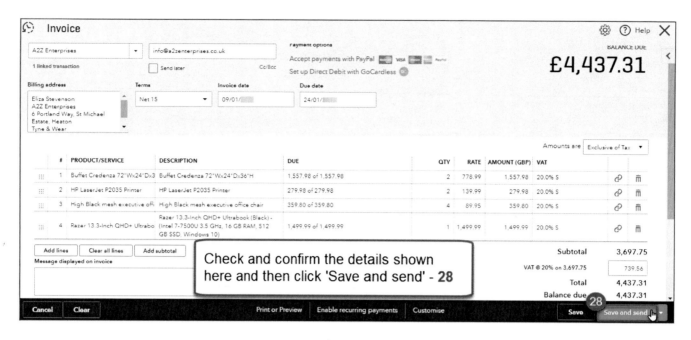

Fig. 197

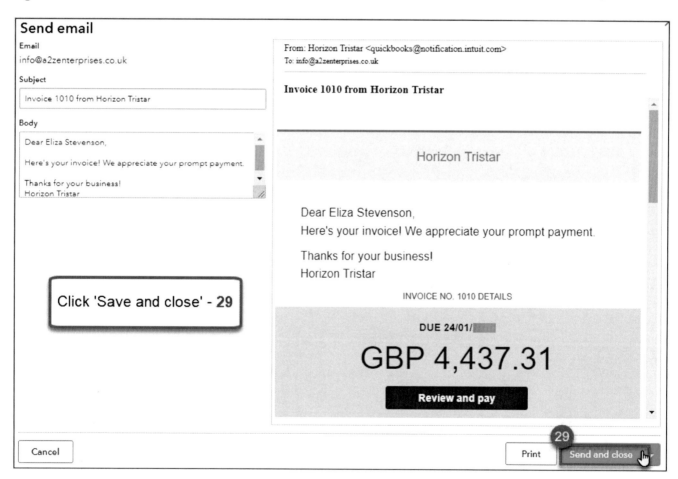

Fig. 198

In the next task, you will have to raise the sales invoice directly from the software instead of going through the sales order/estimate route like we did in the previous sales invoices.

Here is how to do it;
Click on the Create (+) button, then click on Invoice

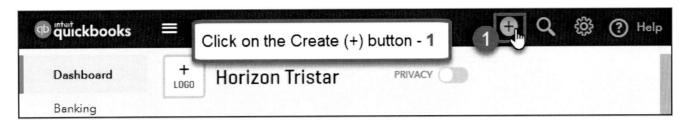

Fig. 199

Fig. 200

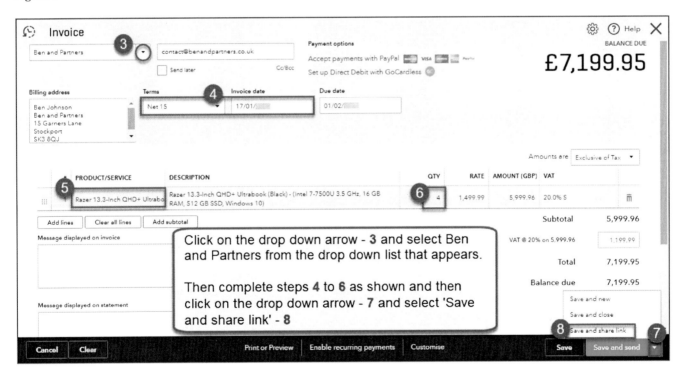

Fig. 201

This space is for notes

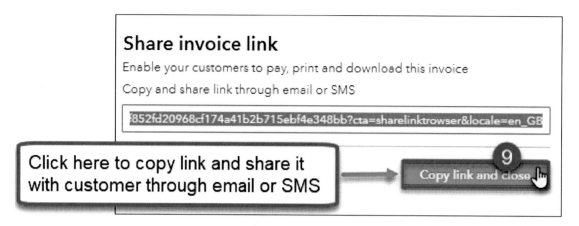

Fig. 202

Click the X at the top right to close the current window and then follow the steps 1 and 2 above to record the next invoice after you have sent the link to the customer for the invoice you have just raised in the previous steps.

Your next invoice window should look like the figure shown below.

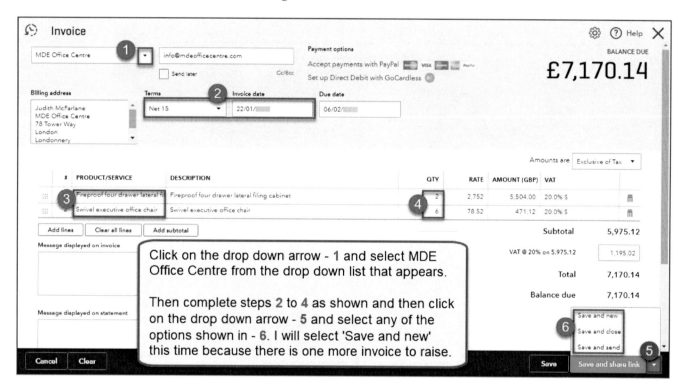

Fig. 203

The next window for the invoice for Peacock Interiors is as shown in figure 204 on the next page.

Notes

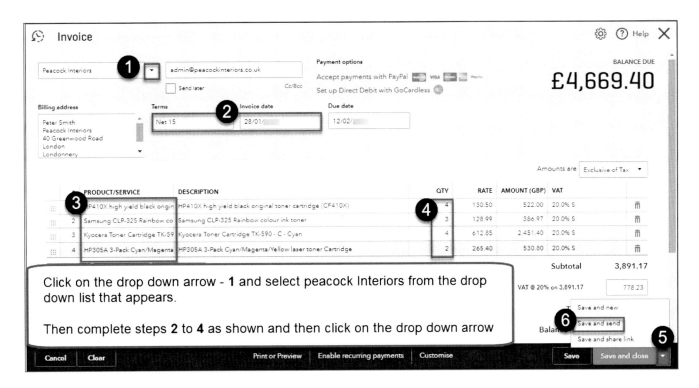

Fig. 204

Fig. 205

Raising a sales credit note

A credit note is a posting transaction which can be applied to a Customer's invoice as a payment or reduction.

Here is how to do it in QuickBooks online;

Click on the Create (+) button, then click on 'Credit Note'.

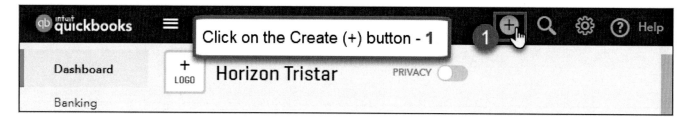

Fig. 206

Fig. 207

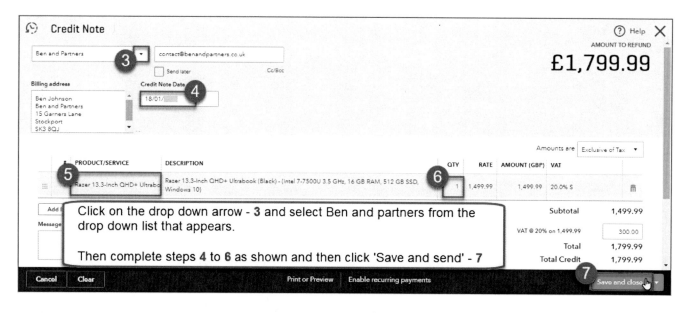

Fig. 208

You now need to apply the credit note you have just raised to the customer invoice to which the returned product relates to. You should do this because just raising a credit note as you did will affect the customer's overall balance, but will not affect a customer's invoice until it is applied to the invoice concerned.

So, here is how to do it.

Click on the Create (+) button, then click on Refund receipt

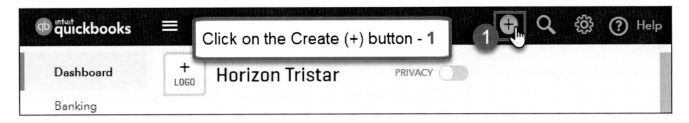

Fig. 209

Fig. 210

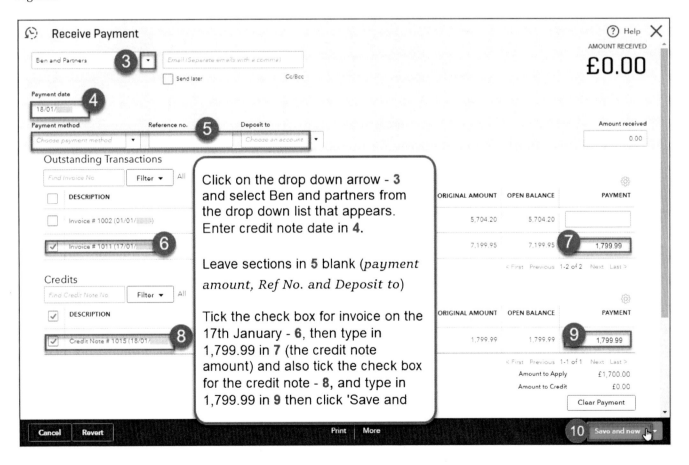

Fig. 211

Task 6b: Recording Customer receipts and a non-customer recept

Two customers; Ben and Partners, and Atomic have made BACS payments and have sent over remittance advice notes. You are now required to update the sales ledger with these details.

But before you that, let's have a look at three ways a customer can make payment for outstanding amounts.

Regardless whether it is customers making payments of their outstanding invoices or the company making payments to its suppliers, there basically three options available to do so:

1. Full payment of an outstanding invoice
2. Part payment of an outstanding invoice
3. Payment on account to reduce any outstanding balance (more like when you pay the minimum balance on your credit card)

See table below for a brief explanation of this a bit further

Payment option	What it means
1. **Full payment**	In this payment option, an outstanding invoice is paid in full. This payment method is specific in that; there is a specific outstanding invoice which the customer is paying for when they send a remittance.
2. **Part payment**	This payment option is similar to a full payment option in that there is specificity as to what invoice is being paid, except on this occasion, not the full amount of the outstanding invoice is being paid but just part of it.
3. **Payment on account**	In this payment option, a customer will just make payment but will not specify which particular outstanding invoice he/she is paying for. It is then left to the accounts receivable department to allocate the payment to the Customers outstanding invoices perhaps with the oldest ones cleared first. Think of the way most credit card bills are paid, most of those payments are payments on account – just to reduce the credit card bill amount each month. The credit card company then makes the payment allocations according to the terms they agreed with you when you signed up for the credit card.

A quick note

To help you keep track of money coming in and manage your cash flow it's important that you record your customer receipts.

The Customer Receipt window helps you easily record receipts and allocate them to the relevant invoices. You can see what the oldest outstanding invoices are so that you can clear these invoices first or you can even spread the receipt value over multiple invoices.

From here you can also allocate outstanding credit notes and outstanding payments on account to invoices.

Let's see how this done in QuickBooks Online

6b(i) Recording customer receipts

Full payment

If you are continuing from step 10 from the previous task, go straight to figure 215 on page 130, otherwise, if you are just starting afresh, Click on the Create (+) button, then click on 'Receive Payment.'

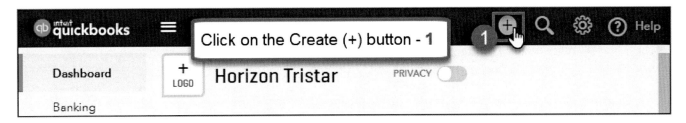

Fig. 212

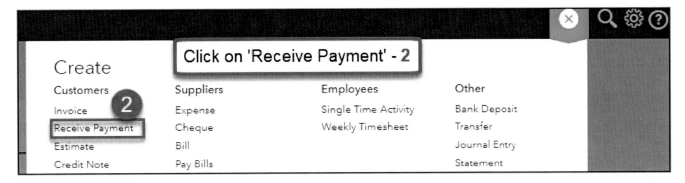

Fig. 213

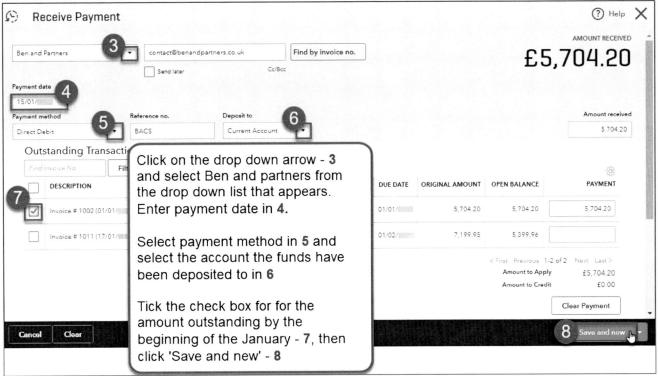

Fig. 214

The next payment is also a full payment by the customer – Atomic Ltd, and your screen should look like figure 215.

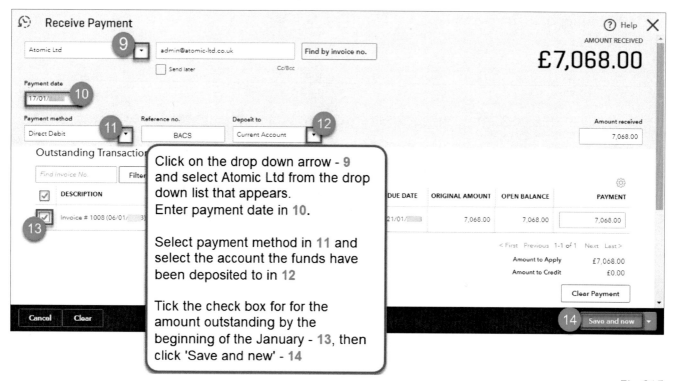

Receive Payment

Atomic Ltd ⑨ admin@atomic-ltd.co.uk   Find by invoice no.

AMOUNT RECEIVED
£7,068.00

Payment date
17/01/ ⑩

Payment method
Direct Debit ⑪   Reference no. BACS   Deposit to Current Account ⑫

Amount received
7,068.00

Outstanding Transaction

Find Invoice No.   Filter

☑ DESCRIPTION

⑬ ☑ Invoice # 1008 (06/01/   3)

DUE DATE 21/01/   ORIGINAL AMOUNT 7,068.00   OPEN BALANCE 7,068.00   PAYMENT 7,068.00

< First Previous 1-1 of 1 Next Last >

Amount to Apply   £7,068.00
Amount to Credit   £0.00

Clear Payment

Cancel   Clear

⑭ Save and new

> Click on the drop down arrow - **9** and select Atomic Ltd from the drop down list that appears.
> Enter payment date in **10**.
>
> Select payment method in **11** and select the account the funds have been deposited to in **12**
>
> Tick the check box for for the amount outstanding by the beginning of the January - **13**, then click 'Save and new' - **14**

Fig. 215

The next payment from the customer is a part payment of the outstanding invoice and continuing from the window that appears after step 14 above, here is how your work should look like:

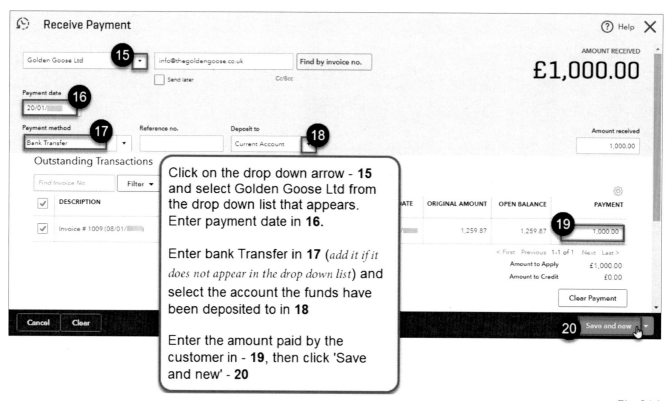

Receive Payment

Golden Goose Ltd ⑮   info@thegoldengoose.co.uk   Find by invoice no.

AMOUNT RECEIVED
£1,000.00

Payment date
20/01/ ⑯

Payment method
Bank Transfer ⑰   Reference no.   Deposit to Current Account ⑱

Amount received
1,000.00

Outstanding Transactions

Find Invoice No.   Filter

☑ DESCRIPTION

☑ Invoice # 1009 (08/01/   )

ATE   ORIGINAL AMOUNT 1,259.87   OPEN BALANCE 1,259.87   PAYMENT ⑲ 1,000.00

< First Previous 1-1 of 1 Next Last >

Amount to Apply   £1,000.00
Amount to Credit   £0.00

Clear Payment

Cancel   Clear

⑳ Save and new

> Click on the drop down arrow - **15** and select Golden Goose Ltd from the drop down list that appears.
> Enter payment date in **16**.
>
> Enter bank Transfer in **17** (*add it if it does not appear in the drop down list*) and select the account the funds have been deposited to in **18**
>
> Enter the amount paid by the customer in - **19**, then click 'Save and new' - **20**

Fig. 216

Follow through with the next part payment from Ben and Partners.

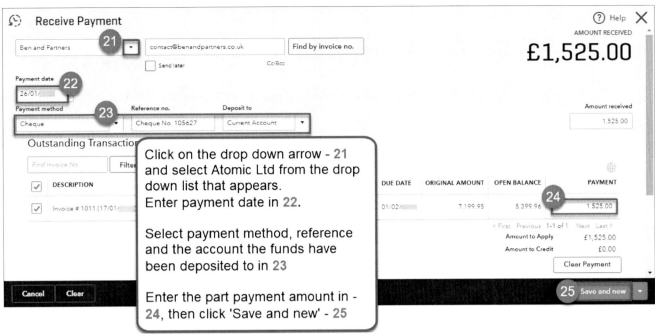

Fig. 217

The next payment made by the customer – A2Z Enterprises is a payment on account and here is how to record it.

From the window following step 25 in the previous task, here is how your screen should look like;

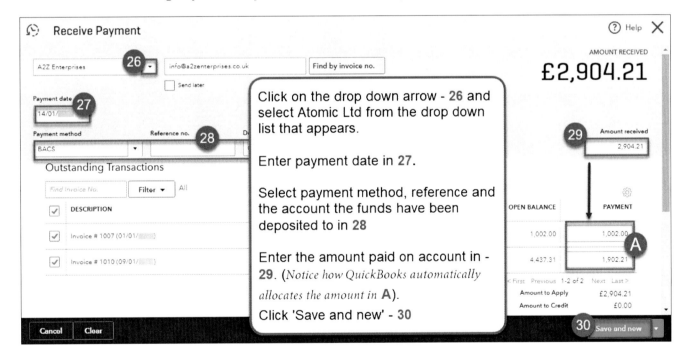

Fig. 218

We are also told that, A2Z also sent a cheque (without specifying which invoice they were paying for) and this cheque was deposited to the bank account on the 22nd January this year. So, you have to record that transaction too.

Here is how your work should look like;

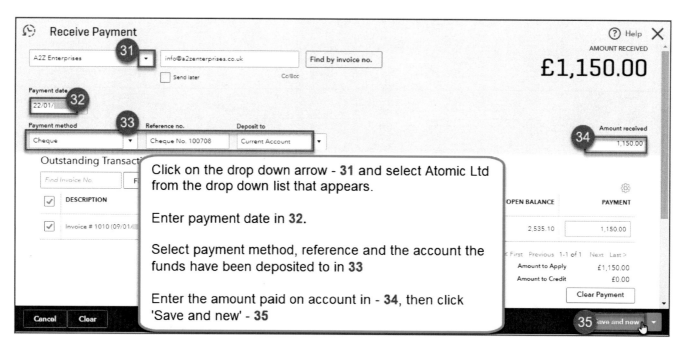

Fig. 219

6b.(ii) Recording non-customer receipts

Recording a VAT refund from HMRC (Tax Authority)

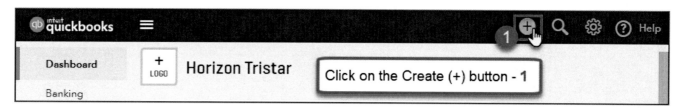

Fig. 220

Fig. 221

This space is for notes

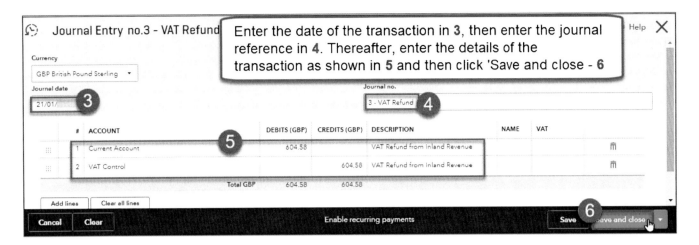

Fig. 222

Recording sales receipts

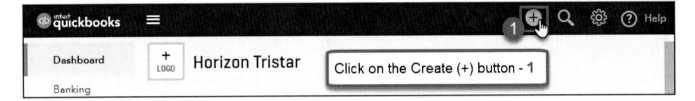

Fig. 223

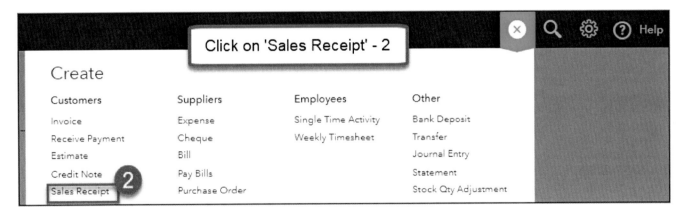

Fig. 224

This space is for notes

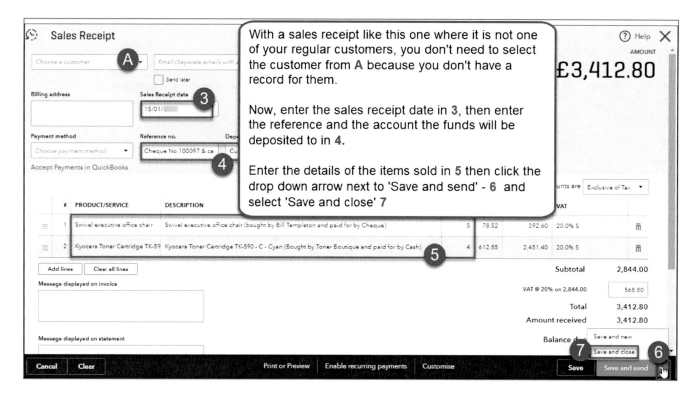

Fig. 225

Recording a drop shipping transaction.

If I am a supplier and a customer comes to me to buy something, and it so happens that I don't have that thing in stock, if I order that item from my supplier ask him to supply it directly to my customer, that would be termed as drop shipping.

We have a situation like that in our work experience to deal with – J.James' transaction. Let's deal with it.

Fig. 226

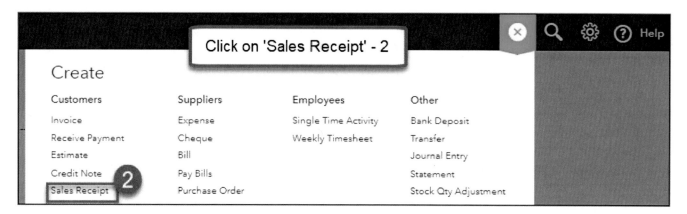

Fig. 227

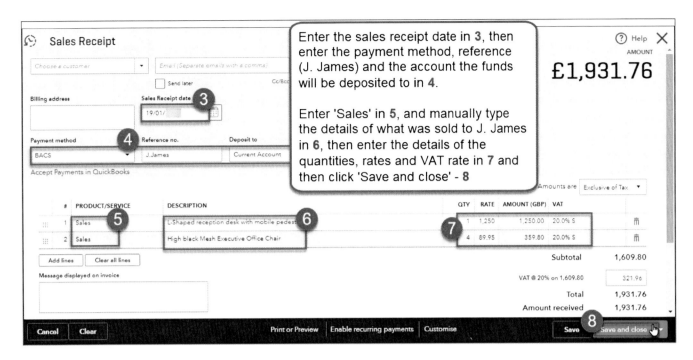

Fig. 228

Remember the items J. James paid for were delivered directly to him from Horizon Tristars supplier – Vandstone plc. The supplier has now sent n invoice for those items and therefore, you need to update the purchase ledger.

Here is how to do it.

Step **1**, click on the plus button - 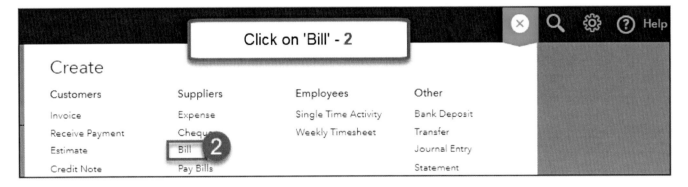 then select "Bill" under the heading of 'Suppliers.'

Fig. 229

This space is for notes

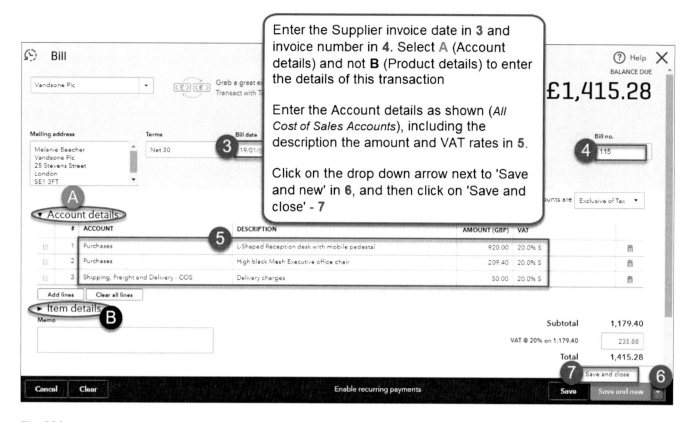

Enter the Supplier invoice date in **3** and invoice number in **4**. Select **A** (Account details) and not **B** (Product details) to enter the details of this transaction

Enter the Account details as shown (*All Cost of Sales Accounts*), including the description the amount and VAT rates in **5**.

Click on the drop down arrow next to 'Save and new' in **6**, and then click on 'Save and close' - **7**

Fig. 230

Task 6c: How to update dishonoured cheques and returned goods.

6c(i): Dishonoured cheque

How do you deal with cheques that the bank has cleared either insufficient funds or mistake on the cheque and how do you update the accounts when customers return goods and want a refund?

Here is how to enter these type of transactions in Quickbooks online.

Step **1**, click on the plus button - ⊕ 🔍 ⚙ and under Suppliers select 'Cheque.'

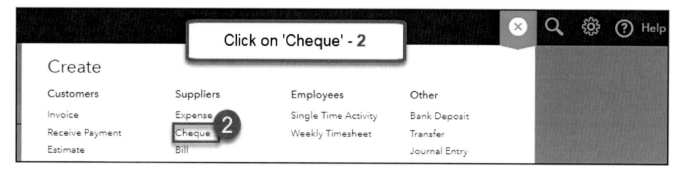

Fig. 231

This space is for notes

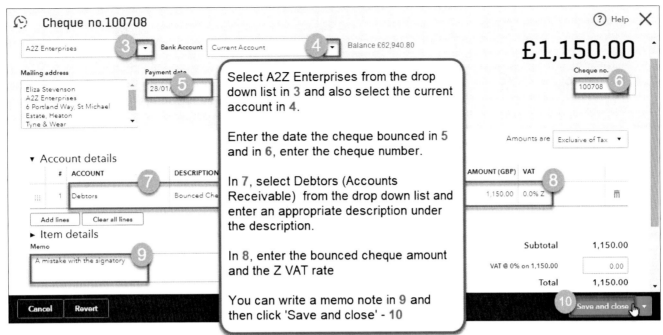

Fig. 232

The bounced cheque is now recorded.

What is a Bounced Check/Cheque

A bounced check/cheque is slang for a check/cheque that cannot be processed because the account holder has nonsufficient funds (NSF). Banks return, or bounce, these checks/cheques, also known as rubber checks/cheques, rather than honouring them, and banks charge the check/cheque writers NSF fees.

Source: *https://www.investopedia.com/terms/b/bouncedcheck.asp*

The next step is to record the service charge from the bank for the bounced/dishonoured cheque.

Step **11**, click on the plus button - , and under Suppliers select 'Expense.'

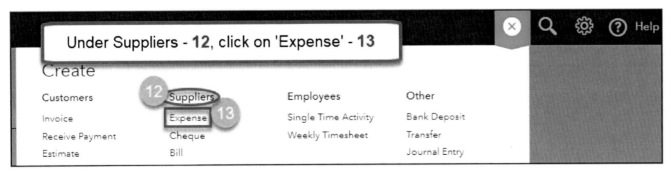

Fig. 233

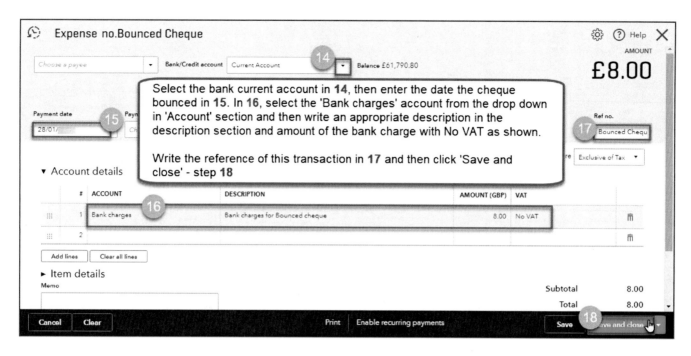

Fig. 234

Now, you need to invoice the customer for the bank charge that the bank charged the company for this bounced cheque.

Here is how to do it.

Next step, click on the plus button - 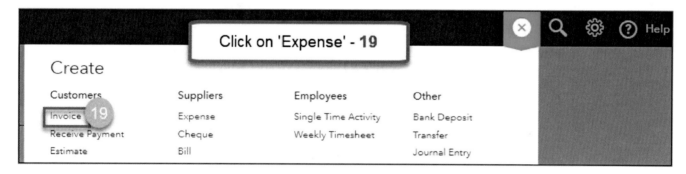, and under Customers select 'Invoice.'

Fig. 235

This space is for notes

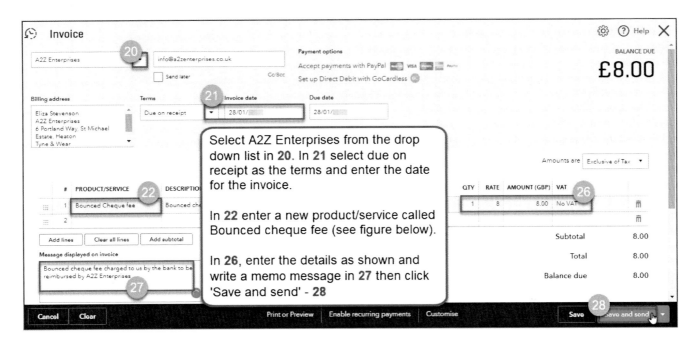

Fig. 236

Step 22 above

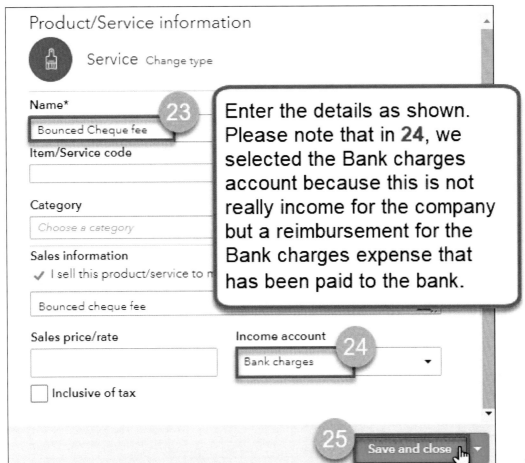

Fig. 237

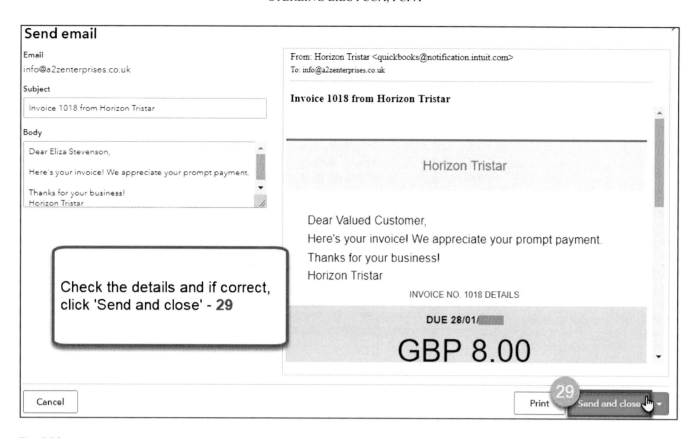

Fig. 238

Task 6c(ii): Dealing with returns in

In this task, you need to record a refund of the sales receipt for the items returned by J. James and also update the stock.

Let's get right to it.

Step **1**, click on the plus button - [⊕ 🔍 ⚙] , and under Customers select 'Refund receipt'

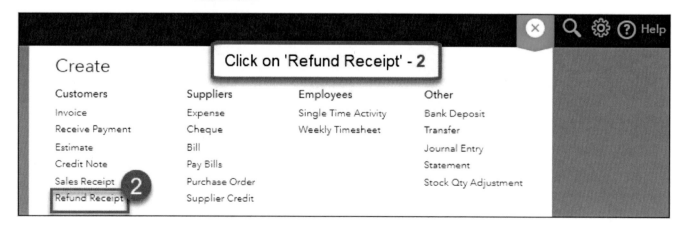

Fig. 239

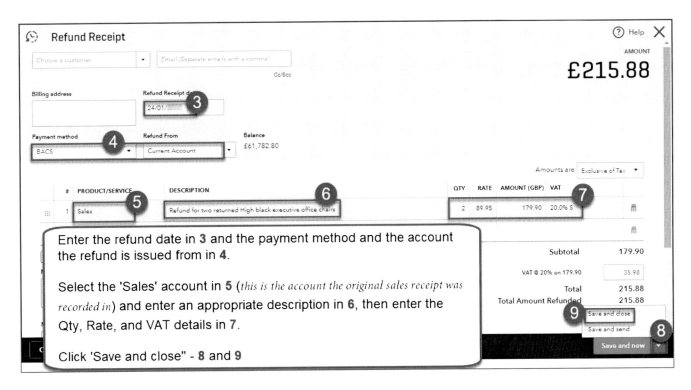

Fig. 240

Here is the confirmation message that the refund has been processed.

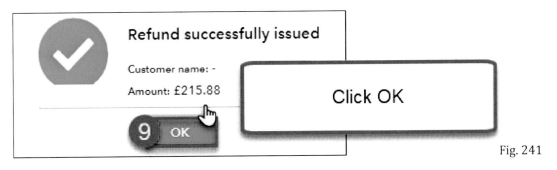

Fig. 241

Let's now update the stock with the chairs that were returned.

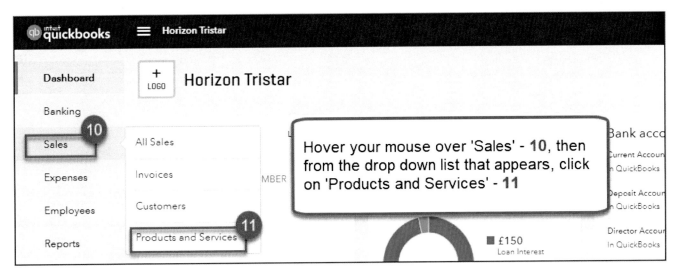

Fig. 242

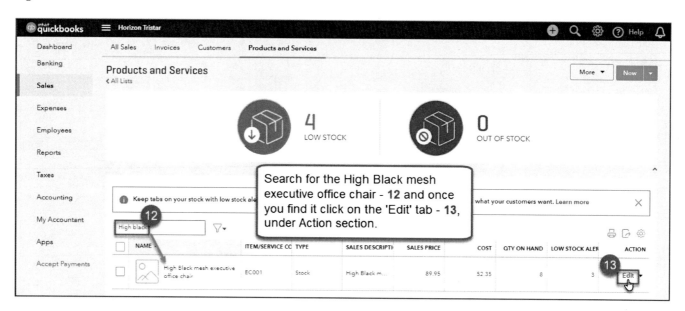

Search for the High Black mesh executive office chair - **12** and once you find it click on the 'Edit' tab - **13**, under Action section.

Fig. 243

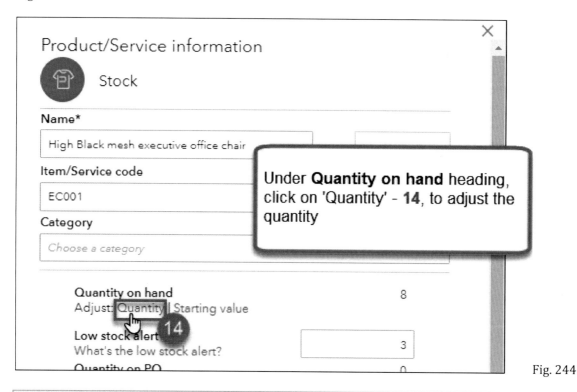

Under **Quantity on hand** heading, click on 'Quantity' - **14**, to adjust the quantity

Fig. 244

Note about Online, mail and phone order sales

Online, mail and telephone order customers have the right to cancel their order for a limited time even if the goods aren't faulty. Sales of this kind are known as 'distance selling'.

You must offer a refund to customers if they've told you within 14 days of receiving their goods that they want to cancel. They have another 14 days to return the goods once they've told you.

You must refund the customer within 14 days of receiving the goods back. They don't have to provide a reason.

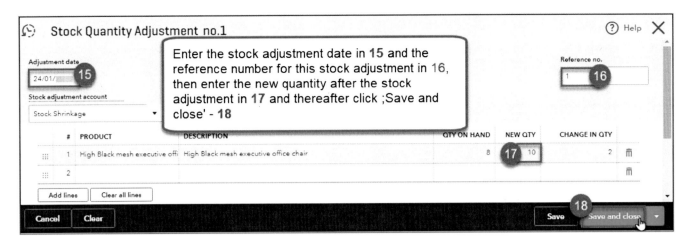

Fig. 245

What the law says about refunds - UK

You must offer a full refund if an item is faulty, not as described or doesn't do what it's supposed to. Under the Consumer Rights Act 2015, consumers may be entitled to a refund, replacement, repair and/or compensation where goods are faulty or not as described; they are also entitled to a refund and/or compensation where the seller had no legal right to sell the goods.

When you don't have to offer a refund

You don't have to refund a customer if they:

- knew an item was faulty when they bought it
- damaged an item by trying to repair it themselves or getting someone else to do it (though they may still have the right to a repair, replacement or partial refund)
- no longer want an item (e.g. because it's the wrong size or colour) unless they bought it without seeing it

You have to offer a refund for certain items only if they're faulty, such as:

- personalised items and custom-made items, e.g. curtains
- perishable items, e.g. frozen food or flowers
- newspapers and magazines
- unwrapped CDs, DVDs and computer software

This space is for notes

Task 6d: How to collect outstanding debtor amounts – part of credit control.

The first thing to do here is to generate a collection report for the accounts that are past their due dates.

Here is how to do it.

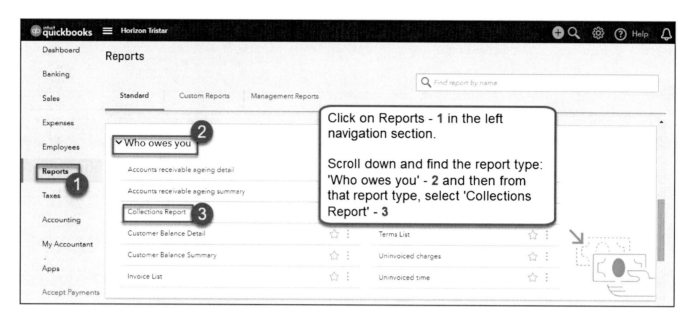

Fig. 246

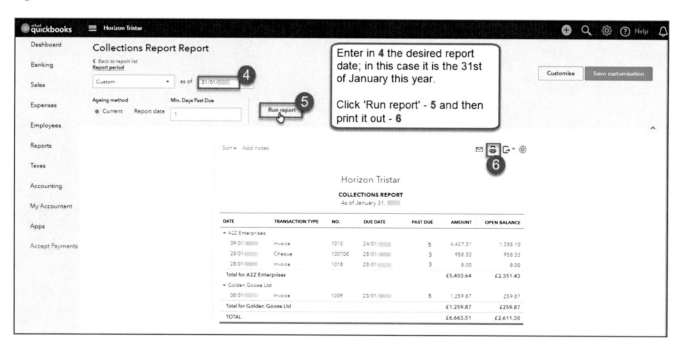

Fig. 247

Once you have the printed report, use the following debt collection procedure to collect the overdue accounts.

14 steps to take to collect outstanding debts from debtors

1. *Send the customer a current account statement or gentle reminder.*

2. *Five working days after sending the statement check to see whether the amount has been paid.*

3. *If the amount has not been paid, telephone the client and discuss the reason for non-payment, remind them of their credit terms, and agree on a payment date.*

4. *Write a letter to the client summarising the telephone conversation and noting the agreed payment date.*

5. *Make a note on the system of the date payment should be received. Use the communication tab on customer record window from Sage to make a note.*

6. *If payment is not received by the agreed date telephone the client and remind them of your previous discussion.*

7. *Agree on a date for payment (or direct debit/credit card if applicable).*

8. *Write a letter to the client summarising the telephone conversation and noting the agreed payment date.*

9. *Make a note on the system of the date payment should be received.*

10. *If payment is not received by the agreed date telephone the client.*

11. *Write a letter to the client summarising the telephone conversation and noting the date court proceedings will commence.*

12. *Make a note on the system of the date payment should be received.*

13. *If payment is not received within the specified time, then continue with the County Court procedure.*

14. *Make arrangements to attend court.*

I do not like to state my opinion on matters unless I know the precise facts

Albert Einstein

TASK 7: JOURNAL ENTRIES AND DOUBLE ENTRY REVIEW

Task 7a: Posting a financial instrument Journal – issue of share capital.

12,000 £1.00 ordinary shares were issued for a cash consideration of £2.70 each, and there were £1,000 of brokers fees to pay.

Here is what to do to enter this transaction in QuickBooks online;

Step **1**, click on the plus button -  , and under Other, select 'Journal Entry'

Fig. 248

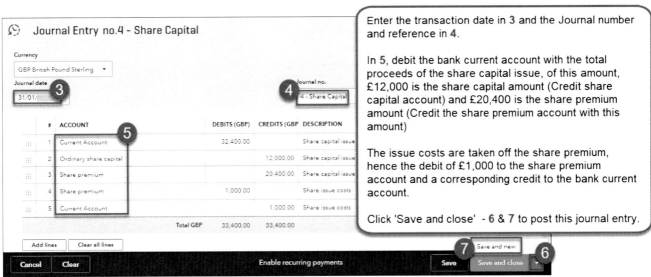

Enter the transaction date in **3** and the Journal number and reference in **4**.

In **5**, debit the bank current account with the total proceeds of the share capital issue, of this amount, £12,000 is the share capital amount (Credit share capital account) and £20,400 is the share premium amount (Credit the share premium account with this amount)

The issue costs are taken off the share premium, hence the debit of £1,000 to the share premium account and a corresponding credit to the bank current account.

Click 'Save and close' - **6 & 7** to post this journal entry.

Fig. 249

Task 7b: Recording Director transactions in a journal.

From the window that appears after step 6 in the previous task, here is how the journal entry for the Director transactions will look like.

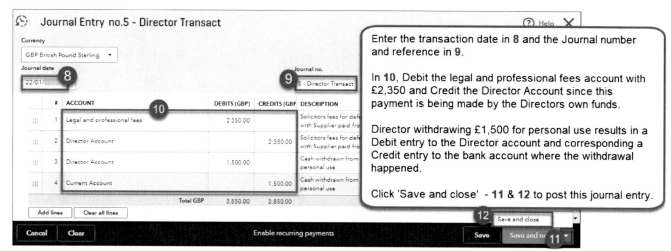

Fig. 250

A brief note about journals

In manual accounting or bookkeeping systems, business transactions are first recorded in a journal...hence the term journal entry.

A manual journal entry that is recorded in a company's general journal will consist of the following:

- the appropriate date
- the amount(s) and account(s) that will be debited
- the amount(s) and account(s) that will be credited
- a short description/memo
- a reference such as a check number

These journalised amounts (which will appear in the journal in order by date) are then posted to the accounts in the general ledger.

Today, computerised accounting systems will automatically record most of the business transactions into the general ledger accounts immediately after the software prepares the sales invoices, processes receipts from customers, etc. The result is, we will not see journal entries for most of the business transactions.

However, we will need to process some journal entries in order to record transfers between bank accounts and to record adjusting entries. For example, it is likely that at the end of each month there will be a journal entry to record depreciation. (This will include a debit to Depreciation Expense and a credit to Accumulated Depreciation.) In addition, there will likely be a need for journal entry to accrue interest on a bank loan. (This will include a debit to Interest Expense and a credit to Interest Payable.)

Task 7c: Double entry review.

Task 7c(i): Double entry to record a cash sale paid for by cash and bank transfer.

Step **1**, click on the plus button - 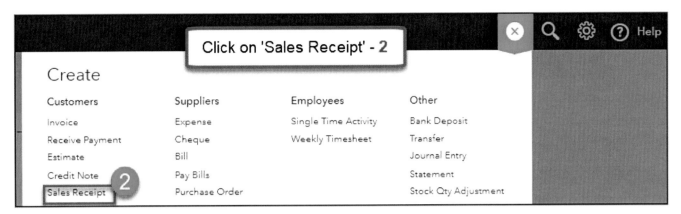, and under Customers, select 'Sales Receipt.'

Fig. 251

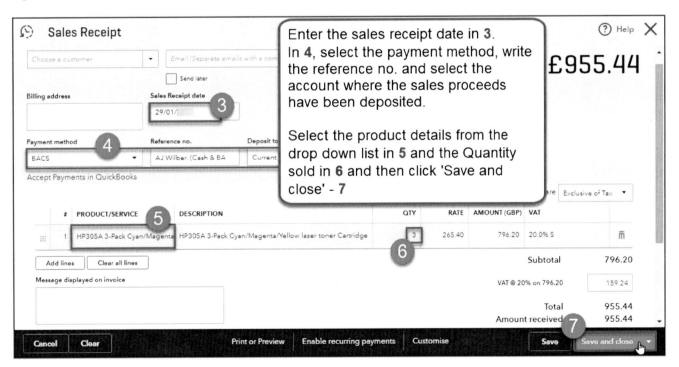

Fig. 252

This space is for notes

Task 7c(ii): Double entry to record a Credit sale.

Step **8**, click on the plus button - ![plus button icons], and under Customers, select 'Invoice.'

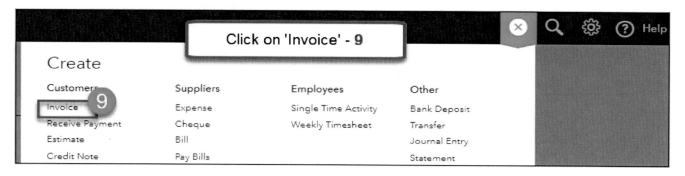

Fig. 253

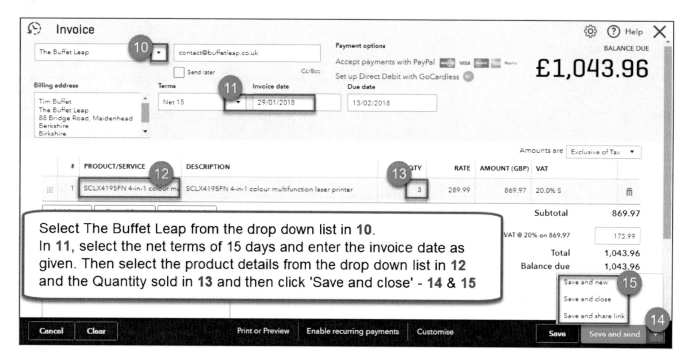

Fig. 254

Task 7c(iii): Double entry to record Company money spent by Director for personal benefit.

Step **16**, click on the plus button - ![plus button icons], and under Other, select 'Transfer.'

Fig. 255

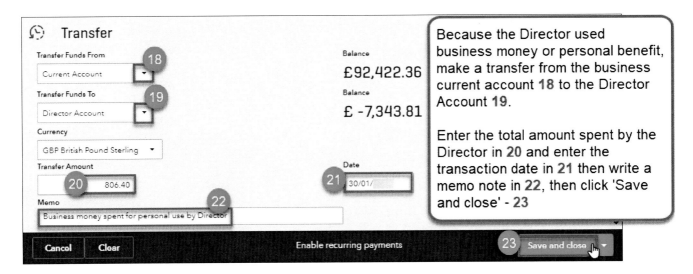

Fig. 256

Task 7c(iv): Double entry to record Directors money spent for business purposes.

Step **24**, click on the plus button - [icons], and under Other, select 'Journal Entry'

Fig. 257

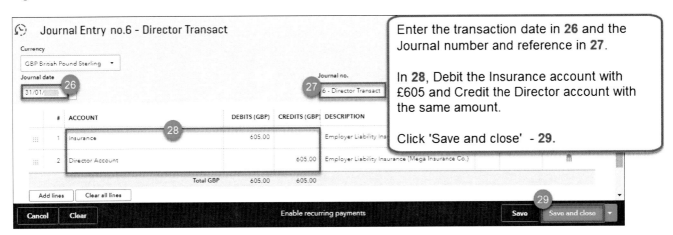

Fig. 258

"If you want to live a happy life, tie it to a goal and not on people or objects"

Albert Einstein

TASK 8: HOW TO ENSURE SECURITY OF ACCOUNTING DATA

Task 8a: How to change your password in QuickBooks online.

Here is how to do it.

Step **1**, click on the gear icon - 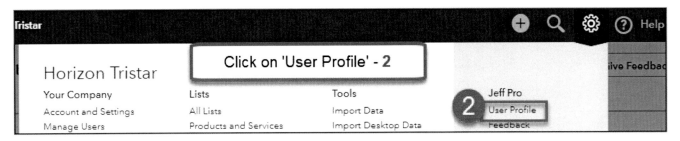 , then select 'User profile.'

Fig. 259

Fig. 260

Task 8b: How to add a new user in QuickBooks online.

We are adding a new user - Caroline McFarlane. Here is how to do it.

Step **1**, click on the gear icon - 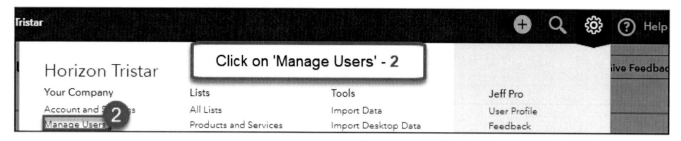 , then under 'Your Company' select 'Manage Users'

Fig. 261

Fig. 262

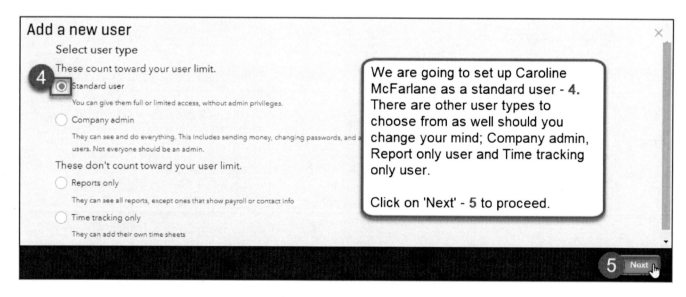

Fig. 263

This space is for notes

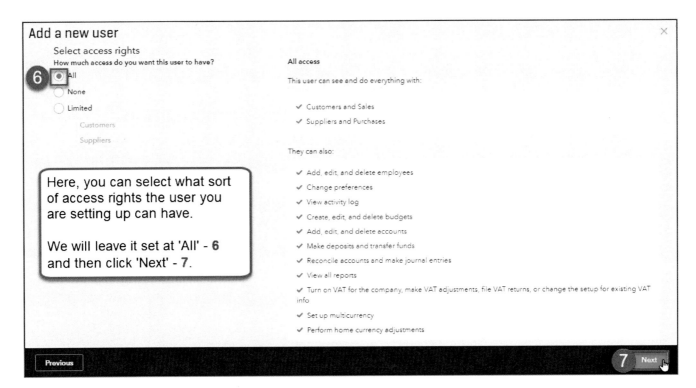

Fig. 264

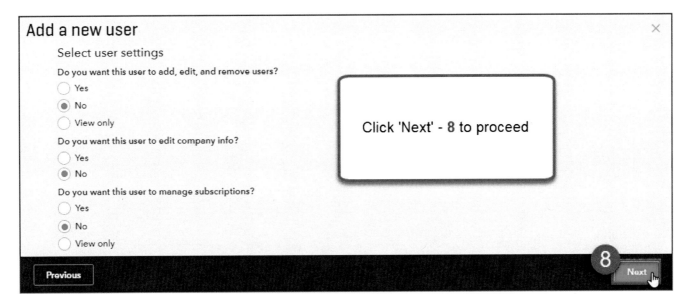

Fig. 265

This space is for notes

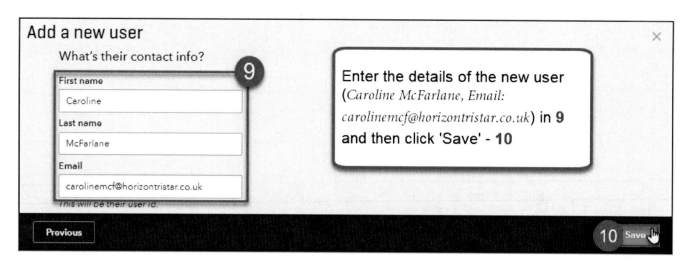

Fig. 266

"Alone we can do so little, together we can do so much"

Helen Keller

TASK 9: BANK RECONCILIATION & VAT RETURNS

Task 9a: How to do bank reconciliation

Reconciling your bank is simply the process of matching your QuickBooks online transactions to those that appear on your bank statement.

Here is how to do it.

Step **1**, click on the gear icon - 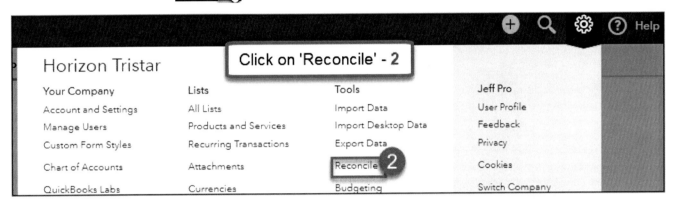, then under 'Tools' select 'Reconcile'. See below

Fig. 267

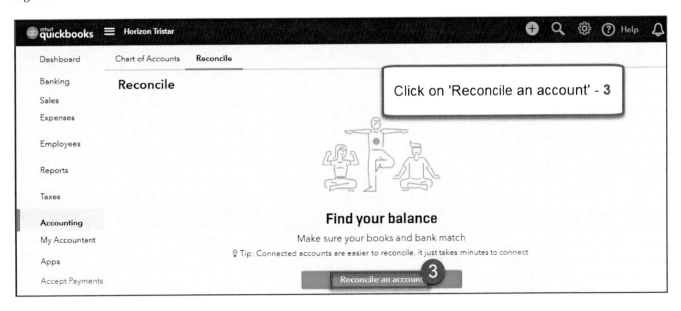

Fig. 268

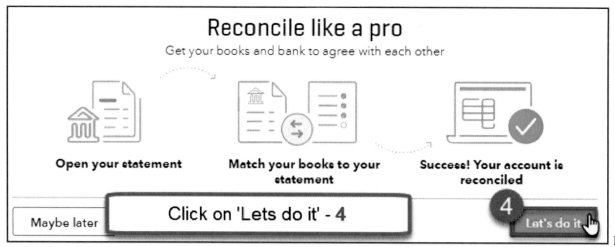

Fig. 269

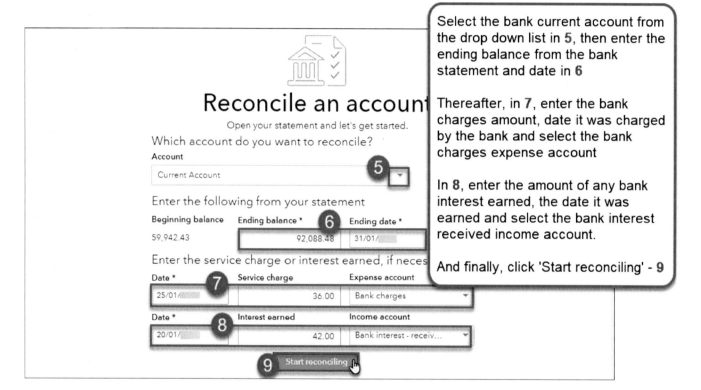

Fig. 270

This space is for notes

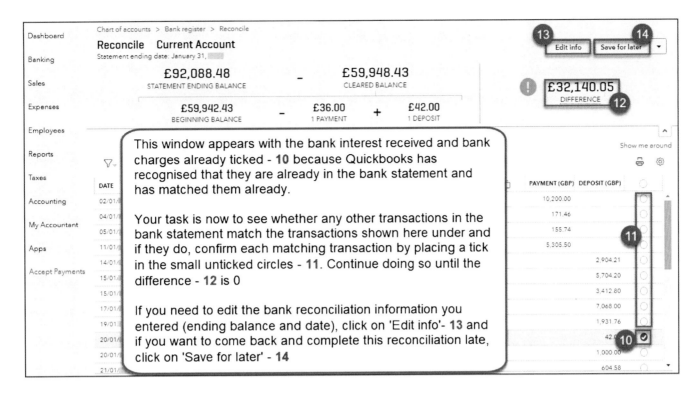

Fig. 271

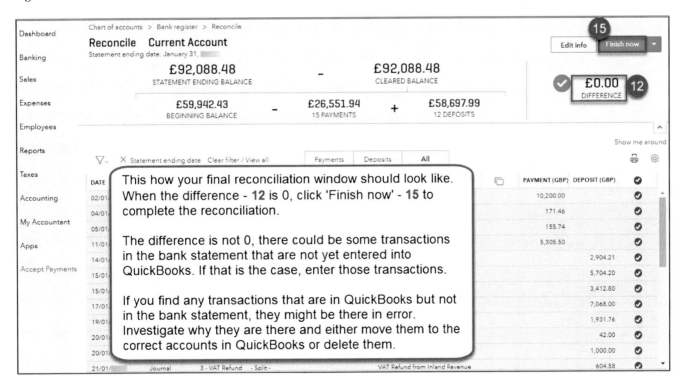

Fig. 272

Bank statement transactions upload to QuickBooks online

You can upload your business bank statement transactions into QuickBooks online in two ways.

1. Manual upload through a csv excel file or
2. Connecting your business bank account to QuickBooks and have automatic downloads of your bank

statement transactions. Please note that the first time you do this, only the latest three months' worth of transactions will be downloaded into QuickBooks online.

Here is how you can upload the bank statement transactions.

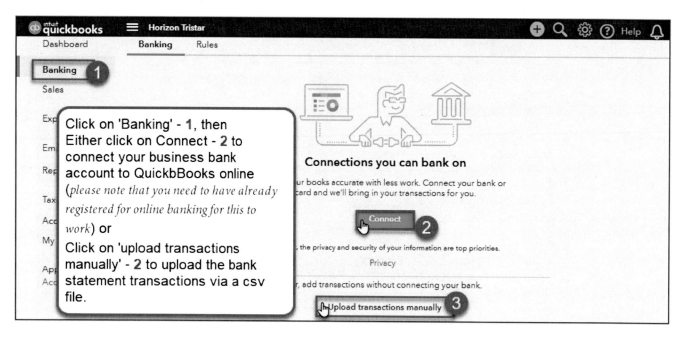

Click on 'Banking' - **1**, then
Either click on Connect - **2** to connect your business bank account to QuickbBooks online (*please note that you need to have already registered for online banking for this to work*) **or**
Click on 'upload transactions manually' - **2** to upload the bank statement transactions via a csv file.

Fig. 273

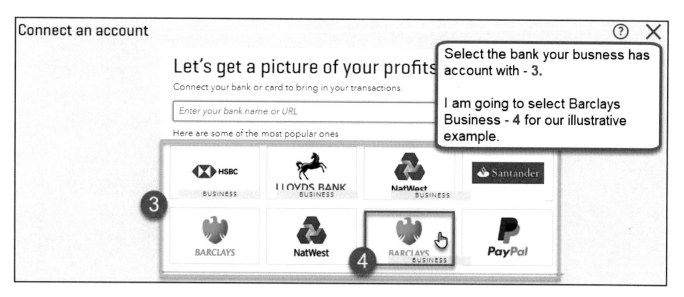

Select the bank your busness has account with - **3**.

I am going to select Barclays Business - **4** for our illustrative example.

Fig. 274

This space is for notes

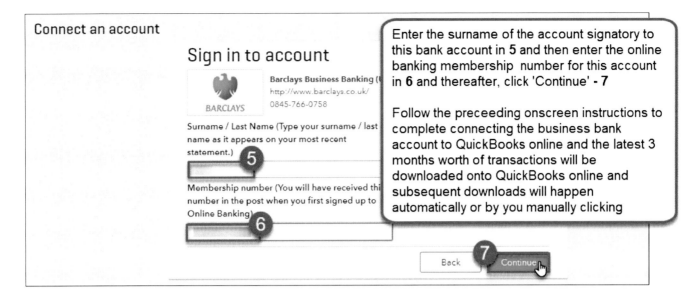

Connect an account

Sign in to account

Barclays Business Banking (
http://www.barclays.co.uk/
0845-766-0758

Surname / Last Name (Type your surname / last name as it appears on your most recent statement.) **5**

Membership number (You will have received thi number in the post when you first signed up to Online Banking) **6**

> Enter the surname of the account signatory to this bank account in **5** and then enter the online banking membership number for this account in **6** and thereafter, click 'Continue' - **7**
>
> Follow the preceeding onscreen instructions to complete connecting the business bank account to QuickBooks online and the latest 3 months worth of transactions will be downloaded onto QuickBooks online and subsequent downloads will happen automatically or by you manually clicking

Back   **7** Continue

Fig. 275

There you have it.

"It has become appallingly obvious that our technology has exceeded our humanity"

Albert Einstein

Let's move on next to look at VAT return preparation in QuickBooks online.

Task 9b: How to prepare, reconcile & submit a VAT Return to Her Majesty's Revenue & Customs (HMRC).

When you register for VAT, HMRC will advise you of the VAT periods, you'll submit for. If you submit quarterly your VAT period falls into one of the following staggers:

- March - June - September - December
- April - July - October - January
- May-August - November - February

If necessary, you can apply to have your VAT period end pattern changed to a different pattern, or request to submit monthly or annual VAT Returns.

Calculating the VAT Return doesn't affect your transactions in QuickBooks online, no postings are made to your nominal codes. This means that you can calculate your VAT Return as many times as necessary. However, when you mark your transactions as being reconciled, this prevents them from being automatically included in a future VAT return calculated in QuickBooks online.

Preparation:

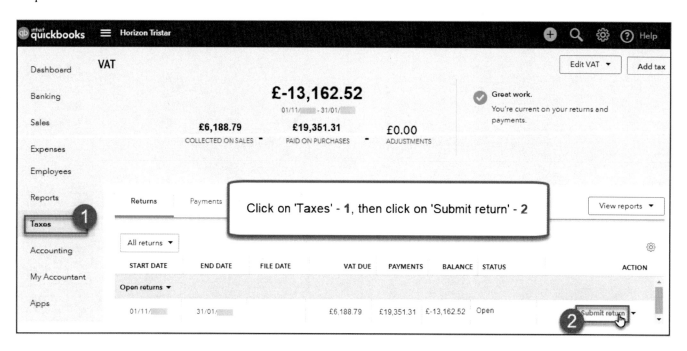

Fig. 276

This space is for notes

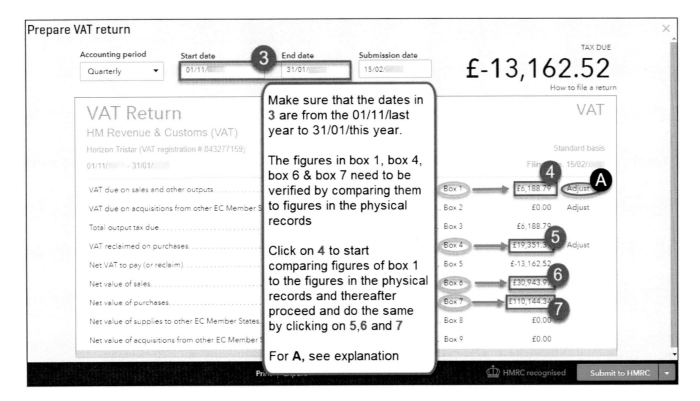

Fig. 277

If you have discovered any mismatch (errors) in the figures in this return, please go to the transactions and amend them.

If you need to make any adjustment to this return due to errors in previous VAT returns that were discovered after the VAT return(s) was submitted, click on Adjust – **A,** to adjust the figures in box 1 or 4.

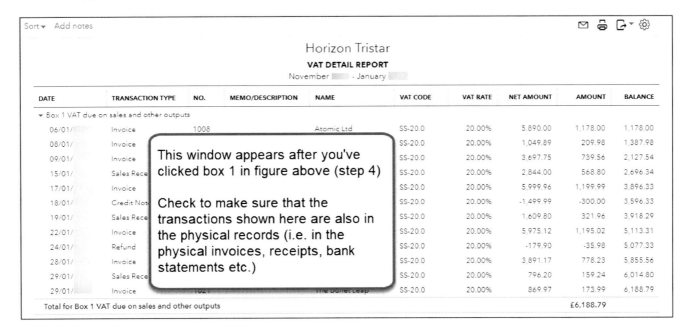

Fig. 278

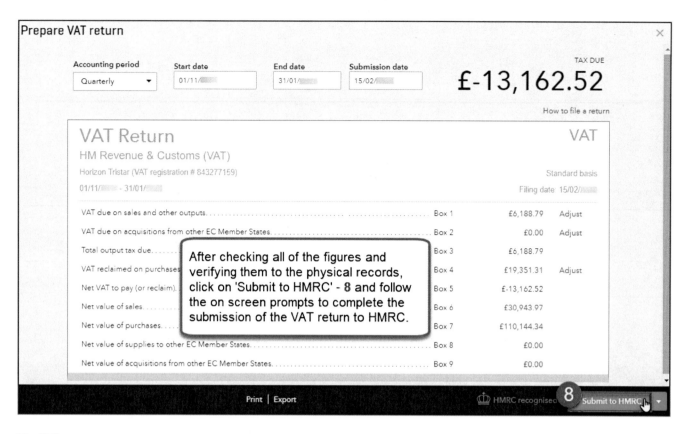

Fig. 279

TASK 10: INTRODUCTION TO MONTH END ACCOUNTING PROCEDURES

There are three steps to take to perform the end-of-the-month accounting process successfully. They are:

Description of the key steps	What to do at each stage (the tasks)
Key step 1: Checking the general ledger accounts for errors & making the necessary corrections	• *Correct the general ledger account errors including mispostings and inaccuracies.*
Key step 2: Doing Adjustments and Reconciliations	• *Financial adjustments, e.g. interest payments adjustments, prepayments, accruals and depreciation* • *Control account reconciliations: Debtors' control account, Creditors' control account, VAT control account, Bank account, Wages account etc.* • *Balance sheet reconciliation (Reconciliation of the Assets, Liabilities, Equity & Reserves)* • *Calculations of closing balances of the accounts after adjustments & reconciliations*
Key step 3: Reporting to senior management	• *Producing a profit & Loss statement and other various management reports if necessary.*

The accounting process can differ slightly from one business to another based on variances in the chart of accounts, revenue and expense recognition, and cost centre breakdown.

Despite these differences, the overall monthly closing process is the same. Following the same standard procedures to close the books each month will help ensure consistent and accurate reporting.

Let's now have a look at how the month end procedures stated in the table above are performed.

How to make nominal account checks & corrections

At this stage:

- ✓ First, establish a closing date by which all expenses and revenue must be posted.
- ✓ Then communicate the closing date to everyone who has access to modify the ledger and
- ✓ Finally lock the ledgers for the month/period as of the date communicated, prohibiting any further changes to the ledgers for that period.

After that,

- ✓ Produce or generate the trial balance report from your accounting software
- ✓ Review the balances in each of the nominal accounts in the Trial balance report to identify any anomalies from what is expected and correct any errors (arithmetical, principle, etc.)
- ✓ Review the transaction details for any accounts you are uncertain of and note any adjustments that need to be made.

To generate your trial balance in follow the steps as illustrated in the figure below.

Fig. 280

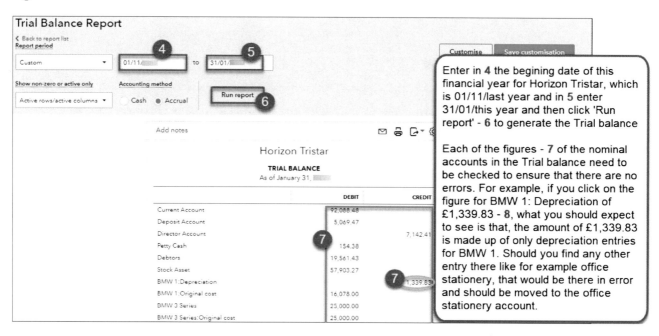

Fig. 281

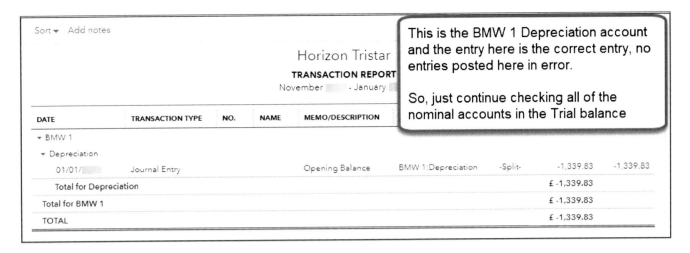

Fig. 282

A Trial Balance is a list of closing balances of ledger accounts on a certain date. It is usually prepared at the end of an accounting period to assist in the drafting of financial statements. Ledger balances are segregated into debit balances and credit balances. Asset and expense accounts appear on the debit side of the trial balance whereas liabilities, capital and income accounts appear on the credit side. If all accounting entries are recorded correctly and all the ledger balances are accurately extracted, the total of all debit balances appearing in the trial balance must equal to the sum of all credit balances.

Purpose of a Trial Balance

- Trial Balance acts as the first step in the preparation of financial statements. It is a working paper that accountants use as a basis while preparing financial statements.
- Trial balance ensures that for every debit entry recorded, a corresponding credit entry has been recorded in the books in accordance with the double entry concept of accounting. If the totals of the trial balance do not agree, the differences may be investigated and resolved before financial statements are prepared. Rectifying basic accounting errors can be a much lengthy task after the financial statements have been prepared because of the changes that would be required to correct the financial statements.
- Trial balance ensures that the account balances are accurately extracted from accounting ledgers.
- Trail balance assists in the identification and rectification of errors.

Making adjustments in the accounts

The common adjusting entries that affect the balance sheet are usually; prepayments, accruals, depreciation & amortisation

Let's look at how you should record each of them:

How to make adjustment for Prepayments

A prepaid expense is an advance payment for a future expense that is recorded as an asset at the time of payment, usually within the year or accounting period. All such costs cover a certain period, e.g. a rent purchase invoice is normally billed a quarter in advance. So, any given rent invoice will cover a period of 3 months. Similarly, business rates are billed in advance and cover a period of 12 months.

Given this, we need to calculate and see how much of the overheads relate to the current month/period and how much again relates to the future. If any of the overhead costs that cover future periods have also been posted to the income statement, you should take them out of the income statement for that month/period and post them to the balance sheet as an 'Overhead Prepayment'.

For example, rent invoice from Office Space Today (invoice number 2308-2847 dated 25th January) was paid on the 28th January. This invoice was for the period of February to April. In that case, the payment made on the 28th January is a prepayment, and you now need to make that adjustment for January month end.

Original Entry when invoice was recorded (Rent & internet charges portion):

Nominal Account	Account Type	DEBIT	CREDIT
Rent	Profit & Loss	12,720.00	
Internet Charges	Profit & Loss	180.00	
Purchase Tax (Input VAT)	Balance Sheet	2580.00	
Office Space Today (Creditor)	Balance Sheet		15,480.00

Original Entry when payment was made:

Nominal Account	Account Type	DEBIT	CREDIT
Office Space Today (Creditor)	Balance Sheet	15,480.00	
Director Bank account	Balance Sheet		15,480.00

Overhead Prepayment Journal to be made on 31 January (prepayment for February to April – 3 months)

N/C	Name	Details	T/C	Debit	Credit
1103	Prepayment	Rent prepayment adjustment	T9	12,720.00	
7100	Rent	Rent prepayment adjustment	T9		12,720.00
1103	Prepayment	Internet Charges prepayment	T9	180.00	
7551	Internet Charges	Internet Charges prepayment	T9		180.00

How to make adjustment for Accruals

The word accrual could mean a transaction in which:
- ✓ Revenue is earned, but no payment has been received – Accrued revenue (an asset), or
- ✓ An expense is incurred, but no payment has been paid – Accrued expense (a liability).

Accrued revenues always create a need to record a new receivable (Debit accounts receivable, and credit revenue/sales).

Let's first of all in this accruals task begin by recording the accrued expense.

In the case of Abacus Enterprises, at the end of January, you realised two issues:

Casual wages for one of the drivers paid on an hourly basis has not yet been paid. His total outstanding hours are 60 hours at an hourly rate of £20 per hour

The accrual adjustment journal to be posted is:

N/C	Name	Details	T/C	Debit	Credit
7005	Casual wages	Casual wages accrual	T9	1,200	
2109	Accruals	Casual wages accrual	T9		1,200

So, let me show you how to post the prepayment and accrual adjustments we have just looked, to QuickBooks online

Step **1**, click on the plus button - , and under Other, select 'Journal Entry'

Fig. 283

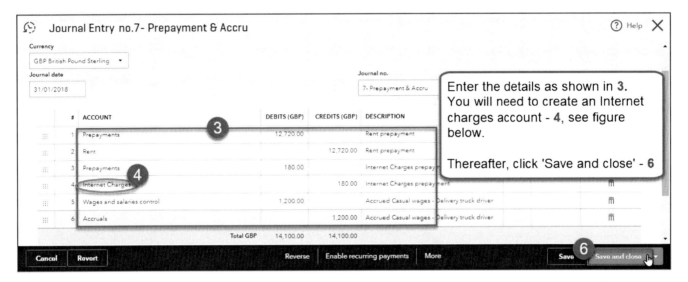

Fig. 284

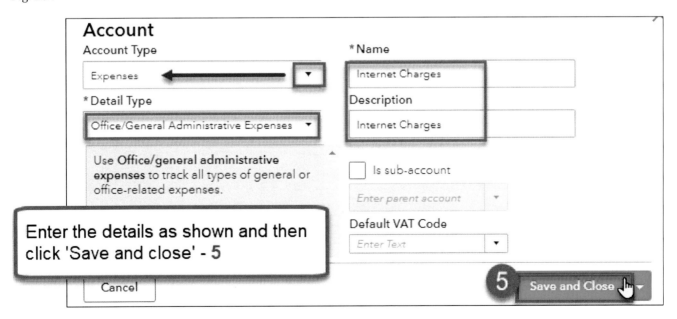

Fig. 285

At the end of February, you will have to reduce the rent prepayment asset by a third (being one month of rent expense incurred). Debit the rent account in the profit and loss and credit the rent prepayment account in the balance sheet.

You also found out that a sale of 2 HP LaserJet printers P2035 to Peacock Interiors on the 23rd January has not been recorded in the books.

Solution: Step **1** is to raise a new invoice to record this transaction. ***Click on the plus(+) sign -***  ***then under Customers, select 'Invoice' .***

Fig. 286

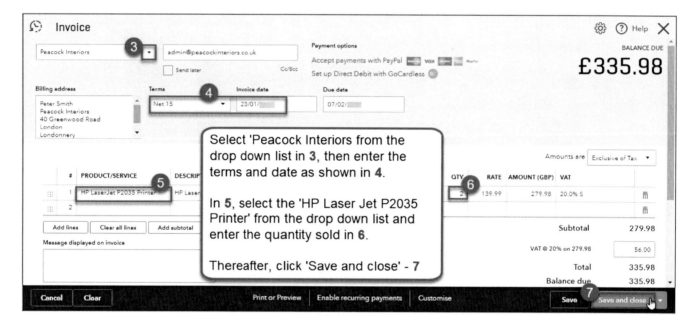

Fig. 287

How to process an adjustment for Depreciation

Depreciation is the process of allocating the cost of plant and equipment assets into expense, during their estimated useful lives, in a systematic and rational way.

In accounting, depreciation means a process of *matching the expense against revenues.* The purpose is to record how much of the original cost of the asset is being used up each period as the asset helps the business to generate revenue. *This has nothing to do with whatever value an asset could be sold for.*

Making a Depreciation adjusting entry:

Calculate the depreciation for all the fixed assets for the Month of January and post them to the ledgers. Your calculation should yield the following depreciation values:

- Furniture and Fixtures: - 140.83
- Motor Vehicles: - £412.68

- Office Equipment: - £595.41

Now post these depreciation charges using a journal. Here are the journal details:

Name	Details	Tax	Debit	Credit
Furniture/Fittings Depreciation Charge	January Depreciation Charge	None	140.83	
Furniture/Fittings depreciation (accumulated)	January Depreciation Charge	None		140.83
Office Equipment Depreciation Charge	Super Workstation Depreciation Charge	None	595.24	
Office Equipment depreciation (accumulated)	Super Workstation Depreciation Charge	None		595.24
Office Equipment Depreciation Charge	iMac 1 Depreciation charge	None	20.24	
Office Equipment depreciation (accumulated)	iMac 1 Depreciation charge	None		20.24
Office Equipment Depreciation Charge	iMac 2 Depreciation charge	None	20.24	
Office Equipment depreciation (accumulated)	iMac 2 Depreciation charge	None		20.24
Motor Vehicle Depreciation Charge	BMW 316si Depreciation Charge	None	133.98	
Motor Vehicle depreciation (accumulated)	BMW 31si Depreciation Charge	None		133.98
Motor Vehicle Depreciation Charge	BMW 1 Depreciation charge	None	208.33	
Motor Vehicle depreciation (accumulated)	BMW 1 Depreciation charge	None		208.33
Motor Vehicle Depreciation Charge	Peugeot Hatchback Depreciation charge	None	70.37	
Motor Vehicle depreciation (accumulated)	Peugeot Hatchback Depreciation charge	None		70.37

Depreciation expense is a noncash adjustment, and you make the adjustment by Debiting depreciation expense – income statement and crediting accumulated depreciation – balance sheet (you can use a journal entry for this)

Here is how to post the depreciation journals above to QuickBooks online.

Step 1, click on the plus button - [icon], and under Other, select 'Journal Entry'

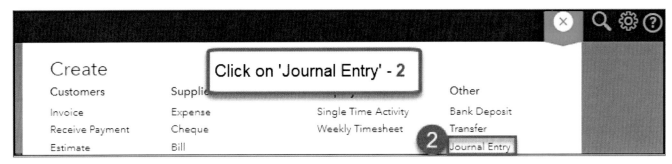

Fig. 288

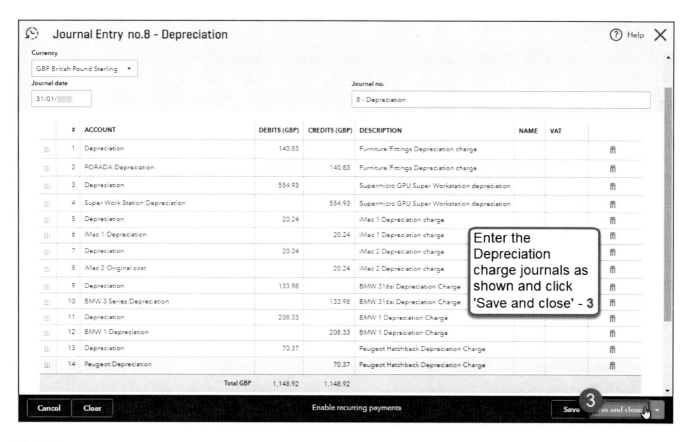

Fig. 289

How to record a sale of a fixed asset (Disposal)

One of the motor vehicles (Peugeot Hatchback) was sold on the 31ˢᵗ January

- A vehicle which was originally purchased for 4,222.00
- Depreciation to date is £822.46.
- It was sold for £2,500.

For example, to transfer the original purchase price from the asset nominal account, post the following journal:

Name	Details	Tax	Debit	Credit
Sale of fixed Assets account	Disposal	None	4,222.00	
Motor Vehicle Original cost account	Disposal	None		4,222.00

You will also need to transfer the accumulated depreciation to date of the asset that has been sold to the Sale of Asset account. Here is the journal to post for that.

Name	Details	Tax	Debit	Credit
Motor vehicle Accumulated depreciation account	Disposal	None	822.46	
Sale of Fixed Assets account	Disposal	None		822.46

Now, the final thing to do is to record the proceeds for the sale of the fixed asset into the accounts.

Name	Details	Tax	Debit	Credit
Bank Current account	Disposal	None	2,500.00	
Sale of Fixed Assets account	Disposal	None		2,500.00

Here is how to enter these set of three journals.

Step **1**, click on the plus button - , and under Other, select 'Journal Entry'

Fig. 290

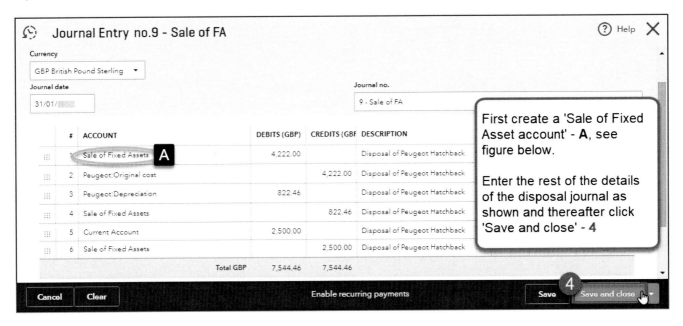

Fig. 291

This space is for notes

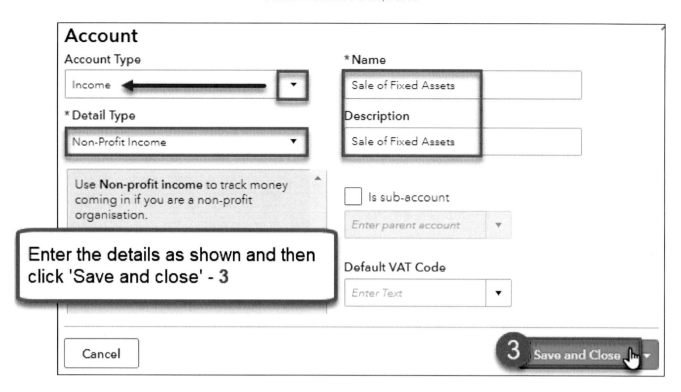

Fig. 292

Bank reconciliation

Bank reconciliation is part of the month end close procedure, and you should do it now. You have done a bank reconciliation before.

How to adjust closing stock

Opening and closing stock transactions are posted to adjust the profit and loss calculation so that the profit figure for a specific period takes into account any unsold stock.

By default, the Profit and Loss report calculates the Gross Profit as Gross Profit = Sales – Purchases

However, if you post opening and closing stock transactions the Profit and Loss report calculates the Gross Profit as:
Gross Profit = Sales - Cost of Sales*
*Cost of Sales = Opening Stock + Purchases - Closing Stock

Why you need to post opening and closing stock journals

If you don't post opening and closing stock journals, then the cost of sales on the Profit and Loss report would include the cost of your purchases and not make an allowance for unsold stock.

In QuickBooks unlike other accounting software like Sage 50 Accounts, there is no closing stock entry or account. QuickBooks inventory is perpetual, the amount in inventory asset is the total of all inventory items presently in stock.

Inventory on hand is an asset and does not show on the Profit and & Loss account.

How to do Debtors' reconciliation

Let's begin by working out what the debtor's balance should be as illustrated in the working below.

	Debit £	Credit £
Debtors at the beginning of the period (Outstanding invoices at the beginning of period equal to closing balances for the previous period)	6,706.20	
Total invoices for the period (Total of sales day book - your list of invoices - gross figure)	33,192.61	
Total receipts for the period (Total from cash book of invoiced income)		18,201.41
***Debtors at the end of period carried forward to the next period** (Balancing figures, which should agree with the prepared list)*		21,697.40
	39,898.81	39,898.81

Compare this debtors figure with the debtors' figure in QuickBooks online; if they match, that's great, move on to do creditors' reconciliation. If they don't match, it might be helpful to go through the checklist below to verify your results and discover any potential errors. Tick the checkboxes on the right of each item as you go along with your checks.

1	Have you listed all your debtors, including invoices only partly paid or outstanding from the beginning of the period, and invoices paid directly after the end of the period, because these receipts would not be in the cash book?	☐
2	Are there any bad debts - invoices you will never receive payment for? These should be entered as a separate credit in your control account.	☐
3	Does your total of invoices in the period include credit notes issued? If not, these must be included on the credit side of the account.	☐
4	Are the receipts from cash book only those that relate to invoiced sales or work done? Exclude any receipts included in the debtors' figure for the sale of a vehicle, loans, refunds etc.	☐
5	Have you included the figure for all un-invoiced sales? - Sales that should have had an invoice raised but by error were not.	☐
6	Have you included as a receipt on the control account any receipts for sales that were not entered into the cash book?	☐
7	Are there any errors of addition of receipts, invoices or debtors' totals, or duplication of invoices, receipts, or debtors in listings?	☐

Once you've gone through the checklist above, start doing your reconciliation with a reconciliation statement that might look something like the following: - see next page

This space is for notes

	£	Debit £	Credit £
Debtors at the beginning of the period		6,706.20	
Total invoices		33,192.61	
Sales not invoiced in error		0.00	
Credit notes			1,799.99
Total receipts	18,201.41		
Sales of vehicle	0.00		
			18,201.41
Addition error(s)	(0.00)		
Receipts banked in private account			2,559.18
Bad debts write-offs and refunds			0.00
Debtors at the end of the period			**17,338.23**
		39,898.81	39,898.81
Reconciliation			
Original debtors figure per accounting software	19,897.41		
Less: Money banked in Directors private account	(2,559.18)		
Bad debt provision	0.00		
Written off invoice/invoice amount included twice	0.00		
Reconciled debtors as above	**17,338.23**		

Well, that's how you do a Debtors reconciliation.

Remember you need to post the entry for the money paid into the Director's private account to clear some of MDE Office Centre invoice of the 22nd January.

Here is how to do it. Step **1**, click on the plus button (+) - 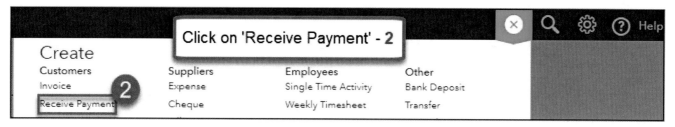, and under Customers, select 'Receive Payment.'

Fig. 293

This space is for notes

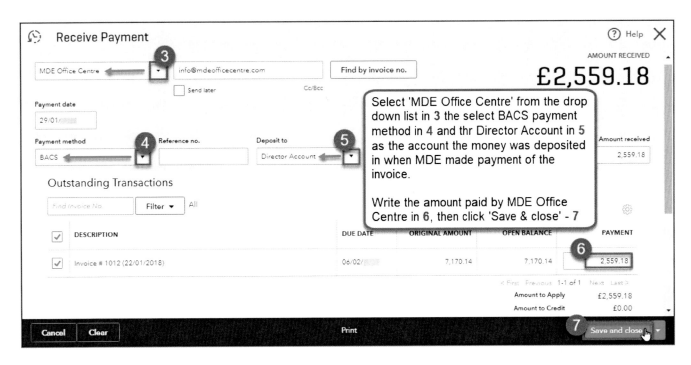

Fig. 294

The next step is to transfer the money from the Director account to the Bank current account in QuickBooks online.

Here is how to do it. Step **8**, click on the plus button (+) -  , and under Other, select 'Transfer'

Fig. 295

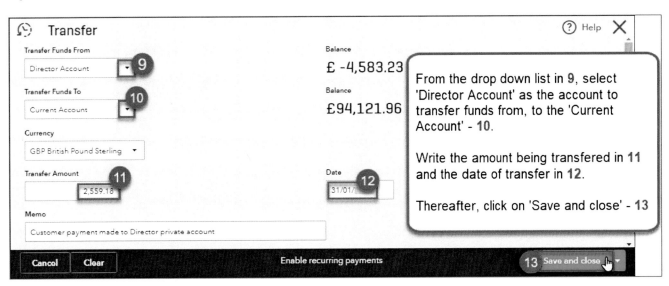

Fig. 296

How to do Creditors' reconciliation

In a purchase ledger control account, the total outstanding invoices at the beginning of a period and invoices received during that period, less payments made for invoiced supplies, will give a balancing figure of invoices still outstanding at the end of the period - your creditors.

You can compare the figure with your listing of unpaid invoices, and the creditor's value should ideally be the same as that of the purchase ledger control account in the software. If they are not the same, then you will need to reconcile them.

Before reconciliation, this is what you might have worked out.

	Debit £	Credit £
Creditors at the beginning of the period (Unpaid invoices at the beginning of period equal to closing balances for the previous period)		44,502.68
Total invoices in the period (Total of purchase day book list of invoices - gross figure)		126,308.80
Total payments in the period (Total of purchase cash book for invoiced expenses)	21,385.96	
Creditors at the end of period (Balance figure, which should agree with the prepared list)	149,425.52	
Total	170,811.48	170,811.48

If you now compare the Creditors at the end of the period value of (£74,659.89) with the creditors' value in the software, they should be the same. If they vary, it could be because of some things, use the checklist below to find out.

1	Have you listed all your creditors, including those invoices only partly paid or outstanding from the beginning of the period, and those invoices paid directly after the end of the period, because these payments would not be in the cash book?	☐
2	Does your total of invoices in the period include credit notes received? If not, these must be included on the debit side of the account	☐
3	Check to ensure that payments from cash book should be only those that relate to invoiced expenses, not items such as wages, interest, etc. If included, these figures should be taken off the payments figure in the control account	☐
4	Make sure that purchases, where a discount reduces the payment below the invoiced amount, should have the discount in the control account	☐
5	Those payments for purchases that were not entered into the cash book will have to be included as a payment on the control account	☐
6	Addition errors of payments, invoices, or creditors totals, or duplication of invoices, payments, or creditors in listings should be noted and recorded	☐

The format of your amended purchase ledger reconciliation statement should look as shown on the next page.

This space is for notes

	£	Debit £	Credit £
Creditors at the beginning of the period			44,502.68
Total invoices			126,308.80
Credit notes		10,297.53	
Total payments	21,385.96		
Addition error	0.00		
		21,385.96	
Payments made from the private account		15,553.72	
Discounts received		0.00	
Creditors at the end of the period		**123,574.27**	
		170,81148	170,811.48
Reconciliation			
Original creditors figure per accounting software	123,574.27		
Creditor paid after a period not on the list	0.00		
Creditor included twice	(0.00)		
Invoice paid short, amount still outstanding	0.00		
Reconciled Creditors as above	**123,574.27**		

At the end of every month or every accounting period, you should work to ensure that the entries in the sales and purchase ledgers (list of individual balances) agree with the entries in the control accounts. The totals in each should be the same, otherwise, follow the above reconciliation steps (debtors & creditor reconciliation steps) to make them the same.

Remember Horizon Tristar Ltd has to pay the director the money he used to pay the rent for the next Quarter.

Here is how to do it. Step **1**, click on the plus button (+) - , and under Other, select 'Transfer'

Fig. 297

This space is for notes

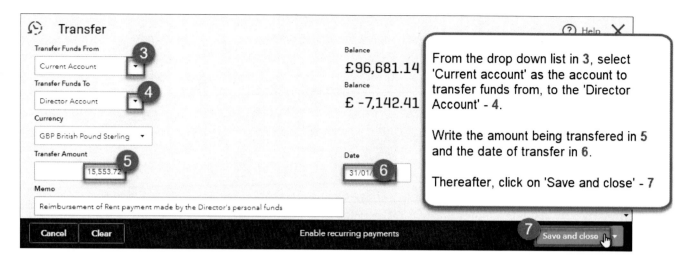

Fig. 298

Other month end notes to deal with include posting the lease rentals, the donation and calculating and posting the tax charge for the year to the accounts

Here is how to do it. Step **1**, click on the plus button (+) - [icon], and under Other, select 'Journal Entry'

Fig. 299

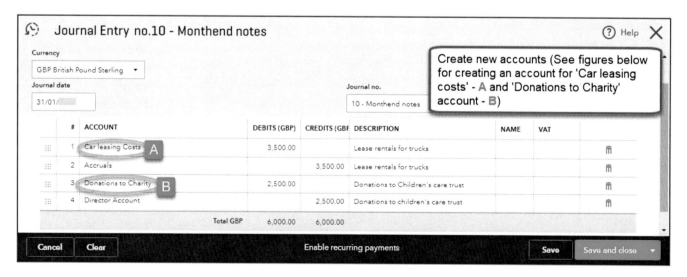

Fig. 300

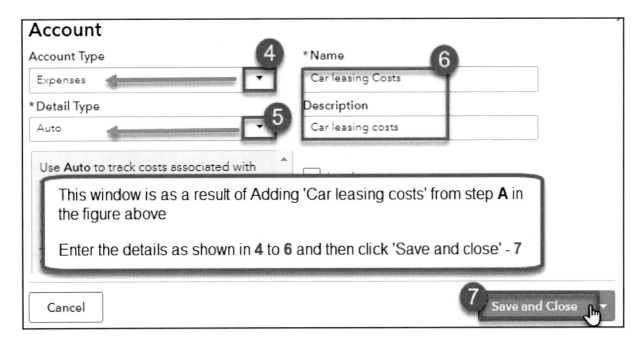

Fig. 301

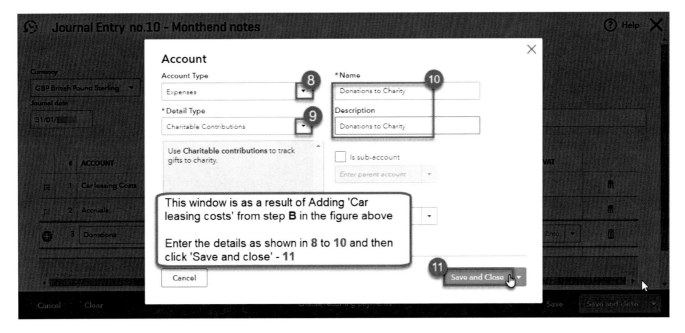

Fig. 302

This space is for notes

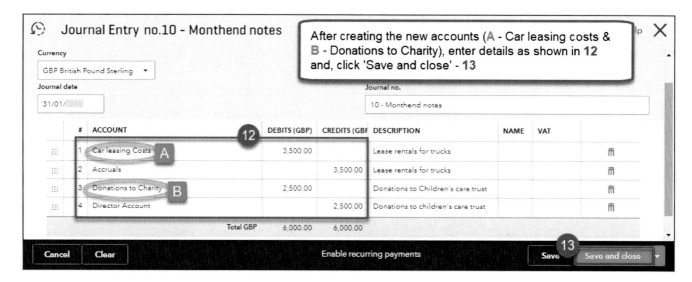

Fig. 303

Calculating the profit chargeable to Corporation tax

Let's assume that this is the year-end (of course this is not the year-end but just to illustrate how to calculate profits chargeable to corporation tax, we will work with the assumption that this is the yearend)

If Horizon Tristar has made a profit, it has to pay Corporation Tax on its taxable profits since it is an incorporated business in the UK (a business which has registered as a company with Companies House). These taxable profits include money that Horizon Tristar Ltd has made from doing business (known as 'trading profits'), rental income from property, investment gains and other chargeable gains.

The rate of Corporation Tax in the United Kingdom is decided in advance and announced in the Chancellor's Budget. The rate of Corporation Tax is 19% from 1 April 2017 and will fall to 17% from 1 April 2020. In Northern Ireland, this rate will fall to 12.5% from 1 April 2018.

If a business is not registered as a company with Companies House, It will not be liable to pay Corporation Tax. Instead, It will be required to pay Income Tax on the profits of its trading activities.

Background to UK Corporation Tax

HMRC requires a company incorporated and controlled in the UK to register for Corporation Tax within three months of starting to trade – i.e. when business transactions begin or when the company starts to receive income. If you don't register within this three month period, your company may be liable to penalties.

Here is what you'll need to tell HMRC:

- The date you began to do business (this will be used as the start date of your company's first accounting period)
- Your company name and registered number (provided to you by Companies House when you incorporated your company)
- The main address you do business from
- That kind of business you do
- The date you'll make your annual accounts up to (see Accounting Periods below)
- The name and home address of the company directors.

HMRC will use this information to work out when your company must pay Corporation Tax and you will receive confirmation to that effect once your registration is completed.

Your company will not be required to register for Corporation Tax if it is dormant – i.e. not trading. For specific guidance from HMRC as to whether your company is considered to be trading, please **click here** or visit -

https://www.gov.uk/guidance/corporation-tax-trading-and-non-trading

Paying Corporation Tax

It is your company's responsibility to calculate how much Corporation Tax it owes HMRC and disclose this by submitting a company tax return to HMRC.

For Corporation Tax purposes, your accounting period is the period covered by your company's tax return and cannot last longer than 12 months. It is important to remember that your Corporation Tax accounting period will not always be the same as your financial period – i.e. the period that your company creates financial statements for. For example, if you have a period over 12 months for financial statement purposes, you will need to submit two tax returns for the period as they cannot exceed 12 months.

Your company's Corporation Tax liability will be calculated in what is known as a Corporation Tax computation. This will be submitted to HMRC along with your company's tax return as evidence that you have calculated your tax liability accurately.

Working out Horizon Tristar Ltd Corporation Tax liability involves calculating a number of different items which will be explained in the section below:

- ✓ Tax-adjusted trading profits
- ✓ Disallowable expenditures
- ✓ Capital allowances
- ✓ Non-trading loan relationships (e.g. bank interest income)
- ✓ Property income
- ✓ Chargeable gains

It is important to remember that HMRC can make enquiries about any company tax return. Therefore you should retain your financial and company records.

Calculating Tax-Adjusted Trading Profits

Horizon Tristar Ltd Corporation Tax will be calculated as a percentage of your taxable profits. The trading profits shown in the profit and loss account (revenue minus expenditure) in the software (QuickBooks online) are not the taxable profits. We must calculate the tax-adjusted trading profits in order to pay the correct amount of Corporation Tax to HMRC.

Let's do it:

We shall begin by producing the profit and loss account statement from the accounting software to see what the reported profit for Horizon Tristar Ltd is.

Here is how to do it: - see next page.

This space is for notes

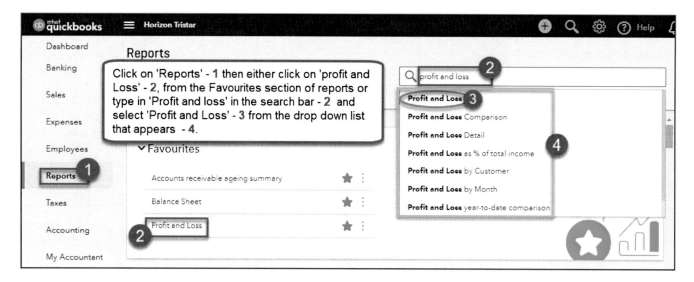

Fig. 304

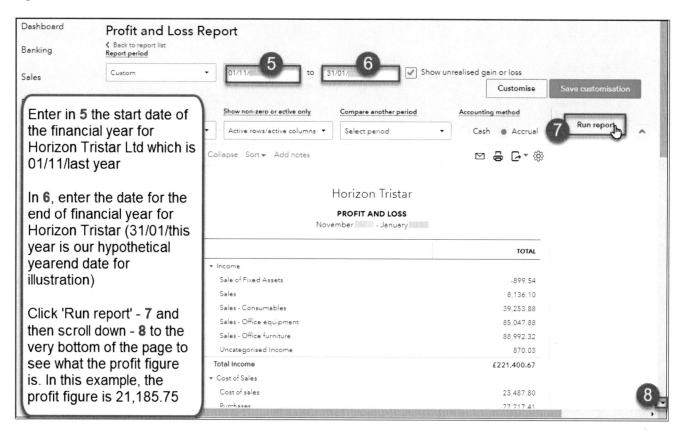

Fig. 305

Now the profit figure of £21,185.75 is the one we will take and start adjusting to compute the profit chargeable to corporation tax.

Here is how it is done: - see next page

Profit/(loss) before interest and taxation	21,185.75
Add back disallowable expenses (see notes below for explanation)	
Entertainment	0.00
Legal & professional fees	0.00
Late Filing Fee	0.00
Donations	0.00
Depreciation and (profit)/loss on sale of assets	2,889.40
(profit)/loss on sale of assets	899.54
Less:	
Capital allowances (see notes below for explanation)	3,056.85
Add back dividends payable on non-equity shares included in interest payable	0.00
Deduct non-trading income	
Interest receivable	54.50
Property income	0.00
Franked investment income	0.00
Other income not taxable e.g Sale of Fixed assets	0.00
Adjusted profit/(loss)	21,863.34
Less:	
Loss brought forward	0.00
Qualifying donations to UK charities	2,500.00
Add	
Chargeable gains	0.00
Taxable profit/(loss)	**19,363.34**

Accounting records

You must keep accounting records that include:

- *all money received and spent by the company*
- *details of assets owned by the company*
- *debts the company owes or is owed*
- *stock the company owns at the end of the financial year*
- *the stocktakings you used to work out the stock figure*
- *all goods bought and sold*
- *who you bought and sold them to and from (unless you run a retail business)*

You must also keep any other financial records, information and calculations you need to prepare and file your annual accounts and Company Tax Return. This includes records of:

- *all money spent by the company, for example receipts, petty cash books, orders and delivery notes*
- *all money received by the company, for example invoices, contracts, sales books and till rolls*
- *any other relevant documents, for example bank statements and correspondence*

Calculating the Corporation tax payable on the £19,363.34

The financial year is 12 months from November to October. November to April is 5 months which is 152 days and from April to October is 7 months which is 213 days out of the 365 days in 12 months.

Days in the accounting period falling in each tax year

Tax year	Days falling in tax year	Days in year
Prior Year	152	
Current Year	213	
	365	365

Corporation tax payable

Tax year	Taxable profit	Tax rate	Corp Tax
Prior Year	8,063.64	19%	1,532.09
Current Year	11,299.70	17%	1,920.95
	19,363.34		
Corporation tax payable			**3,453.04**

The 3,453.04 now needs to post this corporation tax amount into the accounts.

Here is how to do it. Step **1**, click on the plus button (+) - , and under Other, select 'Journal Entry'

Fig. 306

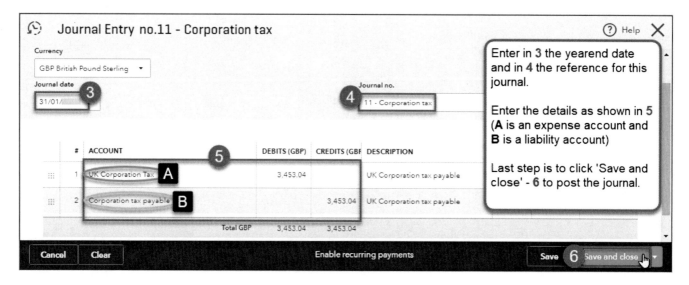

Fig. 307

Notes for the items in the corporation tax calculation

Disallowable Expenditure

Expenditure is a complicated topic within tax. HMRC does not allow you to deduct certain expenditure from your revenue (known as disallowable expenses). You must add 100% of the value of these expenditures to your profits, increasing the amount you're required to pay Corporation Tax on.

Some common expenditure which HMRC disallows include:

- Depreciation of assets
- Entertaining clients and suppliers
- Movements in general provisions

Capital Allowances

As we've already seen, depreciation of fixed assets is not allowable (can't be deducted from profits) for Corporation Tax purposes. This is because depreciation can only ever be an estimate of the reduction in value of your assets and can be subjective. However, capital allowances may be available to take account of the cost of plant and machinery used in the business.

There are two main types of capital allowances:

i. Annual Investment Allowance

Firstly the annual investment allowance (AIA) allows you to deduct 100% of the value of certain qualifying assets from your taxable profits, up to a value of £200,000 (from 1 January 2016). The amount of qualifying investment in plant and machinery made on or after 1 January 2019 until 31 December 2020 will go up from £200,000 to £1m. Capital purchases such as machinery, fixtures, fittings and computers qualify for AIA. It is worth noting that land, buildings and cars do not qualify for AIA. Some types of energy-saving equipment also qualify for a 100% first year allowance.

ii. Writing Down Allowance

Those assets which don't qualify for AIA, or where you have purchased assets in excess of the AIA limits, may still qualify for capital allowances if they fall into one of the following 'pools':

- Main pool (18% WDA)
- All plant and machinery assets are added to the main pool unless they specifically qualify for a separate pool such as the special rate pool.
- Special rate pool (8% WDA) This will reduce to 6% from 6 April 2019.
- A new 2% non-residential structures and buildings allowance (SBA) is available where contracts for physical construction works are entered into on or after 29 October 2018.
- Assets qualifying as 'integral features' to a building, high emission cars or assets with an expected useful life in excess of twenty five years.

Please note that there are special rules relating to cars used in the business.

The writing down allowance (WDA) is the percentage of the value of the asset which is deducted from trading profits each year.

After you have deducted the WDA from the original value of the asset, this residual value (known as the tax written down value) is carried forward into the next year. The tax written down value (rather than the original value) is then used as the basis for calculating capital allowances for that particular asset for the next year.

Calculation of capital allowances for Horizon Tristar Ltd.

Summary	**£**
General pool (a)	56.85
Special rate pool (b)	0.00
Expensive car pools (c)	3,000.00
Short term asset pools (d)	0.00
Total capital allowances	3,056.85

(a) General Pool		**£**
Written down value brought forward		3,715.36
Disposal receipts		-2,500.00
Balancing allowance		-899.54
Balancing charge		0.00
Expenditure qualifying for writing down allowance		0.00
		315.82
Relevant first year expenditure		0.00
Other expenditure qualifying for first year allowance		0.00
Expenditure qualifying for annual investment allowance		0.00
FYA in respect of relevant FYA expenditure	0.00	
Other first year allowances	0.00	
Annual investment allowance	0.00	
Writing down allowance @18%	56.85	
		56.85
Written down value carried forward		258.97

(b) Special rate pool		**£**
Written down value brought forward		0.00
Disposal receipts		0.00
Balancing allowance		0.00
Balancing charge		0.00
Thermal installation expenditure		0.00
Integral feature expenditure		0.00
Expenditure on a car that is not a main rate car		0.00
Expenditure on cushion gas		0.00
		0.00
Expenditure qualifying for annual investment allowance		0.00
Annual investment allowance	0.00	
Writing down allowance	0.00	
		0.00
Written down value carried forward		-

(c) Expensive car pool	
Number of single asset pools	1
	£
Written down value brought forward	0.00
Disposal receipts	0.00
Balancing allowances	0.00

Balancing charges		0.00
Additions		25,000.00
		25,000.00
Writing down allowances		-3,000.00
Written down value carried forward		22,000.00

(d) short life asset pools

Number of single asset pools	0
	£
Written down value brought forward	0.00
Disposal receipts	0.00
Balancing allowances	0.00
Balancing charges	0.00
Expenditure qualifying for written down allowance	0.00
	0.00
Relevant first-year expenditure	0.00
Other expenditure qualifying for first-year allowance	0.00
Expenditure qualifying for annual investment allowance	0.00

FYA in respect of relevant FYA expenditure	0.00	
Other FYA	0.00	
Annual investment allowances	0.00	
Writing down allowances	0.00	
		0.00
Written down value carried forward		0.00

Further detail on capital allowances can be found **here**.

Chargeable Gains

You have made a chargeable gain when you sell a chargeable asset for more than it cost. This is a profit which you pay Corporation Tax on.

HMRC does allow you to deduct any costs associated with the initial acquisition of the asset from your chargeable gain, as well as costs incurred in selling the asset. These can include items such as legal fees and auction fees. Indexation allowance is also available, which reduces the gain according to the expected increase in value of the asset over time.

Chargeable gains can be a very complex area of corporation tax, particularly in relation to the disposal of plant and machinery, shares and intangible assets. It's common to seek professional advice in this area.

Further detail on chargeable gains can be found **here**.

Corporation Tax Losses

Let's just say for illustration purposes that Horizon Tristar made a loss of £25,000 in last financial year which actually was its first year of trading. This loss can be rolled forward and offset against profits made in future accounting periods.

Corporation Tax losses can accumulate for more than one year. The following example helps illustrate how losses can be used:

This financial year as you have just calculated, Horizon made a profit of £21,863.34.

Horizon Tristar can choose to offset its loss from the last financial year in order to reduce its profits chargeable to tax for the current financial year. If that was the case, £21,863.34 profit minus £25,000 of losses = £0 taxable profit. This means that Horizon Tristar Ltd corporation tax liability will be nil for this current financial year. It also means that the It will have £3,136.66 of tax losses left over to continue to roll forward into future accounting periods.

Relief in the form of offsetting losses from earlier years is claimed by including the claim amount in your company tax return – box 4 in the 'Company Tax Calculation'.

It is also worth noting that for accounting periods from 1 April 2017, the way trading losses are set off will depend on when they arise.

For further detail on how your company can offset its Corporation Tax losses, please **click here** or visit: https://www.gov.uk/guidance/corporation-tax-calculating-and-claiming-a-loss

Research and Development (R&D) Relief

You can claim R&D Corporation Tax relief on expenditure which aims to achieve an advance in science or technology through the resolution of a scientific or technological uncertainty. R&D relief is only available to incorporated businesses as it is a Corporation Tax relief.

There are two schemes – one for large companies and one for Small and Medium Sized Businesses (SMEs). If you qualify for the SME scheme, then from 1 April 2015, the tax relief on allowable R&D costs is 230% - that is, for each £100 of qualifying costs incurred, you may deduct £230 from your trading income. Also, if your company is loss-making, then you can choose to surrender the enhanced loss for tax credits. The rate of credit is 14.5% on the R&D relief amount from 1 April 2015, and this is paid to you in cash, which can be very valuable to new businesses.

- ✓ Qualifying R&D expenditure includes revenue expenditure on:
- ✓ Staff directly or indirectly engaged in R&D
- ✓ Consumable or transformable materials
- ✓ Computer software
- ✓ Power, water and fuel.

Horizon Tristar Ltd has no R&D to claim in this financial year.

For further detail on R&D tax credits, please **click here** or visit: https://www.gov.uk/guidance/corporation-tax-research-and-development-tax-relief-for-small-and-medium-sized-enterprises

Creative Sector Relief

Creative industry tax reliefs are a group of eight corporation tax reliefs that allow qualifying companies to claim a larger deduction or, in certain circumstances, claim a payable tax credit when calculating their taxable profits.

This applies to companies operating in the following areas:

- Film
- Animation
- 'High-end' television
- Video-gaming
- Theatre.

Horizon Tristar Ltd has no R&D to claim in this financial year.

For further detail and guidance on Creative Sector relief, please **click here** or visit: https://www.gov.uk/guidance/corporation-tax-research-and-development-tax-relief-for-small-and-medium-sized-enterprises

TASK11: HOW TO PRODUCE ACCOUNTING REPORTS FROM QUICKBOOKS ONLINE

There are three key fundamental stages in practical accounting; First, you analyse the financial documents. Secondly, you record the details in the financial documents into your accounting system, and thirdly you produce financial reports after correcting any errors of the analysis and recording stages and also after making some crucial adjustments to the accounts.

Accounting reports are compilations of financial information that are derived from the accounting records of a business. These can be brief, custom-made reports that are intended for specific purposes, such as a detailed analysis of sales by region, or the profitability of a specific product line. More commonly, accounting reports are considered to be equivalent to the financial statements. These statements include the following reports:

- *Income statement*. States the revenues earned during a period, less expenses, to arrive at a profit or loss. This is the most commonly used accounting report, since it is used to judge the performance of a business.
- *Balance sheet*. Shows the ending asset, liability, and equity balances as of the balance sheet date. It is used to judge the liquidity and financial reserves of a business.
- *Statement of cash flows*. Shows the sources and uses of cash related to operations, financing, and investments. Can be the most accurate source of information regarding the cash-generating ability of an entity.

Several disclosures may accompany the financial statements, in the form of footnotes. This is more likely to be the case when the financial statements have been audited.

The next task is about producing accounting reports.

Trial balance report

A trial balance is a list of all the general ledger accounts (both revenue and capital) contained in the ledger of a business. This list will contain the name of each nominal ledger account and the value of that nominal ledger balance.

Each nominal ledger account will hold either a debit balance or a credit balance. The debit balance values will be listed in the debit column of the trial balance, and the credit value balance will be listed in the credit column. The trading profit and loss statement and balance sheet and other financial reports can then be produced using the ledger accounts listed on the trial balance.

To produce a trial balance in QuickBooks online is really easy. Here is how to do it:

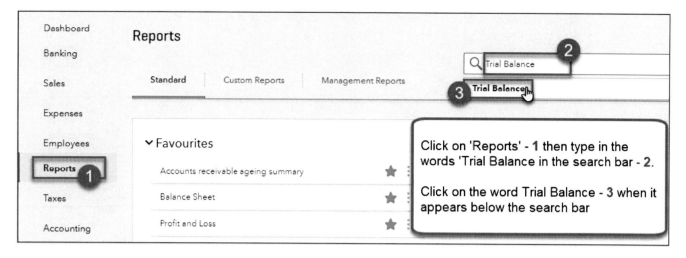

Fig. 308

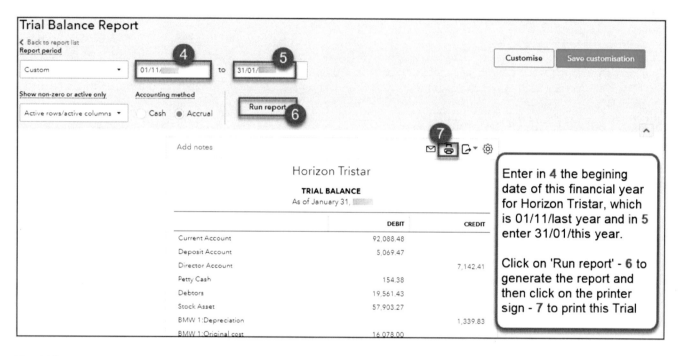

Fig. 309

Income statement – also known as Profit and Loss account report

A profit and loss statement (P&L) is a financial statement that summarises the revenues, costs and expenses incurred during a specific period of time, usually a fiscal quarter or year. These records provide information about a company's ability – or lack thereof – to generate profit by increasing revenue, reducing costs, or both.

The P&L statement is also referred to as "statement of profit and loss", "income statement," "statement of operations," and "income and expense statement."

Here is how to produce the Income statement report in QuickBooks online

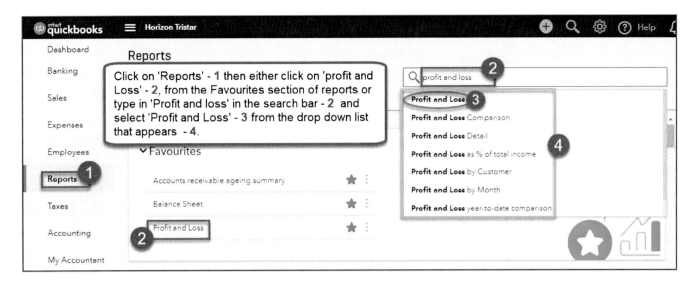

Click on 'Reports' - **1** then either click on 'profit and Loss' - **2**, from the Favourites section of reports or type in 'Profit and loss' in the search bar - **2** and select 'Profit and Loss' - **3** from the drop down list that appears - **4**.

Fig. 310

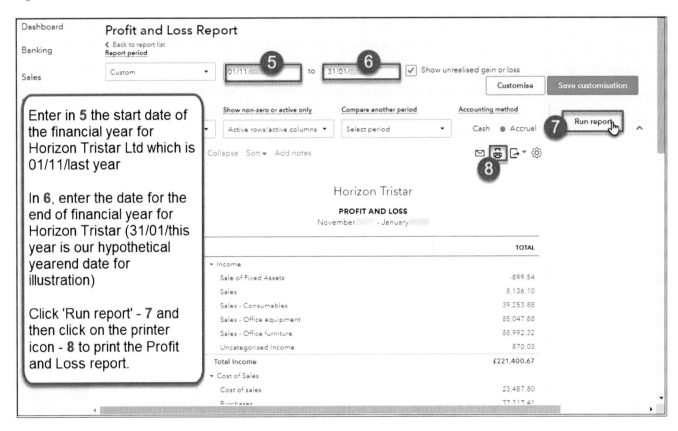

Enter in **5** the start date of the financial year for Horizon Tristar Ltd which is 01/11/last year

In **6**, enter the date for the end of financial year for Horizon Tristar (31/01/this year is our hypothetical yearend date for illustration)

Click 'Run report' - **7** and then click on the printer icon - **8** to print the Profit and Loss report.

Fig. 311

The components of the income statement

Small business owners use the income statement, also known as the profit and loss statement or the P&L report, for understanding the company's revenues and expenses over a period of time. The five components of the income statement are sales (or revenue), cost of goods sold, gross profit, operating expenses, and net income or loss.

> **What the Income Statement is useful for**
>
> Analysts use the income statement for data to calculate financial ratios such as return on equity (ROE), return on assets (ROA), gross profit, operating profit, earnings before interest and taxes (EBIT), and earnings before interest taxes and amortisation (EBITDA). The income statement is often presented in a common-sized format, which provides each line item on the income statement as a percent of sales. In this way, analysts can easily see which expenses make up the largest portion of sales. Analysts also use the income statement to compare year-over-year (YOY) and quarter-over-quarter (QOQ) performance.
>
> The income statement typically provides two to three years of historical data for comparison.

Balance Sheet

A balance sheet is a financial statement that summarizes a company's assets, liabilities and shareholders' equity at a specific point in time. These three balance sheet segments give investors an idea as to what the company owns and owes, as well as the amount invested by shareholders.

All accounts in your General Ledger are categorized as an asset, a liability, or equity. The relationship between them is expressed in this equation: **Assets = Liabilities + Equity**

Here is how to produce the Balance sheet report in QuickBooks online

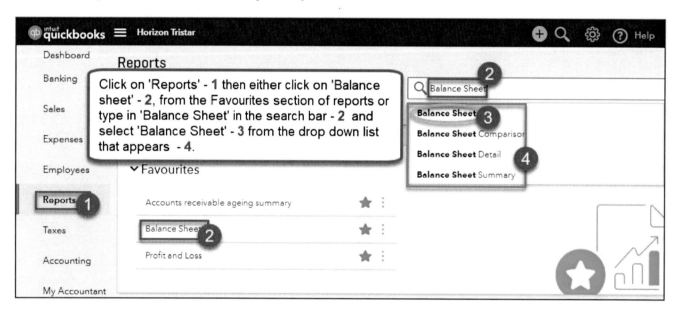

Fig. 312

> **A brief note on the Balance Sheet from QuickBooks online**
>
> *The balance sheet provides business owners with a snapshot of what is owned, what is owed, and how much the business is worth. QuickBooks makes it easy to regularly review your balance sheet in order to spot the strengths and weaknesses in your business, helping you to make smart decisions about how to invest and grow in the future.*
>
> *Because QuickBooks tracks and organizes all of your business's accounting data, it's easy to access your balance sheet and other financial statements. QuickBooks does the appropriate calculations and generates the balance sheet for you, providing you with a snapshot of your business's financial health.*

Fig. 313

Make sure that each of the title headings in the balance sheet like Office equipment's, deposits & cash, etc. and the corresponding figures are correctly reconciled to the general ledger (GL) accounts.

Accounts payable ageing report.

The accounts payable ageing report categorises payables to suppliers based on 'time frames'. The report is typically set up with 30-day time frames so that each successive column in the report lists supplier invoices that are:

- 0 to 30 days old
- 31 to 60 days old
- 61 to 90 days old
- Older than 90 days

This is meant to help the user of the report in determining which invoices are overdue for payment depending on what the companies credit policy with suppliers is.

Here is how to produce the report in QuickBooks online – see next page.

This space is for notes

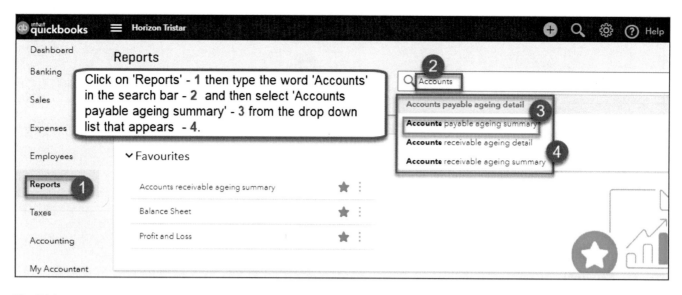

Fig. 314

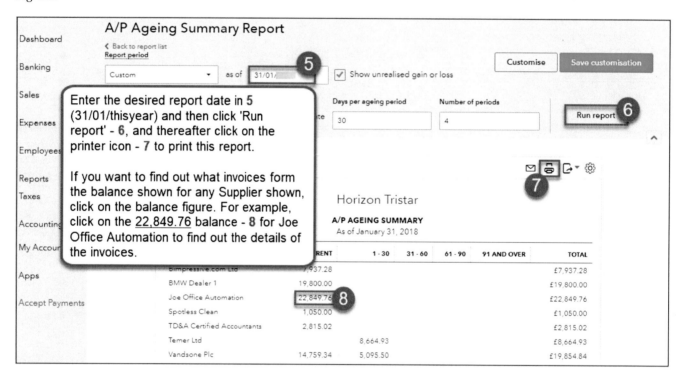

Fig. 315

Accounts receivable ageing report.

An accounts receivable ageing is a report that lists unpaid customer invoices and unused credit memos by date ranges. The ageing report is the primary tool used by credit control collections personnel to determine which invoices are overdue for payment. A typical ageing report lists invoices in 30-day "time frames," where the columns contain the following information:

- The left-most column contains all invoices that are 30 days old or less
- The next column contains invoices that are 31-60 days old
- The next column contains invoices that are 61-90 days old
- The final column contains all older invoices

Here is how to produce an accounts receivable ageing report in QuickBooks online;

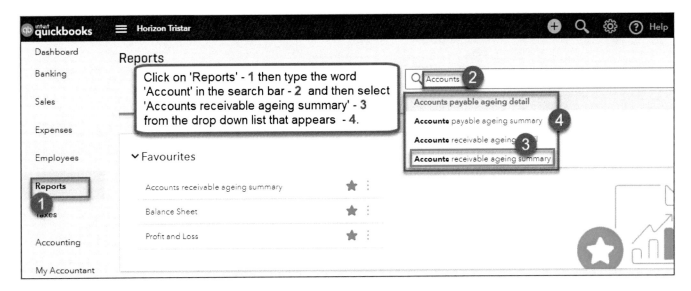

Fig. 316

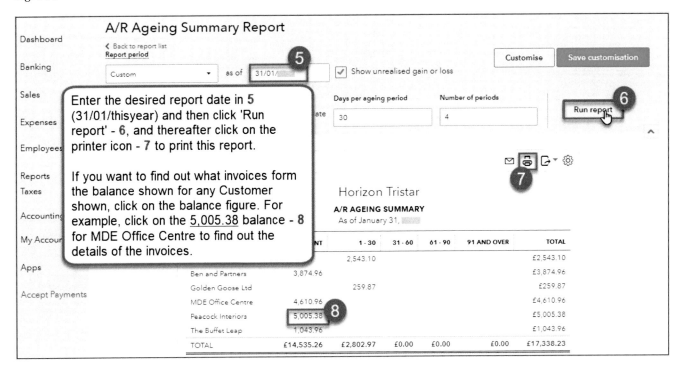

Fig. 317

Management Accounts Reports

Management Accounts should only contain what the Board or Leadership Team really needs to see to allow for informed decision making. Don't waste time producing what is not needed by the management team.

Although every company is different the following are somewhat standard pages or tabs that should be expected in a management accounting report.

1. **Cover sheet**: clearly stating the name of the company and the period in question.
2. **Executive Summary**: on one page pull together all the key items from the rest of the pack
   - ✓ *Summary narrative* — one-liners on the main highlights and lowlights in the month;
   - ✓ *Actual Turnover*, Gross Margin, Overhead, and Operating Profit for the last 3 months, broken out by product or service lines with % growth to give a view to what is performing well or not;
   - ✓ *Aged Debtors* – £ and % — a summary of how the ageing looks. A high % of old debt is cause for

concern;

   Headcount — A summary of numbers by department for the last 3 months to see at a glance movement in heads;

✓ *Cash at bank* — show the bank balance for the last 3 months and include any overdraft facility as headroom;

✓ *Capex* — any material asset purchases in the period;

✓ *KPI's* for the last 3 months — show the breakeven turnover, the burn or cash generation rate, sales per head, overhead per head, and if you're losing money your 'cash zero month' if— this is the cash balance divided by the monthly burn to tell you how many months of cash you have left

For all of the above show the forecast and variance so it's easy to see if you're on track.

3. **P&L Forecast v Actual**: put your p&l headings down the centre of the page and break them out into the right level of detail to make sure the information is meaningful to the reader. Too little or too much detail will mean important movements or trends will be missed. On the left side of the narrative show actual against forecast for the month completed and compare this if relevant to the same month last year. On the right side of the narrative repeat for the Year to Date cumulative numbers actual against forecast and show the full year forecast which will be the year to date actual plus the forecast for the rest of the year. The forecast should be revised at least quarterly;

4. **Monthly P&L Forecast v Actual** this is simply the same p&l as in 3 above but monthlies put side by side so you can see how the different lines of revenue and cost are trending. This is helpful to spot any obvious errors or concerns. For example rent should not change month to month unless you are moving office. It's good to keep the history from inception here all in one place as it is often asked for. One line commentary should be given against material movements in the month;

5. **Budget**: Again the same p&l format broken out by month or by quarter for the full year. Budgets typically go stale soon after they are produced, especially for a dynamic SME but it's a good reference point on what was decided and may help to refine future budgeting exercises when the Board sees how far off they were in their planning;

6. **Balance Sheet**: The monthly balance sheet should be presented with the key headings you would expect to see — Fixed Assets broken out by asset class; Current Assets broken out by Stock, Debtors, Cash, Prepayments; Current Liabilities broken out by Creditors, Taxes, Accruals, and other liabilities; Debt; Net Assets; Shareholder Funds;

7. **Detailed Aged Debtors Listing**: a full listing by customer rank sorted by largest oldest debt first of who owes the business money. Commentary for the oldest debt should be provided; and

8. **Cash flow forecast**: a summary of monies in and out for the next 12 months, 6 months minimum.

The **Management Accounts** should not be published without sign off from the **Finance Director**. To review the accounts timely and efficiently I require **Management Accounts** to be presented with reconciliations for the balance sheet. The Board do not have to see this detail but it is there if they want to and it will show the rigour adopted in preparing the financials.

In this work experience, we are going to produce four separate reports which in a way will cover most of the above points.

The reports we will produce are:

A. Company Overview report
- Profit & Loss report
- Balance sheet report

B. Sales Performance report
- Accounts receivable ageing detailed report
- Sales by Customer Summary report

C. Expenses Performance report

- Accounts payable ageing detailed report
- Expenses by supplier summary report

D. Ratio Analysis report

Here is how to get report A & B in QuickBooks online.

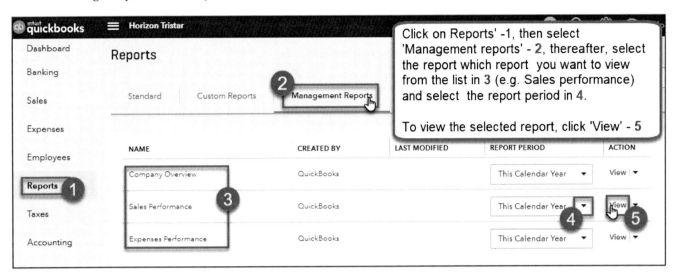

Fig. 318

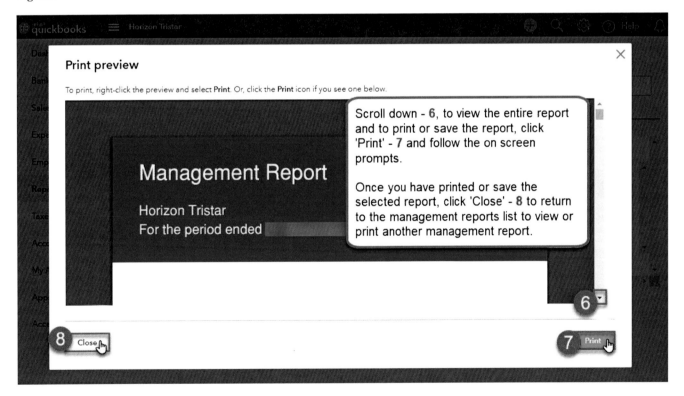

Fig. 319

QuickBooks Online Management Reports feature allows you to customise a professional looking reporting package complete with cover page, table of contents, preliminary pages, reports and end notes.

The Management Reports feature will save you precious time on running business reports – you won't have to export out individual reports to software for assembly and finalisation.

Ratio Analysis

Ratio Analysis - Key Ratios for Horizon Tristar Ltd		
	Prior Year	Current year
Balance Sheet		
Cash	55,250	92,729
Accounts receivable, net	16,100	19,338
Total current assets	120,512	70,563
Total long-term assets	17,150	126,982
Total current liabilities	65,180	130,949
Total long-term liabilities	1,601	12,905
Total shareholders' equity	98,286	163,759
Income Statement		
Total sales	119,142	222,300
Gross profit	87,254	121,398
Total operating expenses	79,250	105,125
Income (loss) before taxes	8,004	22,280
Net income (loss)	6,403	18,827
KEY RATIOS		
Profitability Ratios		
Return on equity	7%	11%
Return on assets	3%	10%
Return on sales	5%	8%
Gross profit margin	73%	55%
Asset turnover ratio	59%	113%
Leverage and Liquidity Ratios		
Current ratio	1.85	0.54
Quick or acid test ratio	1.09	1.47
Long-term debt to asset ratio	0.008	0.065
Debt to equity ratio	0.679	0.878

Ratio analysis

What is ratio analysis?

Ratio Analysis is a form of financial statement analysis that is used to obtain a quick indication of financial performance of a business in several key areas.

The ratios are categorised as:
- ✓ Short-term Solvency Ratios, e.g. *Current ratio and Quick or acid test ratio.*
- ✓ Debt Management Ratios, e.g. *Debt to equity ratio*
- ✓ Asset Management Ratios, e.g. *Receivables turnover*
- ✓ Profitability Ratios, and
- ✓ Market Value Ratios. E.g. *Price earnings ratio*

Return on Equity and Return on Assets

The Return on Assets Ratio indicates the pound (£) in income earned by the company on its assets and the Return on Equity Ratio indicates the pounds (£) of income earned by the company on its shareholders' equity. It is important to remember that these ratios are based on accounting book values and not on market values. Thus, it is not appropriate to compare these ratios with market rates of return such as the interest rate on Treasury bonds or the return earned on an investment in a stock.

Formula

$$\text{Return on Assets (ROA)} = \frac{\text{Net income}}{\text{Total Assets}}$$

$$\text{Return on Equity (ROE)} = \frac{\text{Net income}}{\text{Total Owners' Equity}}$$

Return on Sales:

Return on sales, often called the operating profit margin, is a financial ratio that calculates how efficiently a company is at generating profits from its revenue. In other words, it measures a company's performance by analysing what percentage of total company revenues are actually converted into company profits.

$$\text{Return on Sales (ROS)} = \frac{\text{Operating profit}}{\text{Net Sales}}$$

Analysis

You can think of ROS as both an efficiency and profitability ratio because it is an indicator of both metrics. It measures how efficiently a company uses its resources to convert sales into profits. For instance, a company that generates £1,000,000 in net sales and requires £900,000 of resources to do so is not nearly as efficient as a company that can generate the same about of revenues by only using £500,000 of operating expenses. The more efficient management is cutting expenses, the higher the ratio.

Investors tend to use this iteration of the formula to calculate growth projects and forecasts. For example, based on a certain percentage, investors could calculate the potential profits if revenues doubled or tripled.

Gross profit margin

Gross profit margin is a profitability ratio that calculates the percentage of sales that exceed the cost of goods sold. In other words, it measures how efficiently a company uses its materials and labor to produce and sell products profitably.

The gross profit ratio is important because it shows management and investors how profitable the core business activities are without taking into consideration the indirect costs. In other words, it shows how efficiently a company can produce and sell its products. This gives investors a key insight into how healthy the company actually is. For instance, a company with a seemingly healthy net income on the bottom line could actually be dying. The gross profit percentage could be negative, and the net income could be coming from other one-time operations. The company could be losing money on every product they produce but staying afloat because of a one-time insurance pay-out.

That is why it is almost always listed on front page of the income statement in one form or another. Let's take a look at how to calculate gross profit and what it's used for.

Formula

$$\text{Gross Profit Margin} = \frac{\text{Total Sales} - \text{Cost of goods sold}}{\text{Total Sales}}$$

Analysis

The gross profit method is an important concept because it shows management and investors how efficiently the business can produce and sell products. In other words, it shows how profitable a product is.

The concept of GP is particularly important to cost accountants and management because it allows them to create budgets and forecast future activities. For instance, Horizon Tristar Ltd GP was £121,398. This means if Horizon Tristar wants to be profitable for the year, all of her other costs must be less than £121,398. Conversely, Horizon Tristar Ltd can also view the £121,398 as the amount of money that can be put toward other business expenses or expansion into new markets.

Investors/management can also use a gross profit margin calculator to measure scalability. Horizon Tristar Ltd investors can run different models with her margins to see how profitable the company would be at different sales levels. For instance, they could measure the profits if 100,000 units were sold or 500,000 units were sold by multiplying the potential number of units sold by the sales price and the GP margin.

Asset Turnover Ratio

The asset turnover ratio is an efficiency ratio that measures a company's ability to generate sales from its assets by comparing net sales with average total assets. In other words, this ratio shows how efficiently a company can use its assets to generate sales.

The total asset turnover ratio calculates net sales as a percentage of assets to show how many sales are generated from each pound/dollar of company assets. For instance, a ratio of .5 means that each pound/dollar of assets generates 50 pence/cents of sales.

Formula

$$\text{Gross Profit Margin} = \frac{\text{Net Sales}}{\text{Average total assets}}$$

Net sales, found on the income statement, are used to calculate this ratio returns and refunds must be backed out of total sales to measure the truly measure the firm's assets' ability to generate sales.

Average total assets are usually calculated by adding the beginning and ending total asset balances together and dividing by two. This is just a simple average based on a two-year balance sheet. A more in-depth, weighted average calculation can be used, but it is not necessary.

Analysis:
This ratio measures how efficiently a firm uses its assets to generate sales, so a higher ratio is always more favourable. Higher turnover ratios mean the company is using its assets more efficiently. Lower ratios mean that the company isn't using its assets efficiently and most likely have management or production problems.

Like with most ratios, the asset turnover ratio is based on industry standards. Some industries use assets more efficiently than others. To get a true sense of how well a company's assets are being used, it must be compared to other companies in its industry.
The total asset turnover ratio is a general efficiency ratio that measures how efficiently a company uses all of its assets. This gives investors and creditors an idea of how a company is managed and uses its assets to produce products and sales.

Current ratio

The current ratio is a liquidity and efficiency ratio that measures a firm's ability to pay off its short-term liabilities with its current assets. The current ratio is an important measure of liquidity because short-term liabilities are due within the next year.

This means that a company has a limited amount of time in order to raise the funds to pay for these liabilities. Current assets like cash, cash equivalents, and marketable securities can easily be converted into cash in the short term. This means that companies with larger amounts of current assets will more easily be able to pay off current liabilities when they become due without having to sell off long-term, revenue generating assets.

Formula

$$\text{Current ratio} = \frac{\text{Current Assets}}{\text{Current Liabilities}}$$

Analysis:
A higher current ratio is always more favourable than a lower current ratio because it shows the company can more easily make current debt payments.

If a company has to sell of fixed assets to pay for its current liabilities, this usually means the company isn't making enough from operations to support activities. In other words, the company is losing money. Sometimes this is the result of poor collections of accounts receivable.

The current ratio also sheds light on the overall debt burden of the company. If a company is weighted down with a current debt, its cash flow will suffer.

Quick or acid test ratio

The quick ratio or acid test ratio is a liquidity ratio that measures the ability of a company to pay its current liabilities when they come due with only quick assets. Quick assets are current assets that can be converted to cash within 90 days or in the short-term. Cash, cash equivalents, short-term investments or marketable securities, and current accounts receivable are considered quick assets.

Formula

$$\text{Quick ratio} = \frac{\text{Cash} + \text{Cash Equivalents} + \text{Short term investments} + \text{Current receivables}}{\text{Current Liabilities}}$$

Sometimes company financial statements don't give a breakdown of quick assets on the balance sheet. In this case, you can still calculate the quick ratio even if some of the quick asset totals are unknown. Simply subtract inventory and any current prepaid assets from the current asset total for the numerator. Here is an example.

$$\text{Quick ratio} = \frac{\text{Current Assets} - \text{Inventory} - \text{Prepaid Expenses}}{\text{Current Liabilities}}$$

Long term debt ratio

A company can build assets by raising debt or equity capital. The ratio of long-term debt to total assets provides a sense of what percentage of the total assets is financed via long-term debt. A higher percentage ratio means that the company is more leveraged and owns less of the assets on balance sheet. In other words, it would need to sell more assets to eliminate its debt in the event of a bankruptcy. The company would also have to generate strong revenue and cash flow for a long period in the future to be able to repay the debt.

This ratio provides a sense of financial stability and overall riskiness of a company. Investors are wary of a high ratio, as it signifies management has less free cash flow and less ability to finance new operations. Management typically uses this financial metric to determine the amount of debt the company can sustain and manage the overall capital structure of the firm.

Formula

$$\text{Long Term Debt Ratio} = \frac{\text{Long term debt}}{\text{Total Assets}}$$

It's also important to look at off-balance sheet items like operating lease and pension obligations. These items are not presented in the long-term liabilities section of the balance sheet, but they are liabilities nonetheless. If you don't include these in your calculation, your estimates will not be completely correct.

Keep in mind that this ratio should be used with several other leverage ratios in order to get a proper understanding of the financial riskiness of a company. Some of other relevant ratios that you can use are the Total debt to total assets ratio, Total debt to Equity ratio, and the LT debt to Equity ratio.

That's how you can use the LT-debt ratio to measure a company's financial leverage and calculate its overall risk. Used properly while considering all the loopholes, this metric can be an important tool to initiate constructive discussion with the management about the future of the company.

Debt to Equity ratio

The debt to equity ratio is a financial, liquidity ratio that compares a company's total debt to total equity. The debt to equity ratio shows the percentage of company financing that comes from creditors and investors. A higher debt to equity ratio indicates that more creditor financing (bank loans) is used than investor financing (shareholders).

Formula

$$\text{Debt to Equity Ratio} = \frac{\text{Total Liabilities}}{\text{Total Equity}}$$

Analysis

A lower debt to equity ratio usually implies a more financially stable business. Companies with a higher debt to equity ratio are considered riskier to creditors and investors than companies with a lower ratio. Unlike equity financing, debt must be repaid to the lender. Since debt financing also requires debt servicing or regular interest payments, debt can be a far more expensive form of financing than equity financing. Companies leveraging large amounts of debt might not be able to make the payments.

Creditors view a higher debt to equity ratio as risky because it shows that the investors haven't funded the operations as much as creditors have. This could mean that investors don't want to fund the business operations because the company isn't performing well. Lack of performance might also be the reason why the company is seeking out extra debt financing.

This space is for notes

TASK 12: HOW TO FILE ACCOUNTS TO COMPANIES HOUSE & HMRC

UNITED KINGDOM ONLY
From: https://www.gov.uk/guidance/corporation-tax-use-hmrcs-free-filing-software

You can use the HMRC online service to file your company, charity or association's:
- Company Tax Return (CT600) for Corporation Tax
- supplementary return pages CT600A, CT600E and CT600J
- statutory company accounts
- Corporation Tax computations
- other attachments (in PDF format) to support your return

The service will:
- help you work out your profit or loss adjusted for tax purposes
- automatically complete most of the form CT600 Company Tax Return for you

You'll be able to report:
- gross income from property up to £5,200 (expenses should not be greater than income)
- income up to £1,000 that does not come from your organisation's main trade
- capital allowances and balancing charges for plant and machinery in the main pool
- Annual Investment Allowance (AIA)
- low emission cars
- trading losses brought forward, set against profits in the same period or carried back from a later period
- share dividends

Companies that can file a Company Tax Return with the HMRC online service

You can use the service if:
- you're a charity and your turnover is up to £6.5 million per year
- a company whose turnover is up to £632,000 per year and are either a:
    - limited company
    - community amateur sports club
    - members club or other unincorporated organisation
    - community interest company

You must:
- have income from the profits of a single UK trade
- only need to make adjustments for:
    - depreciation
    - disallowable entertaining

- donations
- legal and professional fees
- net losses on the sale of fixed assets
- penalties and fines
- unpaid employees' remuneration

Companies that cannot use the service

You cannot use the service if your company is:
- in liquidation or receivership
- not registered in the UK
- part of a group
- an insurance company, not including independent insurance brokers
- an investment company
- a credit union
- a commercial property management company

You also cannot use the service if your company has had more than 12 company directors at any one time in the return period, or:
- your accounts need an audit or have been audited
- the Corporation Tax accounting period for the return is covered by more than one set of statutory accounts
- your company pays its Corporation Tax in instalments
- you need to claim a repayment of a loan to a participator (for example, a director's loan) more than 9 months after the end of the accounting period
- you need to report:
  - adjustments for something reported in a previous year
  - called up share capital not paid
  - capital allowances (except for specific plant and machinery, AIA and low emission cars)
  - chargeable gains or losses
  - complex loan-relationship entries
  - contingent assets
  - financial instruments
  - foreign currency transactions
  - foreign trade income
  - income or expenditure from investment assets
  - leased cars
  - non-trading income (except interest received)
  - research and development costs
  - restructuring costs
  - share-based payments
  - share premium

What if you cannot file a Company Tax Return using the HMRC online service

If you cannot use the HMRC online service you can send your Company Tax Return online using commercial software. Visit: https://www.gov.uk/government/publications/corporation-tax-commercial-software-suppliers

---

A brief note from - gov.uk

Your company or association must file a Company Tax Return if you get a 'notice to deliver a Company Tax Return' from HM Revenue and Customs (HMRC).

You must still send a return if you make a loss or have no Corporation Tax to pay.

You do not send a Company Tax Return if you're self-employed as a sole trader or in a partnership - but you must send a Self Assessment return.

The process of filing statutory accounts and tax return using HMRC online software

This task assumes that you will be using HMRC online software as opposed to third-party comercial software to file your accounts and tax return.

Here is what you'll need before you start:
   a) Your Accounts (Profit and Loss account, Balance sheet & Trial Balance) prepared using your accounting software.
   b) Your Government Gateway user ID and password - register for a HMRC online account if you don't have one by visiting this web address: *https://online.hmrc.gov.uk/registration/newbusiness*
   c) Your Companies House password and authentication code if you're filing your accounts with Companies House at the same time - register online with Companies House if you haven't already by visiting this web address: *https://ewf.companieshouse.gov.uk/runpage?page=webfilingRegister*

Once you have those details handy (a, b and c), type *https://www.gov.uk/file-your-company-accounts-and-tax-return* to a web browser.

Here is what you will see once that page loads up – see figure below.

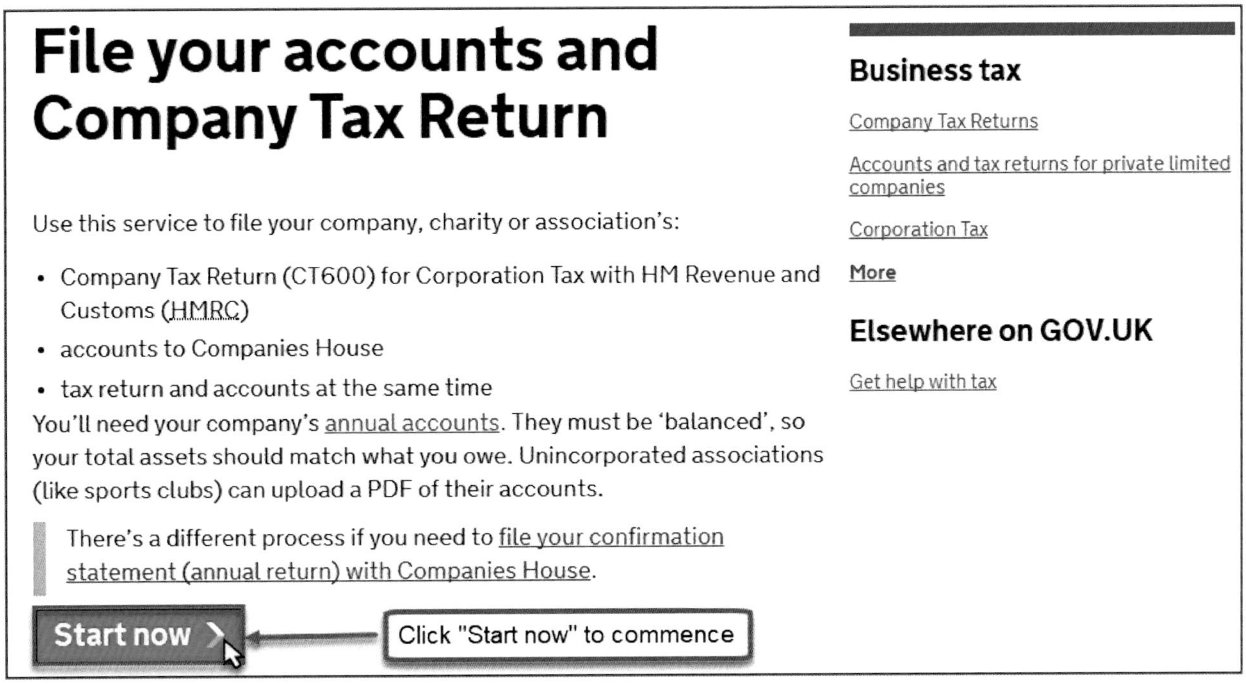

File your accounts and Company Tax Return

Use this service to file your company, charity or association's:

- Company Tax Return (CT600) for Corporation Tax with HM Revenue and Customs (HMRC)
- accounts to Companies House
- tax return and accounts at the same time

You'll need your company's annual accounts. They must be 'balanced', so your total assets should match what you owe. Unincorporated associations (like sports clubs) can upload a PDF of their accounts.

> There's a different process if you need to file your confirmation statement (annual return) with Companies House.

Start now >   Click "Start now" to commence

Business tax

Company Tax Returns

Accounts and tax returns for private limited companies

Corporation Tax

More

Elsewhere on GOV.UK

Get help with tax

Fig. 320

Once you click start now as illustrated in the figure above, you will be directed to the sign in page.

When you file your tax return, you work out your:

- *profit or loss for Corporation Tax (this is different from the profit or loss shown in your annual accounts)*
- *Corporation Tax bill*

You can either get an accountant to prepare and file your tax return or do it yourself.
If you have a limited company, you may be able to file your accounts with Companies House at the same time as your tax return.
Source: https://www.gov.uk/company-tax-returns

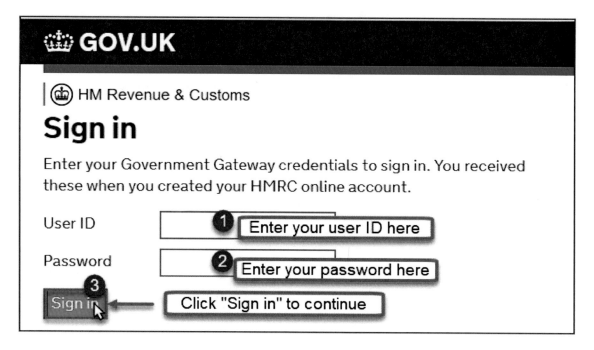

Fig. 321

For security reason, once you have signed in an access code will be sent to the mobile phone number you have registered for this purpose.

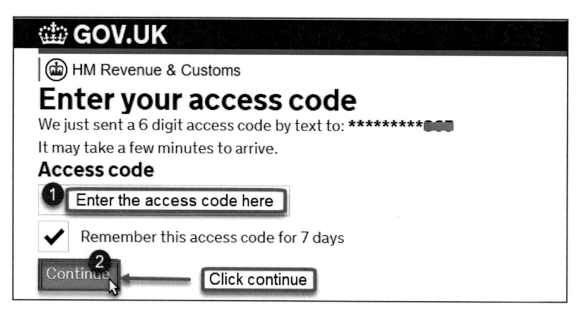

Fig. 322

You will then be directed to set up security back up – see figure on the next page.

Tax Return deadlines

The deadline for your tax return is 12 months after the end of the accounting period it covers. You'll have to pay a penalty if you miss the deadline.

There's a separate deadline to pay your Corporation Tax bill. It's usually 9 months and one day after the end of the accounting period.

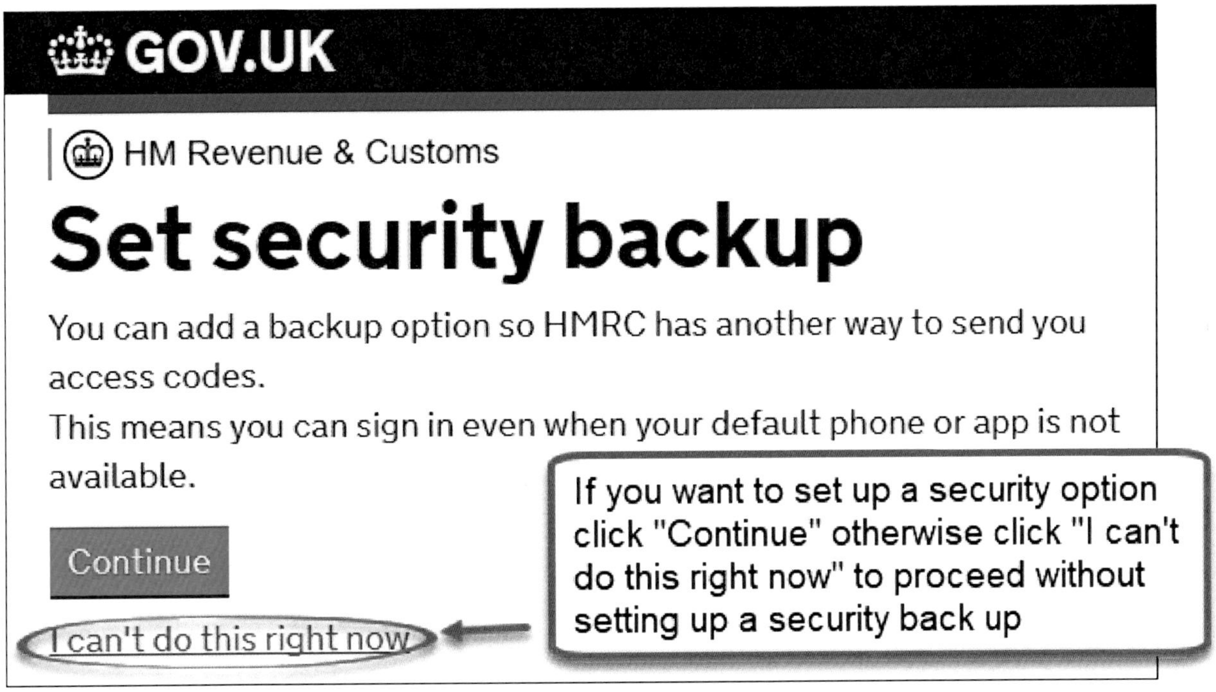

♔ GOV.UK

♔ HM Revenue & Customs

Set security backup

You can add a backup option so HMRC has another way to send you access codes.

This means you can sign in even when your default phone or app is not available.

Continue

I can't do this right now

> If you want to set up a security option click "Continue" otherwise click "I can't do this right now" to proceed without setting up a security back up

Fig. 323

♔ HM Revenue & Customs

Backup not set

You didn't set your security backup today.

We'll remind you next time you sign in.

Continue

> This is the page you will be directed to if you choose not to set up the security back in the previous page. Click "Continue" to proceed

Fig. 324

You will then be directed to the dashboard of your tax account when you click continue.

This space is for notes

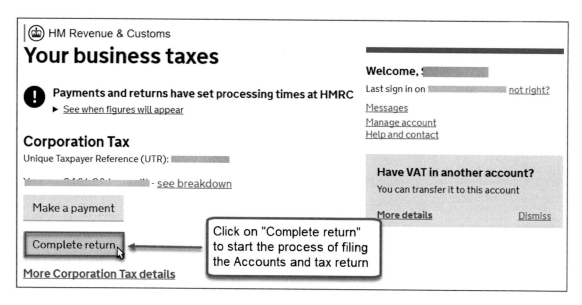

Fig. 325

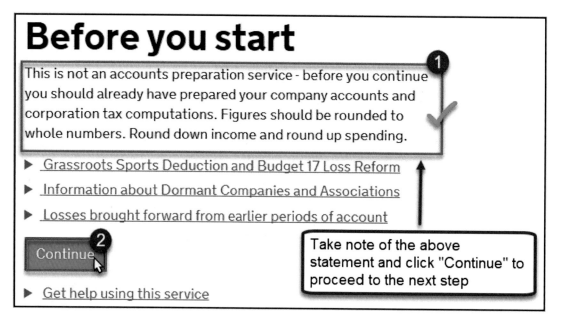

Fig. 326

Having got your accounts (Trial balance, Profit and Loss account and Balance sheet) ready and handy, when you click continue as illustrated in the figure above, you will then be led through a series of questions requiring mostly yes or no answers.

Once you have answered the questions accordingly, you will come to the profit & loss and balance sheet pages where you will then be able to use the figures of the profit & Loss, Trial balance and balance sheet produced from your accounting system to complete the profit & Loss and Balance sheet details within HMRC software and eventually once you have completed filling in the profit & Loss account details and the balance sheet, you will then be directed to a page where you can submit the accounts and tax return to Companies House & HMRC.

ABOUT THE AUTHOR

Sterling Libs FCCA trained as a Chartered Accountant and has written several practical accounting books that have helped many accounting students and graduates in their accounting career journeys to getting accounting jobs. He studied and qualified for his professional accountancy career in London England and is now a Fellow of the Association of Chartered Certified Accountants. He currently lives and works in London, United Kindom.

Sterling is pragmatic, motivational and hard working. He has been very instrumental in training many accounting students, and graduates in gaining work-based practical accounting experience and many of his trainees have been able to get accounting jobs in the UK and abroad. His passion for practical accounting and training is profound, and he loves mentoring individuals to discover, develop and deploy their talents and gifts to make the world a better place for all.

He is passionate about inspiring confidence for work, and life in general, among all those he meets and interacts with.

The Author can be contacted by sending an email to sterling@sterlinglibs.com

Made in United States
North Haven, CT
18 June 2022

.20379570R00124